The Sacristy Manual

By G. Thomas Ryan

Illustrations by Adam Redjinski

LTP
LITURGY
TRAINING
PUBLICATIONS

Acknowledgments

Visit our website at www.ltp.org

This book was edited by David Philippart, with the assistance of Jerry Reedy and Sarah Huck. It was designed by Mary Bowers. Kari Nicholls set the type in Futura and Sabon. *The Sacristy Manual* has been printed in Canada.

Library of Congress Cataloging-in-Publications Data
Ryan G. Thomas, 1947–
The sacristy manual/G. Thomas Ryan : illustrated by Adam Redjinski
270 p. cm.
Includes index.
1. Sacristans — Handbooks, manuals, etc. 2. Catholic Church-Liturgy — Handbooks, manuals, etc. I. Title.
BX1972.R83 1933
247 — dc20 93-29863
CIP

ISBN 0-929650-92-1
SACMNL

Table of Contents

Part 3. ◆ EQUIPPING THE SACRISTY

Part 4. ◆ CHECKLISTS

Preface

Like the work of sacristans, this manual is full of details. Small items can deter or facilitate public actions. Particular customs in the sacristy can do one of two things for the liturgy: help it to be the act of the whole church, or keep it the province of clerics. Correct attention by sacristans to liturgical details is fundamental to healthy liturgy.

Checklists and procedures, ordos and norms impede our liturgy or become trivia if our attention to them is not deeply rooted in a commitment to the liturgical life of the local church. We need more than intellectual assent to the church in its actions. We need a passion for the local community as sacred reality, a passion for the communal rites as sacred interactions, a passion for the shared physicalities—from grand architecture to the tiniest artifact—as sacred art.

While reflecting on these basic beliefs and requisite details, I visited a parish across town for Sunday eucharist. I had never been in the building, but had read about its fine architecture. Upon entering, it became obvious that something strange was in the air. I joined a cluster of people standing to the side of the sanctuary. They were staring at a life-sized, marble statue of St. Anthony of Padua, toppled from its pedestal, and headless. The image of the baby Jesus in Anthony's arms had been similarly mauled. The stone showed evidence of powerful thrusts of the axe wielded by the one who had stolen the heads. Surely the act of a deranged person, we might say, but amazing in its power to render speechless an otherwise intelligent, articulate group of city-dwellers.

The statue had been no artistic match for the far superior architecture of the church; furthermore, it had been placed a bit too close to the altar area. Decapitated, it made such thoughts impertinent. The parishioners felt violated. Their sacred art had been desecrated; their house of prayer had been profaned.

In the presence of these primal emotions, I recalled a moment from my youth in a large urban parish where the church and parish school were the central points of energy. One day, while gazing from our back porch, my friends and I saw smoke rising from the church. We rushed to the sacred place, a haste made all the more purposeful by the shrill sounds of sirens as fire engines sped down the streets.

Police blocked our access, but we were all altar boys and knew well the back alley that would provide us with an unobstructed view of the smoking church. When we got there we saw the priests carrying out the treasures of our community's prayer. Their varying degrees of clerical dress bespoke their haste as they carried out the monstrance, some black boxes we knew encased chalices, and smaller containers that we guessed were for the sacred oils. We heard that the hero of the day was Father Hankins, the priest who had taught us our Latin responses. He had just rescued the blessed sacrament. We knew that this was a priest's duty, no matter the risk to life and limb. In hushed tones and nervous laughs, we thanked God that Father Hankins had survived.

With grave solemnity and fear we awaited the collapse of our church. What a relief—and momentary disappointment—that the fire was doused and all was well within a few minutes. Everyone went back home, figuring out how to make the final story more exciting than a ten-minute fire. Still, it was exciting—to see the sacristy saved, the eucharist rescued. Over the past few decades, liturgical reforms and progressive teachers have helped most Catholics pass beyond the understanding of the parish church as the sacred throne-room for the tabernacled Lord. Calling our objects sacred is dangerous. We know that the church complex is sacred because the people who meet there are sacred and are engaged in sacred rites. Yet, the physical elements that are within, from the reserved eucharist to the chalices, from the altar to the various statues, are not just neutral matter.

When parishioners lose their church building to fire, when statues are decapitated by vandals, when vessels are stolen or strewn about, the reactions are primal, strong, far beyond the "rational." One could remind members that chalices can be replaced for a few hundred dollars, that the building can be rebuilt in a more glorious and energy-efficient way, that Saint Anthony (of all the saints) will find his head again. But if you were to say these things out loud, you would sound foolish. The emotions surrounding any violence to the place of worship tell us that the very objects of our common prayer are strong symbols of our life together. The building itself, even when empty, is a sustaining symbol of our identity. The given parts of a church complex come to represent the topography, the cosmology of the sacred for the local community. How fitting it is that the sacred assembly, the church, has lent its name to the building itself.

Our attention to the details of the sacristy and our passion for full community meet here. We tend to the implements and artifacts worthy of a sacred people. True, they are mortal things—everything in the sacristy is either consumed and replenished or conserved. Yet the importance of these things is what makes our ministry in the sacristy so rewarding. Because the community of mortals needs frequent interactions, our work is never ending. Because the requisites themselves are transitory, our ministry of providing and preserving is year-round. If the community finds its immortal future through the physical interactions of sacraments, then our attention to the physicalities of those sacraments makes this sense of sacredness possible.

The first chapters of this manual form an introduction, setting the later details into this framework of church and liturgy. Part 2 is a long tour through the different parts of the church complex, showing the relationship of the items in the sacristy to the actions and places of community. Part 3 describes the sacristy's holdings and functions; it is a review and background for experienced sacristans and a suggested program for those building a new sacristy. Finally, Part 4 is a series of checklists for major feasts and rites. These are just lists—the principles and norms are found in the main body of the manual.

Sacristans may want to use the various chapters for reading or for group study. Then the checklists can be referred to as events are scheduled. In any construction or renovation, and even in the planning of decorative programs for parts of the parish church complex, the pertinent chapters provide some framework for shared discourse.

No single sacristy manual can be all-inclusive. For example, the various documents that set norms for sacristies are not reprinted here. The central ones are found at the front of each official liturgical book, like the *General Instruction of the Roman Missal* at the front of the sacramentary. (These documents are sometimes a bit dense, full of odd vocabulary, or preoccupied with now-defunct problems, but they are our common ground for sacristy work. They spell out the shared rites that our work must support.) Some details hinted at here, but not covered in depth, will be found in a companion volume, a building manual to be published in 1994 by Liturgy Training Publications. There one will find comments on matters of a more architectural nature—access for the physically challenged, ideas for renovations, and tools for making a liturgical audit of the property.

As a server during the 1950s in Saint Gregory's parish in Dorchester, Massachusetts, I looked over the junior curate's shoulder to see the notes that he consulted. They were the richly detailed notes of a young commentator, Frederick McManus. I owe much to this generous man, this high school classmate of my father, this man who introduced so many of us to the reformed holy week, this capable administrator under whom I served at The Catholic University of America, the man who epitomizes the best of the local church from which I come, the archdiocese of Boston. I also praise and thank all of the sacristans with whom I have been privileged to work, not the least of whom was Adam Redjinski, the illustrator of this volume and a gifted sacristan at the Cathedral of the Holy Cross. Richard Butler—gifted pastor and pastoral liturgist and another Bostonian—also has been a docent and support to me. To them, and to all who have taught me that we can come to know the Lord through the concrete details of the sacristy, this volume bears witness.

PART ONE • *Preparing for the Sacred Mysteries*

1◆ The Church

The Action of the Church

"For these sacristans, that the preparations they make for the celebration of the liturgy may remind us to prepare our hearts for worship. . . ." This petition, from the blessing of sacristans *(Book of Blessings,* chapter 62), captures the essence of sacristy work. The joys and concerns, the moments of energy-rush, the hours of painstaking details—all are part of this ministry of preparing the action of the church.

The word "church" itself comes from Greek words for the "gathered people" or "the Lord's holy congregation." When two or three or a thousand Christians gather, we constitute much more than a gathering of volunteers who have chosen to work together. We are a gift of God, the people gathered together by Christ, the Risen One, through his death and resurrection. The Lord's death and resurrection also have been described as Christ becoming the perfect temple and building a temple of living stones. The First Letter of Peter summons every parish: "Like living stones, let yourselves be built into a spiritual house, to be a holy priesthood, to offer spiritual sacrifices acceptable to God through Jesus Christ." (1:5)

The Action of Christ

Whether described as the holy people or as the temple of living stones, the congregation is engaged in the action of Christ. We pray as a community through, with and in Christ. This liturgy is the act of Christ. To say that Christ is the progenitor of a people may sound like mere abstract theology when a parish community seems to resent liturgies that take more than 45 minutes. Jesus, the perfect temple, may seem frightfully distant from the inattentiveness of many congregations. Yet we nonetheless cling to this affirmation: The liturgy is the act of Christ.

Millions of God-fearing worshipers know this. Gathering Sunday after Sunday, we know the holy power of Christ. We know that this power is at work in a holy meeting of ministries. We look forward to being shaped by an interaction with fragrance and oil, water and ashes, bread and wine. Our best and most memorable liturgies may or may not be marked by brilliant preaching and artfully arranged furnishings. But they are invariably marked by the profound interaction of holy people and holy symbols. Even if we do not use these exact words, we know that our mystery is not like the "mysteries" of pagan temples, not a mystery of divine magic and secrets. In the Christian mystery we perform revered actions together.

This interaction equips us to live in the world. Though old mysteries seem to have helped adherents escape from the world, we know that Christ's action was and is one of saving the world. If we "leave the world" at liturgy, it is not an escape, but a plunging deeper into the promised transformation of this very flesh, this very world.

The thousands of alienated Catholics who, despite their distance, seek ashes one day each February are not looking for a fast cure. The teaching and popular imagination of our century never have given ashes the power of a talisman. No, the thousands come forward for some signal of their identity, as mortal beings even now called to new life. The ashes, worn back to work or home, signify involvement with the coming transformation of the world.

In just such a way, week after week, the material elements of our holy gatherings, the vessels and elements set up by sacristans, provide the matrix in which we interact. Water, fire, oil, ashes, bread and wine are the archetypal elements that form the environment of our interaction. These elements accompany the many artifacts that facilitate such basic actions as cup-sharing, lamp-lighting, incense-burning, moving in procession, and committing our deceased to the earth. Catholics and many other Christians find that words are not enough for the sacred interactions that occur on Sundays and feasts. We need these elements and artifacts, too.

Our assemblies are far more complex than those that take place in schools, sports arenas and city halls. But the complexity of our rites does not exist for the sake of complexity. Our ancestors never sat down to see how difficult they could make the work of future sacristans. The complexity comes from the rich repertoire of rites that respond to the varied needs of our assemblies. People are born, those who marry stand before us, the sick ask to be prayed over, and people die. Through seasons and days, each served by the proper artifacts, we act as Christ. We realize that we are Christ's holy people, the new temple of living stones.

A Building for Action

From the earliest centuries, the people of Christ have found appropriate buildings to house these sacred actions. To distinguish themselves from other religions, they were quite careful, from the beginning, to say that they had "no temple" but Christ, that their buildings did not contain their God. Over the centuries, the name of the people—"gathered people," "church"—came to denote the building in which the people met to perform their actions together. Thus, the building was called "church." Our official liturgical books and the origins of the name itself suggest the felicitous nature of this double meaning: Even the name of the building reminds us of the people gathered there. Church buildings exist for the sake of the church people, for the God who called this people into being, for the holy interactions that mark the passage through a year.

In tracing our history, we might ask: Is the church building the "house of God" or the "house of God's people"? The question can be answered with a resounding "Yes!" It is both. The church building is the house or temple of God because the church assembly is the house or temple of God. God is not contained by these walls; we do not come to the church complex to see a magical epiphany or pageant of the Risen One. Instead, we gather so that we can engage—with Christ—in the liturgical rites of our community. The intensity of these rites and the holiness of our union in Christ are what make this place holy.

When empty of its members, a church of stone should stand as a constant sign of the living stones who are now in the world, preparing the world for its transformation. And, just as surely, the church is also a sign of the generations gone before us, those who worshiped here, the communion of saints.

When enlivened by the presence of its assembly, a church building provides shelter and images for liturgical actions. If Christianity were just a set of beliefs to be transmitted, then a classroom would do. If the holy people became holy and remained so by sheer will power, then there would be no need for a public place. If we did not believe in the incarnation, then fleshy matters would be peripheral. But we are a holy people who find communion and identity in our public interaction, who shape this action with very traditional material elements. We cannot be church without our shared water and oil, bread and wine; we would find it difficult to be the church without our churches.

This relationship of the people and their place for liturgy comes to beautiful and intense expression in the rite for the dedication of churches. For example, the rite calls for the interior walls to be anointed at twelve (or four) places. Crosses and candles can later be installed at these points along the perimeter. Those illuminated by baptism will gather here week after week, the lights will embrace them in their gathering and lead them to recognize their identity.

The Second Vatican Council devoted a lot of attention to the need to make liturgical architecture responsive to the liturgical actions that take place within it. This functional approach is the only one that half the population knows. Those middle-aged enough to remember the days before Vatican II (and those who have visited spaces that have not been renovated in the wake of that convocation) know that older church interiors were ill-suited to the reformed rites. Some buildings looked like show palaces for pageants. Others looked like throne rooms for the reserved eucharist. The older buildings needed renovations to make them suitable for the sacred action of the members. Unfortunately, some attempts at renovation consisted merely of rearranging the seats to adjust the view, to create a new "theater in the round." The more successful renovations created space for the assembly to move and interact.

Yet church buildings need to be more than functional. If the buildings of stone are to signify the living stones, then they should look like something more than a fortress or a commercial sales hall. Architecture, furnishings and decor play an important role in our churches. The document that gives authoritative directions for the celebration of the eucharist offers a summary:

> For the celebration of the eucharist, the people of God normally assemble in a church or, if there is none, in some other fitting place worthy of so great a mystery. Churches

and other places of worship should therefore be suited to celebrating the liturgy and to ensuring the active participation of the faithful. Further, the places and requisites for worship should be truly worthy and beautiful, signs and symbols of heavenly realities. *(General Instruction of the Roman Missal, #253)*

The Local Church

In the church community, in the local church building, one comes before these "heavenly realities." In this very place, in nooks and crannies, in the midst of this community of this altar, God and church are engaged in a saving interaction. This manual provides background information and set-up lists, explanations and advice; readers must then adapt these guidelines in light of local conditions. Though written with the Catholic parish in mind, this book can be used and adapted for monasteries and chapels and for other Christian communities.

Local conditions and the adaptations they require should not be seen as burdens. There is no church where an ideal or universal set of conditions applies, where local characteristics are unimportant. Sacristy work, much as the church itself, is founded on this saving truth: In each specific community of the altar, with all of its unique qualities, the fullness of Christ is present. The people who come together here—relatives and neighbors, strangers and friends—are the "gathered people," the "temple of living stones."

2◆ History of the Sacristy

Before Christianity

Sacristies are privileged places where the liturgical rites are prepared, where the treasured objects that facilitate that prayer are stored. Every place of public assembly has side chambers that shelter the objects used by the assembly. Archaeologists have identified many sites with these support rooms along the sides of both ancient temples and theaters. The Bible contains many references, especially in the two books of Chronicles, to side chambers at the Jerusalem Temple. These rooms were used by priests and other officials to store treasures and cultic materials, to receive and distribute gifts. The Septuagint, an early Greek translation of the Bible, used the term "pastophoria" to designate these auxiliary rooms.

Early Christian Centuries

An early Christian document from Syri used the same term for the side rooms in its description of an ideal worship site: "First, let the building be long, with its head to the east, with its vestries on both sides at the east end, and so it will be like a ship" *(Apostolic Constitutions,* II.7). Long before the civil legitimation of Christianity in 313, local communities met in specially designated and equipped buildings for liturgy. Sites now identified as early churches throughout the Mediterranean basin show that the communities utilized several interconnected spaces: eucharistic hall, baptistry, atrium, catechumeneon, and auxiliary rooms not unlike our sacristies. For example, in 303 the church of Cirta (regional center in current Algeria) was closed by the government. Possessions confiscated from the sacristies are listed on an extant portion of the local court's proceedings. They describe the chalices and lamps that were taken, but they also tell how the church's ministers took the scriptural books from the sacristy and hid them.

Documentary evidence of such ministers is rare. Every Christian assembly had some equivalent of sacristans, but the work of preparing the environment and the artifacts has always been quiet and untrumpeted. Yet we know that, among the ministries related to the early sacristies, there were both porters and sacristans. A porter *(ostiarius)* tended the doors, and in later centuries rang the bells and performed other works of liturgical preparation. This ministry later became codified as a "minor order." Long before it was eliminated in 1971, it had become just a title conferred on seminarians. Yet, through all the centuries, every local church has entrusted its keys to dedicated members who served as porters, as janitors, or simply as the first one up in the morning.

Sacristans were listed by writers (Jerome, for example) and by church councils as "ministers of God." When recounting his life in the fourth century, Bishop Paulinus of Nola wrote, "I call the Lord to witness that I longed to begin my holy service with the name and office of sacristan." *(Epistle 1)*

Such holy service is suggested by several stories told in the sixth century by Pope Gregory the Great *(Dialogues* 1 and 3). They sketch out examples of sacristans privileged to work in the midst of a sacred people on Sunday, and in the places of celebration and burial throughout the week. Holy sacristans are also cited as healers and wonder workers. Constantius of Ancona was known far and wide as a pious man. When the supply of oil for the lamps ran out, he took water, poured some into the lamps, fixed the wicks and lit them as usual. They all began to burn as if they were fueled by oil. As Gregory noted, "Try to imagine now how great must have been the merits of the man who could change the nature of a physical element." Acontius is also said to have healed a girl who was paralyzed. In our rationalist times, we tend to be embarrassed by such stories, explaining them away. But the evidence of the early centuries tells of sacristans' holiness and of their work in relationship to the entire body of the faithful.

While taking great care to stress the holy nature of this work, leaders of the churches also passed on detailed lists to describe the practical work of sacristans. Isidore of Seville (seventh century) described the ministry as the care of security, access, vestments, sacred vessels, codices, oil, lamps and candles.

Sacristans, bishops and builders found various systems for organizing these materials and the rooms in which they were kept. A wide range of local names was used for these sacristies, often reflecting the particular items that were kept there. Rooms that held liturgical vessels and the elements for the eucharist were often called treasuries—a name that conveys the esteem in which the eucharist was held, not just the value of any precious metals that might have been kept there. Churches in some regions contained rooms equipped to store and distribute gifts (clothing and food, for example) to the poor. Such social services were deemed highly appropriate for a liturgical space, and the rooms took on names equivalent to "service center." Separate sacristies (or portions of rooms) were set aside for vesting and became known as vestries. Still other zones, separate rooms or not, were established for the reservation of sacred objects (especially the eucharist for the sick and the holy oils). Before Christians ever began to use tabernacles in the main worship hall, the eucharist was reserved in the sacristy.

One such system for organizing the sacristies is known from seventh-century Constantinople. The Great Entrance (presentation of gifts) was a full and grand procession with bread and wine. Leaving a separate treasury building where the vessels were stored, the procession moved to and then through the assembly area of the church. The faithful were not lined up in pews; commentaries from that time describe them surging toward the arriving gift-bearers and then processing with them. This dramatic entrance, movement and interaction with the assembly would be replaced in the medieval period by a brief appearance of the gifts as they were transferred to the altar table from a newly constructed sacristy (called a *prothesis)* next to the altar. The transfer of the side chamber, from a separate building to a zone right by the altar, signalled the end of participatory processions as well as a growing clericalization or privatization of the eucharistic liturgy (Thomas Mathews, *The Early Churches of Constantinople: Architecture and Liturgy,* Penn State, 1971).

Middle Ages

In the Eastern churches, it was fairly standard practice to have two sacristies. On one side of the altar was a *prothesis* for the preparation of eucharistic elements; on the other side of the altar was a *diaconicon* for vesting and the storage of oil lamps and the like. Two separate rooms also became the custom in Western churches. One was for the clergy (with vestments and eucharistic vessels), the other for items tended by sacristans and other ministers (candles, flowers, incense).

In the eleventh century, a man by the name of Guy became sacristan in Anderlecht, a district of Brussels. His zeal for the care of the place for worship was so great that he was memorialized as a saint and as patron of sacristans. A remarkable number of legends about him grew up and spread. They tell us little about his humble life, but a lot about the esteem with which sacristans continued to be held. The descriptions of his work and documents of that era indicate an important shift in the way that the role of sacristans was perceived. More and more, their role was being confined to the sanctuary section of the church complex. The sacristans' work was viewed more as a service to the clergy than to the whole assembly, and the rites were becoming more and more standardized.

Before and After the Council of Trent

The Middle Ages, the Renaissance, and the reformations of the sixteenth century are not remembered with great fondness by liturgists. By then, liturgical actions had shriveled, and the liturgy itself was largely a pageant of clerics. As "low" Mass became the norm, the celebration was often colorless. After the Council of Trent in the sixteenth century, liturgies with minimal involvement of the faithful were codified and made even more universally standard. For hundreds of years before and then for hundreds of years after that council, sacristans served the clergy and the sanctuary with lists that were virtually the same in Madrid, Paris, London, and in the American colonies.

By the time Christianity was brought to this continent, Catholics of the West (and other Christians who kept eucharistic rites after the Reformation) were familiar with two sacristies. All but the tiniest chapels had one room for vessels and vestments, another for candles, vases and servers' robes. The first room was called, variously, the "priests' sacristy," the "secretarium," the "vestry" or the "sacristy." The second room, usually on the other side of the sanctuary, was the "servers' sacristy," the "second sacristy" or the "work sacristy."

Sacristies near the altar facilitated the changing of altar cloths and the provisioning of the credence table. This placement also worked with the minimalistic liturgical practices of the era—"processions" that just popped out from sacristy to altar steps, a sense that the clergy rather than the assembly were the beneficiaries of sacristy work, a sense that all of the sacred actions were unfolding at one end of the building screened off by a communion railing. Liturgists of old accepted this placement of the two sacristies. One of the very few improvements they fostered was the provision of separate doors from the assembly area and from the exterior to the sacristies so that no one would need to pass through the sanctuary on the way to the sacristy.

The Decades before Vatican II

Many scholars and pastoral ministers formed a liturgical movement in the decades before the pontificate of John XXIII (1958-1963). They shared new research and fresh appreciation of the liturgical heritage. Patristics experts produced definitive editions of ancient liturgical texts and homilies; scriptural scholars adopted new methods of critical research; theologians began formulating a vision of church that was more community-centered; pastors and catechists discovered the power of the liturgical year in structuring domestic prayer and religious education; daring pioneers envisioned a liturgy in the languages of the people; activists saw the power of the liturgy for reshaping the world. These were but a few of the trends in the air. They signaled that well before Vatican II many leaders within the church had already agreed on the need for reforms.

In terms of the environment for worship, pioneering scholars and pastors of the liturgical movement highlighted the material forms of the community's interaction. They fostered participatory ceremony, art that followed the canons of beauty and liturgy, and the use of vesture and vessels that truly facilitated the "sacred action" of the church.

Among the most progressive activists were church architects, especially in Europe during the rebuilding of cities after World War II. It was as if some architects saw the future and called the rest of the church to it. They designed spaces for "Mass facing the people" before most even heard of it. They foresaw the end of communion rails, the end of tabernacles on center altars, the end of side altars for devotions, the end of bird-bath-sized fonts. They embraced modern art, new technologies, an appreciation of the active assembly undivided by pillars and screens, and an aesthetic that preferred simplicity to gratuitous ornamentation.

Vatican II and the End of the Twentieth Century

Pope John XXIII was certainly mindful of the reform movements when he called the Second Vatican Council. Neither he nor any observer could have failed to notice the new and daring church architecture that had appeared in his diocese of Venice and in post-war France (where he was nuncio), not to mention in dioceses all over Europe. As Roman preparatory commissions sought out agenda items and drafted documents for the council, leaders of the liturgical movement became active in their diocesan offices and at the Vatican. Progressive liturgists were appointed as experts to the bishops; the architects with the new ideas were also heard, as new norms for church buildings were debated. The council itself only formulated the call to reform and its broad parameters. The actual reforms were left to Vatican commissions.

No document was issued then, or since, outlining the rearrangement of sacristies for the reformed rites. But implications can be drawn from the official liturgical books. Most notably, the *General Instruction of the Roman Missal* contains several sections on vesture, vessels and other artifacts that relate directly to the work of sacristans. In and between the lines of these books, and in the currents of change that are often a step ahead of the documents, sacristans are finding both reform and invention.

The reforms are substantive, marking a return to the fullness of texts, ceremonial, and participation that seemed to mark the earliest church. Sacristy work is seen as a service to the whole temple of living stones and to the whole church complex. The role is once more described in the terms of ministry and holiness. With all of the changes, it is no wonder that the quality of liturgical practice varies. In certain areas, the idiosyncratic interpretation of one bureaucrat or liturgist has set the pace. In other places, broadly based programs of education and power-sharing have allowed for the implementation of the post-conciliar reforms in a much fuller way. Thus, we are at an exciting moment in the history of sacristies. Now that the rites have been reformed, certain directions seem clear and we are able to figure out the kind of setup that works best in each place. While absolutes are few, we do have some pretty clear directions to pursue. For them we can thank the architects who led the way after World War II, the liturgists who have attended to the impact of the new rites on our buildings, and the artists and sacristans who have contributed to the church-wide discernment.

Through the shifting forms of rites over the centuries, sacristans have always responded to their communities' needs—securing and cleaning meeting places, setting up and maintaining proper materials, providing images and decorations. Despite the paucity of historical stories about this ministry, the few that we have bespeak the holiness found through the performance of these tasks. This is one job in the church that puts to rest the foolish thought that spirituality rises as attention to the physical or material diminishes. It is precisely in these everyday, practical concerns where you will find the holiness of Christian people. Sacristans do not need time off from their work to find God. They need the insight to find God in the very act of preparing the way for public prayer.

The Current Position of Sacristies within the Church Complex

The word "church" has come to mean the place in which we celebrate the eucharist. But it also can refer to other areas within the building, as well as to other buildings on the parish property. That is why this manual uses on occasion the more precise, if unusual, term "place of eucharistic action." We need to see the meeting place of the parish as a network of spaces—assembly hall, baptistry, sacristy, chapel for the reservation of the eucharist, meeting rooms, reconciliation chapel, social hall, shrines, and so much more. In like manner, planners and sacristans need to think through the ways that the various spaces and their functions interact. For symbolic reasons, is the reconciliation area near the font? Do the baptistry and entranceway relate to each other? In terms of the Sunday liturgies, do the areas for vesting promote a full processional entrance? Are the musical leaders and instrumentalists in a place that allows them to be leaders rather than soloists?

Shifts in vocabulary are both important and inevitable. A few decades ago, the terms "epistle side" and "gospel side" were commonly understood. With our current furniture and ceremonial, these designations have disappeared about as quickly as maniples. Other familiar distinctions will have little meaning in the future. Within contemporary assembly places, especially those with circular forms, terms like "right and left" or "front and rear" are of little or no use. In some cases, there might be several terms that would accurately describe an area of a church building. For example, the lobby could be called the narthex, the vestibule, the commons, the gathering place or the entranceway. As for terms in this manual, some may appear strange, owing to regional or academic differences. They should become clear in their context.

Current Division into Two Sacristies

We inherited church buildings with two sacristies, usually located on either side of the sanctuary. We can still use two sacristies, but with a different division of materials and perhaps new locations. On this matter, the *Ceremonial of Bishops,* issued by the Vatican for the bishop's liturgies, is quite applicable to all parish churches:

> The cathedral church should have a *vesting room,* that is, a suitable place, as close as possible to the church entrance, where the bishop, concelebrants, and ministers can put on their liturgical vestments and from which the entrance procession can begin. The sacristy, which should normally be separate from the vesting room, is a room where vestments and other liturgical materials are kept. . . . (#53)

One simplification of this scheme for parishes is to store the vesture in the vesting room itself. This is the "ideal" form of two sacristies that will orient the advice contained in this manual. It will not be possible everywhere, but there is a surprising number of places where it can be done.

Note that the vesting room is placed close to the entrance, so that processions (and greetings) are facilitated. Besides these benefits for Sunday Masses, imagine the ease with which mourners and the remains of the deceased might be greeted at the entry. Consider how the full greeting at the door of bride and groom will unfold without peeking through the sacristy door and peering down the nave of the church.

The functions of the two support-rooms should no longer be divided between clergy in one sacristy and servers in the other. The vessels do not need to be in the room of the clergy, with the flower vases in the lesser sacristy. Now the division of materials is related to the rooms' functions within the building complex. The ordained and all of the other ministers who vest can do so in the one vesting area, forming processions together. The eucharistic vessels and all of the other materials needed for good liturgy can be maintained together elsewhere, closer to where they are used.

3◆ The Sacristan

Ministry in the Sacristy

Whether or not there is a person bearing the title of sacristan, many things need to be done before liturgy can take place. The building must be opened and lit, cleaned and decorated for the feast. Bread and wine must be in place, vessels and vestments available, books and candles set out.

The ordained ministers often do some of this work. The lectors, acolytes, ushers and eucharistic ministers usually have responsibilities for making ready the materials that they themselves use. Other individuals and groups that might be involved include sextons, janitors, altar guilds, liturgy committees, decorators and members of the pastoral staff. In parishes with a large number of volunteers, a great number of members may be involved in the work of the sacristy. In these parishes, good communication is required to make sure that all the tasks, performed by so many, will be done well. To make sure this happens, the pastor or liturgist will need to provide overall supervision and support. Individuals and groups need to be given clear mandates and power to do the varied tasks. In most cases, this work will be enhanced by designating a sacristan, who will assure continuity and accountability in the performance of these tasks and will train new volunteers.

Other parishes, especially smaller ones, follow other models for the accomplishment of sacristy-related chores. Even in the smallest liturgical community, however, it's a good idea to have someone other than the priest undertake this ministry. The assembly needs to appreciate that the gathering and the tasks leading up to it are holy duties for the whole community, not just quick visits to get what the pastor has prepared.

Job Description for Sacristans

1. *Supervise the calendar.* There can be only one master calendar, with definite rules that specify who can add an event to it, who can commit facilities and personnel. Local festivals need to be added early so that their

hours will be kept clear of other events. Optional memorials need to be selected, and certain restrictions need to be set up far in advance (for example, clear rules against booking weddings during the Easter Triduum). During the course of the year, procedures for booking funerals and other last-minute events need to be made clear and then followed by all concerned.

2. *Prepare specific seasons and liturgies.* Sacristans should prepare for planning meetings by reviewing the liturgical texts and options, by reviewing previous years' files, and by noting sacristy-related questions. At these meetings sacristans will note any objects that need to be borrowed or purchased. After the meetings, they will prepare lists of things that the parish will need in order to perform the agreed-upon ritual. They will prepare all of the objects that will facilitate the celebration.

3. *Establish standard operating procedures.* Sacristans, in collaboration with presiders and committees, should negotiate a clear flow chart of responsibilities for the daily and weekly operation of the sacristy.

4. *Maintain the church complex.* Every part of the building (including the exterior) needs regular maintenance and cleaning. The sacristan might well be the one to enlist volunteers for this and negotiate the responsibilities of a custodian in relationship to other ministers.

5. *Prepare liturgical materials.* The lectionary, the sacramentary or other ritual books need to be set up (with any previously-agreed choices marked). Locally-prepared texts such as the intercessions need to be available. Vestments, vessels and other materials need to be maintained, cleaned or replaced as necessary, and set up for each rite.

6. *Maintain images and decorations.* Permanent and seasonal images need maintenance and cleaning. Either sacristans or another group of volunteers need to plan and care for flowers or other seasonal decorations. Whenever flowers are brought into the church complex, responsibility needs to be taken for their watering and disposal.

7. *Take inventory.* Sacristans set up and supervise the regular replenishment of materials like wine, bread, candles, charcoal. They procure annual items like palms and the paschal candle. Every few years, they take an inventory of church property. This might include a review of insurance policies, appraisals of old objects, and setting priorities for acquiring new things or replacement items.

8. *Minister at major liturgies.* All involved need to know who will be present at each given liturgy to assure the proper flow of work. Responsibilities include the opening and closing of facilities, setting up objects, welcoming other ministers, participating in certain parts of the rite (ringing bells from the tower or lighting new charcoal at various points of a Mass) and returning all objects to their proper place after a liturgy.

9. *Perform other administrative duties.* Prepare budgets, participate in the drafting of visitation reports, and attend certain meetings of the pastoral staff or parish pastoral council.

Close Collaboration

When members of a parish volunteer for the first time, especially when they enter into committee-based deliberations, they are often surprised at the tension and discord that exist at the heart of the parish, even when the sacred rites are involved. Good pastoral leaders make the lessening of tension one of their highest priorities. Yet the church will continue to deal with life-and-death issues, with symbols that are central to faith. These are never easy to negotiate. Friction and emotion are guaranteed. We must resist the temptation to pine away for a perfect church where all tensions are resolved. It is better to find God in the actual local church. Our communion is not often marked by passive tranquility; our love is measured by the amount of tension it can stand. Within a community of frail and holy ones, sacristans need to relate to these specific groups:

PARISH MEMBERSHIP: Sacristans serve the entire assembly. This relationship should never become a them-and-us division, with parishioners considered a force outside there somewhere.

PASTORS: Pastors serve as coordinators of the various ministries, reducing tensions or directing them to healthy and holy ends. Earlier in this century, the priest was the only one who mattered to the sacristan. The priest celebrated the liturgies in his own style, outfitted the church complex according to his own designs, and generally made all of the decisions. That model of leadership was continued by some "new wave" priests, who made up the rites as they went along, according to their own desires of the moment. Priests and sacristans need to see beyond themselves and adhere to the advice of the *General Instruction of the Roman Missal* (#313): "The priest should consider the general spiritual good of the assembly rather than his personal outlook."

PASTORAL STAFF: Larger churches benefit from the work of other leaders—education directors, liturgists, musicians, social activists, counselors and others. Depending on local custom and personal preferences, a person in charge of a given area might bear the title of "minister," "director" or "coordinator." Lutherans or Episcopalians will find in this and other sections of this book equivalent titles in their own traditions. If there is a parish liturgist, then she or he is the liaison with the sacristan. The sacristan and all of these ministers must have full and open communication with one another.

PARISH COMMITTEES: Most parishes have a parish pastoral council and a finance committee. Sacristans might attend some of these meetings, but most of their "committee time" should be invested with the liturgy committee. There are no hard and fast rules in place for liturgy committees. They may plan every major liturgy in great detail or they may simply supervise the standard operating procedures. Sacristans have an important role here, especially when budgets and difficult decisions are under discussion. Sacristans also should work closely with building committees to ensure that the church complex is not only well maintained, but that it also functions efficiently as a liturgical site.

ACOLYTES OR SERVERS: Acolytes or servers are the traditional allies of sacristans. For centuries, they have passed on traditions about how to set up wine and water, how to fix wicks and otherwise deal with candles, and how to get the maximum smoke from a parish's thurible. The work of these individuals and that of others who prepare the symbols and artifacts of ritual is supervised by sacristans. Because sacristans and acolytes work together so closely, they must necessarily have great respect for one another. When a parish draws its servers only from the earliest grades of elementary school, some of this collaboration is limited by the inability of the children to interact maturely with the greatest symbols of our rites. Nevertheless, sacristans can be patient and firm educators in the proper decorum and respect that children can show toward the public action of the parish assembly.

OTHER MINISTERS: Other ministers have roles in preparing for Sunday eucharist. Musicians often take care of their area of the church as well as the microphones. Lectors often set up the lectionary. Eucharistic ministers sometimes set up the various patens and chalices (and clean them afterward). Ushers often assume a great deal of responsibility—opening and closing parts of the complex, setting out materials, preparing the assembly area before people arrive. The roles of these individuals should be understood by all involved, and be subject to periodic evaluation and reform.

SEXTON OR CUSTODIAN: Whatever the title, a church complex can benefit greatly if the budget will sustain such a position. Parishes with both sacristans and janitors have always had to define territories for the two. It would seem incorrect in the reformed liturgy to have the sacristan do everything in the sanctuary, the janitor everything in all of the other zones. A better division might be more along these lines: The sacristan takes responsibility for all liturgical items; the janitor takes responsibility for the physical maintenance of the church complex.

ALTAR GUILDS AND OTHER VOLUNTEER GROUPS: Under this heading, or that of tabernacle societies, church members have been volunteering for centuries. Clear guidelines need to be established and maintained to ensure that the members of such a group not only contribute to the liturgical life of the parish, but that they also take satisfaction in their roles. In parishes where these groups do not exist, sacristans might set up new groups of dedicated volunteers. Rather than calling them "altar" or "tabernacle" societies, titles that relate more closely to their work might be chosen instead. For example, some might act as "environment ministers," seeing to the proper use and placement of church decor and furnishings. Others in this general category might work on seasonal or festival decorations—flowers, outdoor luminarias and the like. Still others, perhaps under the heading of "housekeeping" or "maintenance volunteers," might clean the church complex on a regular basis. A "textile" or "vestment" group might take care of the vestments (cleaning and repair) or the linens (laundry and ironing). The list could go on and on—bread bakers and candle makers to name but two more.

DECORATORS: Some parishes have formed "environment and art committees" or have otherwise deputed certain individuals as decorators for the parish. These, too, would be expected to work closely with the sacristan.

ARTISTS AND ARTISANS: In procuring new materials, the first source considered should be artists and artisans who are members of the parish. The benefits of such collaboration are great, but not so great that inferior work should be commissioned or accepted. This can lead, at times, to awkward situations. For example, what if the person sitting in the second row makes a new but ugly altar cloth and it is never used? Situations of this kind have caused some pastors to retreat to the pages of commercial church goods stores, rather than risk offending a parishioner whose heart is in the right place, but whose skills fall short. That's unfortunate, because problems of this kind can be avoided by establishing a careful process of research, evaluation and commissioning.

VISITORS: This special category of persons should be close to the heart of every sacristan. Visitors should be welcomed during off hours and given tours of the sacristy and church complex. School groups, and especially middle-grade children, love to explore the recesses of the sacristy, gaining wonderful insights into the richness of the liturgical tradition. By making these opportunities available, sacristans can help to enhance the participation of these children at liturgy.

VENDORS: Thousands of activists throughout America participated in the liturgical movement prior to 1963. With their colleagues in other countries, they declared a sort of holy war against the monopoly of Latin, against rites that had become encrusted with too many secondary elements—and against the purveyors of church goods that flooded sanctuaries with cheap materials and "pious rubbish." At Vatican II and in the reforms thereafter, they won all of these battles, except the last one. To this day, some church goods companies still know little of the liturgy and less about art, as the items they sell continue to demonstrate.

Artists and artisans, bread bakers and candle makers, either from the parish or the local community, should be the primary sources of materials. Some needs can be met by shopping wisely in nearby towns and at retail outlets other than those that specialize in church goods. Fine cruets, for example, often can be found in such retail outlets. For certain items, however, a general church goods catalog may be utilized—for example, when purchasing fine liturgical linens. Other items, like wine and regular candles, might be procured on a sort of standing order once a good choice of source has been made. In general, the specialized catalogs of vestment makers and vessel artisans are better sources of quality items than are the general catalogs that offer everything. In no case should a catalog be used to purchase the major art and furnishings of the church complex.

DIOCESE: The sacristan's relationship with the diocese normally will be centered around the worship office or liturgical commission of the diocese. These entities can be enormously important to sacristans, because they usually have lists of reliable local purveyors. They also often sponsor workshops and consultation services.

CIVIL AUTHORITIES: Either sacristan or pastor will, on occasion, need to go before various offices and boards. In some localities, permits are often needed for outdoor fires, as at the Easter Vigil, as well as for street processions and outdoor sound systems (even when they're on church property). Codes also may govern the use of candles, straw in mangers and cut Christmas trees. If decorations will cut across walkways, the legal egress specifications should be consulted.

Attention to these kinds of things not only can lessen the risk of injury to persons, but also can reduce the potential legal liability of the parish, an important consideration in the increasingly litigious times in which we live. At the same time, if civil officials and the codes they administer seem unduly restrictive, then sacristans and pastors should be prepared to do some negotiating. This can be done by, or in consultation with, diocesan personnel or local lawyers.

Qualifications

Those who coordinate the ministries of a parish need to take the role of sacristan seriously and have clear ideas about the kinds of persons they will engage to assist them in this work. Here are some qualifications:

1. We need sacristans who are regular and alert communicants, women and men who sing with gusto and throw themselves into the liturgical actions. From such regular participation, they should be attuned to the flow of seasons and of rites. What they do not know in the area of vocabulary and sacristy practice, they should be able to learn.

2. Complementing this dedication to the liturgy, sacristans must be zealous in their commitment to fostering the growth of the local church. This happens through the setting up of liturgical elements, but also through the sharing of responsibilities with children and adults, the friendly supervision of all aspects of the work. With the gifts of all members so central to the vitality of the church, the days when a sacristan could claim the sacristy as a personal fiefdom are long gone.

3. Sacristans should be free to work at the highest festivals. Prospective volunteers and paid sacristans must plan their schedules around the long hours of the Easter Triduum. They will be needed on Christmas, as well as on days such as New Year's, Ash Wednesday and Thanksgiving.

4. Sacristans may be of any age and either gender. All that counts is the ability to perform and enjoy the tasks. The role of sacristan was once reserved to the ordained. By this century, it had been taken over mostly by women—boys were servers and girls were junior sacristans. Now all are welcome—young and old, male and female—and the diversity of our individual gifts brings fresh approaches to this work. Parishes that engage large numbers of volunteers in such projects as decorating for Christmas and Easter will want to include whole households.

In-Service Training

LOCAL READING AND DISCUSSION: Sacristy volunteers, liturgy committees, or groupings of all the liturgical ministers should spend a considerable part of their donated time learning more about the liturgical heritage. Some of the topics might be:

1. History of the liturgical reforms of this century or a general history of liturgy, using published commentaries.

2. The rites used in a parish, with study materials from the official ritual books. Use the introductions at the chapter headings along with an outline of the rites or a sampling of the texts themselves. The Mass can be studied with its *General Instruction.* The liturgy of the hours, initiation, funerals, pastoral care of the sick, penance, marriage and blessings frame a parish's life and should be studied in turn over the years.

3. The central furnishings and symbols of our liturgy. The church building itself and the altar can be studied by using the dedication rite. The actual local church complex can be studied using printed copies of the homily and press reports at its dedication, anniversary books and archive copies of parish bulletins. The baptistry, oils, chair, ambo, tabernacle, reconciliation area, doors, bells, chalice and paten can be studied using their respective chapters in the *Book of Blessings.*

4. Images of the church complex. Use the introduction and blessing texts at chapter 36 of the *Book of Blessings.* The cross, stations of the cross, Advent wreath, Christmas tree, and manger can be studied along with their own blessing rites. Liturgical arts in general can be studied from modern commentaries. Studies on the name of the church (saint or title of the Lord) will yield ideas about existing or future images.

5. The liturgical year. The general norms, printed in the sacramentary, can be supplemented by other articles. If parish leaders do not have such sources at hand, call the diocesan worship office.

FORMAL INSTRUCTION: Beyond local discussions, training can take place in several venues. The diocese or region may have occasional classes or workshops on the liturgy; the parish budget should allow for an ample number of ministers to participate in these programs. Art museums usually have art history classes that shed light on the evolution of liturgical art. Programs of continuing education in one's own city or town should be reviewed for worthwhile classes. These are often the best places to learn the technical side of sacristy work: the care of materials found in sacristies, floral arrangements and interior design.

VISITING: Even if there is little time given to group education at the parish level, even if the formal classes of a particular region are few and far between, people's love of travel should provide a final and fruitful arena for training. Alone or in groups, sacristy workers should visit other churches (especially ones recommended by the diocesan office). By means of these trips, sacristans can see good renovation and construction work, along with creative alignments of furniture. Most of all, a visit to another environment fosters fresh insights into the relationship of the various parts of the church and the dynamics of liturgy. The local cathedral should be a model of such liturgical fullness. Even if it is not, a visit there will allow some items to be seen in their unique setting, such as the bishop's chair and the repository of oils for the entire diocese. Often, the art of the cathedral reveals much about the history of the diocese, as well as that of the region.

Two very specific types of visits are available to those who live near or in our largest urban areas. Art museums with medieval collections have "church treasuries." Visits to such places, complemented by readings suggested by education departments, can imbue ministers with a sense of the richness of our heritage and offer clues to the evolution of the rites we celebrate today. Some few places have wonderful museums that feature liturgical items from our American heritage. Some examples are the Spanish missions of the West and Southwest, St. Augustine, New Orleans, the diocesan museums of Quebec and Montreal, the earliest churches of Philadelphia, and the sanctoral shrines of American saints such as at Emmitsburg and Auriesville. It is no exaggeration to say that in traveling to these places we are seeking ways to prepare for the holy city that is to come.

4◆ Sacred Mysteries and Liturgical Art

The Local Church

The unique characteristics of the local church should guide sacristans and decorators in every part of the church complex. There are several ways to appreciate each church's character.

1. *The assembly:* The architecture and interior of the building are usually related to the kind of community that uses the building. In this manual, unless otherwise specified, the focus will be on parish church sacristies. Because of this, sacristans who work in other worship environments—convent chapels, monastic churches, campus centers and urban "chapels of convenience"—may have to adapt some of the ideas found in this manual to their specific circumstances. The number of sacraments and rites observed in a given chapel will vary as well. For example, the rites of initiation and marriage are performed regularly in the typical parish, but very seldom in the other worship environments mentioned.

One parish church in each diocese is designated as the place for the bishop's chair (cathedra). In many dioceses, this church serves as the liturgical model for the other parishes (cf. *Ceremonial of Bishops,* #46). The questions specific to these centers of diocesan ministry will be handled in this manual under such headings as the Chrism Mass and ordinations. In dioceses where such episcopal liturgies occur outside the cathedral, these notes should help the parish sacristans involved in preparations. Some parishes and some non-parochial worship sites are visited by large groups of pilgrims during the year. Such transient groups, with their size and devotional interests, present special tasks for sacristans. Though some special accommodations may need to be made, liturgical principles should never be compromised. (Some of the more renowned of these centers, after proving to the Roman authorities that their liturgies are exemplary in the fullness of participation and that their artistic quality is revered, have received the honorific title of "minor basilica"—a confusing term unrelated to the basilican style of architecture.)

2. *The title of the church:* This is another factor that will specify some of the work in the sacristy. Churches can be named after the Trinity, the Holy Spirit, Christ (invoked according to a mystery of his life or a title in the liturgy, such as the Triumph of the Cross), one of the angels, Mary (according to an appellation already in the liturgy), or one of the other saints *(Dedication of a Church,* #4). The rather unfamiliar term of "titular" is used here, avoiding the imprecise term "patron." (The Holy Spirit and the Holy Cross, for example, are not patrons.) The title has implications for the calendar (the annual solemnity for the local titular) and for decorations.

3. *The age of the church building:* The treasures sometimes discovered in the sacristies of old churches would amaze many finance committees. Sadly, because of ignorance or carelessness, many valuable objects have been discarded over the past few decades. As custodians of the materials in a church, sacristans should discard old objects only after consulting reputable experts, such as preservationists or museum curators. Nothing should ever be sold or given away until its value and historical significance have been ascertained.

4. *Architectural style:* The exterior style, the architectural shape and the interior decoration of a church edifice should have an enormous influence on the work of sacristans and other environmental ministers. Throughout this manual, the parish church will be referred to as a complex of spaces or areas. Even in a tiny chapel, the place of reserving the eucharist should be perceived as a separate zone from the altar itself. Sacristans need to consider how each chapel, room and hallway is decorated and how it serves the particular action for which it was designed. Further, we need to see how each place is connected to the other places, and how real people, whether at Sunday Mass or at a wedding or funeral, move between the places. Even if the areas of word (ambo) and eucharist (altar) are only a few feet away, we still need to know how each looks and how each is used.

Sacred Mysteries

We must prepare the church complex for the sacred mysteries. But there are different mysteries. Some "new age" followers and progressive decorators have embraced new styles but have kept an unfortunate notion of mystery. In an attempt to foster an experience of "mystery" or the "Mysterious One," they play with windows and lights, shadows and surfaces, framing the liturgical furniture in hushed and secret and "mysterious" zones. Or they devise an elaborate display of symbols that flow from a given day's gospel passage. The congregation is awed and attentive, impressed and edified, enveloped in a hushed atmosphere. For many others, the same effects can be produced by a church that is merely quiet, well-decorated and filled with the smell of yesterday's incense.

From the start, when pagans held to a sense of mystery that was atmospheric and unintelligible, Christians have held that mystery is not an atmosphere but a sacred reality, the paschal mystery. We are engaged in these sacred mysteries. In Christ, the assembly does the actions that are our mystery.

Preparing for the sacred mysteries is not a matter of atmospherics, but of enabling ritual actions, the action of the holy assembly in Christ. The arts foster the sacred mysteries of Christian liturgy when they empower a congregation to be a truly active assembly, when they entice all present to move with the rites from word to eucharist, or from word to font, or from the funeral eucharist to the place of committal.

These actions embrace the material world and images and elements like bread and wine, fire and water. Unlike those who denigrate the senses and consider the spiritual to be apart from the world, we find our holiness incarnated. Differing with those who think that beauty softens or corrupts, we find in beauty our very identity—in and through words, actions, images and spaces that are beautiful. When we come to know every zone of liturgical action, when we discover the unique life of this local church, then we are prepared to celebrate the sacred mysteries.

Art for the Sacred Mysteries

Before considering the varied parts of the church complex, we can consider the arts that serve the sacred mysteries throughout the building. Sacristans are often called upon to be the chief decorators for seasons and feasts. At the very least, they must keep in close communication with separate planning groups for the environment and decorations. After the permanent, seasonal, or feast-day images or flowers are set up, sacristans are usually in charge of maintaining, cleaning or watering them. Throughout all phases of the decoration/design process, sacristans should be advocates for arts that enhance the liturgical action.

DISTINCT FORM OF ART: As wise commentators have been saying for centuries, there are many works of religious art and many decorations that do not qualify as liturgical art. Just because a painting shows Jesus doesn't mean it's appropriate for the liturgy. Liturgical art is a distinct form of art. It is related in style, content, and placement to liturgical action.

By its presence in the given space (baptistry, eucharistic action hall, reconciliation chapel), a work of art must facilitate the action of that space. It also should express the ethos of the community's liturgical tradition. Lutheran churches should express the ethos of the Reformation. Roman or Latin rite churches should be decorated and served by art that is congruent with liturgical language and forms of the Roman rite. Over the centuries and in the current reforms, this has meant that Roman Catholic church buildings and artifacts should have an inherent beauty, be made from honest and natural materials, demonstrate a certain restraint of exuberance (so as not to overwhelm the actions) and avoid both private perspectives and gaudiness.

ANCIENT FORMS: Liturgical art is part of a long tradition. As our earliest Christian ancestors were sharing ritual practices in cities around the Mediterranean, and as these practices then spread to more distant frontiers, certain scriptures also were shared as the most appropriate for given days. Many images were shaped at that same time, often drawn from Jewish and pagan precedents. They came to adorn catacombs, cemeteries, eucharistic vessels, fonts and manuscripts. Just as the ritual outlines and assigned scriptures were passed on from generation to generation, so too were these formulas for images. Certain symbols and forms have come to bear particular emotions and meanings in our long heritage.

Liturgists of our own time have drawn on early Christian prayer texts and lectionary lists as important parts of the reform. This has not been motivated by mere antiquarianism, but by the need to recover the full tradition, by the need to see how rites looked before they were clericalized in the Middle Ages. In the same way, liturgical artists can draw upon the ancient images. But these earliest texts, rites and images have not been repeated as if by a photocopier. In every century, they have received fresh life from the technologies and tastes of the time. The lamb at Easter, the ox and ass at Christmas, the palm of martyrs, the great image of Jonah coming from the whale, the wondrous power of a tree of life—these are but a few of the ancient forms that have entered our subconscious, our literature, our folkways, our Western heritage. They sprang from our scriptures and liturgical actions, and they can continue to be the best way to decorate our holy places.

No one sacristan, whether new or experienced, can be expected to know all of the traditional forms and systems. Yet all are cordially invited to see and learn the treasured images of our faith. Just as in liturgy, the visual arts call us not to invent, but to enter into and interact with the pool of life-giving images that have come down to us from our rich tradition.

CURRENT NORMS: The standards set by our own official liturgical documents foster art forms flowering from and serving the liturgical action. In 1952, the Holy Office in the Vatican forbade "second-rate and stereotyped statues" (*AAS*, 44, p. 545). Vatican II, in its Constitution on the Liturgy (1963), called for the removal of all works of art that offend by "the deficiency, mediocrity, or sham in their artistic quality" (#124).

Environment and Art in Catholic Worship (1978), the justly popular and authoritative guide from our Bishops' Committee on the Liturgy, provides a fine summary of the demands made by liturgy on the arts (#19–23). There are two demands: the *quality* of genuine materials, a harmonious whole, a well-crafted work; and the *appropriateness* that is capable of bearing the awe and wonder in liturgy and that serves the ritual action.

ROOTED IN LITURGICAL ACTION: In 1963, Daniel Berrigan was characteristically prophetic as he commented on arts and the liturgy:

> With regard to the past, it would serve no real purpose here to detail the centuries of vapid, dissociate art which we are in the process of disowning. Since the late middle ages, religious art has been largely and progressively shunted to the studio and drawing room; it has become the adjunct of the prie-dieu, instead of the impassioned flowering of a public, virile, and believing mind. . . . If it served for anything, it was only to heal over the wounds by which Christians were marked, the wounds of their amputation from their greatest possessions, the altar and the word of God. . . . Since the fourteenth century, the Western Christian community has been quite simply ill—not irrecoverably, but still seriously; and its religious art is the syndrome of its illness. . . . It was an art designed quite literally for the sick room. It kept alive Christian memories and hopes in a subjective, devotional way. But its cumulative effect was disastrous, because it beckoned (Christians) further and further into their sick reveries. It helped them forget that there had ever been realities like community, anamnesis, sanctuary action. ("The Spirit of Modern Sacred Art" in *Liturgy for the People*, edited by W. Leonard [Milwaukee: Bruce Publishers], 157)

His analysis followed in the tradition of the great commentators of this century's liturgical movement. Citing but two of the more obvious leaders, one can see their consistent cry for an end to vapid art and pious trash, a rooting of liturgical art in the communal traditions of word and altar, the actions of the sacred mysteries.

In 1930, E. A. Roulin wrote:

> Everybody knows the sort of use that is made of pennons, banners and flags on certain feastdays to decorate, or rather to uglify, our churches, even the best of them. . . . Our churches are not worthily decorated by masses of these cheap bannerets. It would be better to abolish all this trashy stuff and to limit ourselves to a couple of great pennons or flags of good shape and proportions and made of silk or damask. Our folk would soon learn to appreciate them and to prefer them to those countless gaudy objects that are really only suited for a country fair. *(Vestments and Vesture,* Newman, p. 289)

Ten years later, Martin Hellriegel addressed the first National Liturgical Week: "Pious rubbish must scrupulously be kept from the church as unworthy of the King of Ages, unworthy of his chosen and kingly priesthood." *(How Firm a Foundation: Voices of the Early Liturgical Movement,* edited by Kathleen Hughes [Chicago: LTP, 1990], 126)

Decorations and Iconographic Programs

PURPOSES OF IMAGES: The liturgical art form that has been discussed the most over the centuries is the representational image. Leaders and thinkers in the church have identified three purposes that representational images should serve (see the current *Book of Blessings,* #1258, 1293). Though you might think that ornamentation would be one of the three purposes, it is not; ornamentation purely for its own sake is not part of our liturgical tradition. The legitimate purposes of representational images are as follows:

1. *The formation of the faithful.* This might well be the most misunderstood reason for having images. Gregory the Great is often quoted referring to images as books for the illiterate. Later leaders called them the catechism of the unlettered. Gregory was not putting down the illiterate, but rather promoting the power and efficaciousness of images. In fact, images do teach people, and not just illiterate persons and children. From the smallest church building to the most exalted museum halls, images teach lessons of history, scripture, cultural differences and much more. We all need the education we receive from the careful viewing of artful images.

When looking at representations of the saints, for example, this instruction can be described as a calling to mind of the saints—their witness or example, the communion we share with them, the Lord whom they served. This purpose of viewing images is truly perpetual in its validity.

This educative function of images is misunderstood if phrased in too didactic a manner. In the fourth century, Augustine of Hippo used broader and more powerful phrases when he wrote that liturgical elements shape our hopes and desires, motivate us to transform the world and seek the city that is to come. In 1948, in his important encyclical on the liturgy, Pius XII spoke of images in churches as stimulating the senses and drawing viewers to reform *(Mediator Dei,* #167). When preparing images for churches, these are the kinds of effects we should be striving for.

2. *Assistance for memory.* This is quite similar to the formation function; the viewing of sanctoral images should always remind Christians of the communion of saints. In one sense, most of us have already been educated in this. All we need is a little prompting, a reminder from time to time that we are part of a broad communion. We have a holy past from which we spring, in which we grow, a holy future toward which we stretch.

3. *Facilitate veneration.* It is not enough to say that we stretch toward full communion with the saints in heaven. The future, the new Jerusalem, pulls us toward that great and holy end. It is not just our efforts, our education, our service to the poor; the fullness of justice and peace comes only from God. Images do not just decorate our places and form our personalities. They can draw us into a sense of the real power of God who is all in all. Through the centuries, we have not just learned lessons from what we have seen; to this day we can feel impelled to kneel in awe and wonder. Theologians and church councils have called this being pulled from the visible (form) to the invisible (the prototypes). The experience of powerful images is not magical; the response is an expression of our deep-seated veneration for the holy. When cynics laugh at people who treat images as if they were living, it is a measure of the critics' fear. When pious ones kiss, touch or place flowers before images, they are providing even further proof of the power of images for focusing prayers and desires.

In the Eastern churches, icons are an integral part of the liturgy. In the Roman church and in other Western churches, images are venerated but rarely incorporated into liturgical action—the veneration of the cross on Good Friday being the notable exception. In both East and West, though, people transact all manner of holy business in church complexes. Catechesis, social service and devout honoring of revered symbols are all part of the public work we do as people. They all form us in ways that lead to and from the liturgical banquet.

SIMPLIFICATION AND FOCUS: It is no secret that representational images and decorations in churches are fewer in number since Vatican II. In some regions, it would appear that we are in the midst of another iconoclastic era. To be sure, the reforms of these decades have called for simplification, but this should not be interpreted as a license to denigrate images or strip our churches bare of them. The reduction of images and their more careful placement are acknowledgements of their power and the concomitant need to keep them from drawing energy away from the sacred rites. The *General Instruction of the Roman Missal* says,

> In keeping with the church's very ancient tradition, it is lawful to set up in places of worship images of Christ, Mary, and the saints for veneration by the faithful. But there is need both to limit their number and to situate them in such a way that they do not distract the people's attention from the celebration. There is to be only one image of any one saint. In general, the devotion of the entire community is to be the criterion regarding images in the adornment and arrangement of a church." (#278)

This attitude, while specifically applied in this instruction to the eucharistic assembly area, permeates all of the rites and canon law. Thus, the other places in the complex—baptistry, reconciliation chapel, reservation of the eucharist chapel, entranceway—need to be clear in their focus, decorated with restraint and dignity. Where parishes elect to create a separate devotional area or shrine, this is never to be just a catch-all chamber for every image, ugly or beautiful, that the parish ever owned. In every corner of the community's house of divine praise, all elements of the environment must contribute to the sacred mysteries, to communal action.

OVERALL PROGRAM FOR DECORATIONS: Within each area of liturgical action, one should review all that is seen, all that creates ambience, all that hinders or facilitates the actual rites that unfold there. *Environment and Art in Catholic Worship* takes such an approach (#98–103). It suggests that sacristans and interior designers look at all of these elements: images in painting or sculpture, tapestries, cloth hangings, banners, other permanent or seasonal decorations, the furniture, objects used in the rites, flowers, plants, trees, and the very restricted use of symbols that identify particular cultures, groups or nations. (Manuals that were published before Vatican II made a distinction between decorations and images. The latter usually meant statues, but also included the altar crucifix. A more integrated view seems to be called for today.)

Planning, commissioning and installing images and decorations is not, for sacristans, a regular privilege. We are instead presented with buildings that are in place, painted or decorated, equipped with some permanent images, and we are already in the habit of using certain seasonal decorations. All of these amount to what our tradition calls the "iconographic program." Whether called this or called a "scheme of decoration," every church edifice has one. It is the total set of what is seen—the order in which forms and colors appear, the congruence or dissonance of shapes and textures with the liturgical actions, the attractiveness or lack thereof, the ways that the images appeal to us or repel us. Too often the program has evolved with little concern for the whole. Pastors or decorators add this or move that; other improvements may be put on hold indefinitely, or implemented with deliberate speed if a parish benefactor happens to be involved. This randomness is dangerous, because the iconographic program continually shapes and orders the church's memory.

Before any changes are made in an iconographic program, sacristans and decorators need to appreciate what surrounds and forms each liturgical zone at the present moment. Only after such an appraisal has been made should additions and changes be contemplated. And in considering such changes, we need to devote primary attention to the architectural surfaces that shelter the assembly, to the central artifacts and images of the liturgy—worthy cups and plates for the eucharist, a font of fine stone and dignified color, vestments and wall hangings of high quality fabric and rich color, a cross that the entire parish will cherish. There is still a place for images and temporary decorations such as flowers, but these are never as central to the liturgical space.

ARCHITECTURAL SURFACES AND PERMANENT DECORATIONS: The most important work of liturgical art is, of course, the building itself. It is the most obvious starting point for identifying the current program of design. Because decorations should relate to the architecture of the building, those who decorate the building, or any of its interior rooms and halls, need to know their building very well. Scale is very important. It would be a mistake, for example, to hang little wicker baskets of pansies from huge gothic pillars.

To know a building well means to be familiar with the full scope of rites that occur in a given space. This requires a careful review of the liturgical texts and ritual action that unfold in that particular area, whether it be the baptistry, the eucharistic reservation chapel, or the eucharistic assembly area itself. For example, colors, shapes and images placed in the baptistry should not overwhelm the brightness of the paschal candle or obscure a wall-mounted repository of holy oils. Our liturgical tradition draws strength from and is complemented by icons, sacred images, architectural forms and the liturgical furnishings themselves. No symbol brought in for a particular

"Mass theme," no pot of cut flowers should trivialize these all-important parts of the worship environment.

Knowing a building well also means knowing it surfaces—walls, supports, ceiling and floor. They either add to or subtract from the liturgical experience. Never are their effects neutral. Usually such surfaces must be "hard," able to sustain a lot of action, rather than soft carpets or acoustical tiles. Soft materials dull the acoustics and just as significantly dull the ambience of public interaction. The finishes for the architectural surfaces can let us know that they are there; we do not need every wall and every ceiling to be off-white. Exact specifications of color would best be determined in light of the architecture itself; stone and wood make different demands.

Lighting the Church Complex

Church lighting is normally handled by electricians and renovation committees, not by sacristans. There is another kind of lighting in churches, though; one that might be evoked by the rich word "illumination." The baptized carried candles and were called the "illuminated" by our earliest ancestors. Ever since, candles have been elements of our liturgical interaction—and the tending of lamps and candles has been an important part of the work of sacristans. Now, as in every century, the illumination of the liturgical space is essential to its decoration.

HISTORY OF CANDLES AND LAMPS: Long before Christianity, ritual candles were used at the Temple in Jerusalem and in the meetings of many other religious communities. They were used not only at night, but during the day as well. Night or day, the controlled fire of the wick flickered as an expression of religious emotions. Before the invention of matches, it was eminently practical to keep an "eternal" flame burning in places where candles were lit regularly. At places like the Jerusalem Temple this seems to have led to a ritual keeping and honoring of such a flame.

When Christians first began holding their meetings, those scheduled at night obviously were lit with some forms of oil lamps or groups of candles. One such occasion is described in the Acts of the Apostles (20:8). As Christian communities developed, the night was often marked by liturgical gatherings, principally the hours spent singing and praying in vigil before Sunday or an important assembly. By the third century, the lighting of the lamps at nightfall and its ritual form, the "lucernarium," gave rise to many beautiful prayers and hymns, some still present in our hymnals—*Phos hilaron,* for example.

Ritual candles and an eternal flame would have been familiar to first-century Christians, both at home and as a part of communal worship, and the same could be said of certain pagan groups. From inscriptions and drawings of the catacombs and ancient cemeteries and from extant homilies and commentaries, we know that two of the earliest uses of illumination in the liturgy were at tombs and in funeral processions, as well as other processions, such as when the gospel book was being carried. When the procession ended, the candles often were placed on floor-mounted stands. A stone inscription found at Aquileia (northeast Italy) shows some third-century Christians praying beside a lighted candle that rests on a floor stand not unlike many seen in modern churches.

The visions described in the Book of Revelation show how candles figured in the dream life and religious meanings of these earliest ancestors in faith (Revelation 1:12, 4:5, 11:4). The use of such primordial forces as fire was never just utilitarian; humans always have used fire to express their emotions, their desires for fullness and the power of life beyond. It was the same in early Christianity. They did not light candles only to be able to see or to create an attractive light. They interacted with these elements of illumination, carrying them in processions and thus forming what was called "liquid fire." They placed the flame by their beloved's tomb, passed light to the illuminated neophytes. In that interaction, they experienced the holy presence, the light of Christ, the joy that we so haltingly say that candles "signify."

The liturgy in later centuries was far less participatory. Members of the congregation saw liturgical fire and candles only from afar. By the late middle ages, the candles that once had graced processions were put on the altar. In the same era, when the eucharist reserved for the sick was moved into a tabernacle in the public prayer zone, a lamp was placed by it. Some commentators began confusing this with the eternal flame that predated matches; some even began to see this late addition as the primary light and identifying mark of Catholic places. As the distance grew, people treated candles as symbols to look at. By the number that were lighted, they were told what kind of Mass was about to be celebrated. Thus were people separated from the action; expressive elements evolved into didactic props.

Despite this impoverishment, many Catholic and Orthodox Christians continued to light devotional candles before statues and icons. While the actions were more individual than communal, they did (and still do) involve choosing a candle, lighting it, placing it before an image, and spending some time in veneration. After Vatican II, many reform-minded pastors did away with votive candles. This may have been a mistake, for the interaction between candles and people was genuine, and the votive candles were all they had left. No longer had they any real involvement with the primordial elements of ritual, with lucernarium lights held by all, with processions of liquid fire.

MATERIAL FOR CANDLES: The principal candles in liturgy were always made of beeswax, clean-burning and obviously a product of nature. When formulating allegorical lessons, commentators could say, "The pure wax extracted by bees from flowers symbolizes the pure flesh of Christ received from his Virgin Mother, the wick signifies the soul of Christ, and the flame represents his divinity." (A. J. Schulte in the 1907 *Catholic Encyclopedia* I, 347) In the decades before Vatican II, various forces caused the Vatican to mitigate this requirement. Exceptions were made for missionaries. For example, in 1850, because beeswax was unavailable in Oceania, the churches there were allowed to use sperm candles. In 1904, the requirement was further modified so that beeswax need constitute only a majority part of the candle. This quickly created a market for candles that were only 51 percent beeswax. In our current *General Instruction of the Roman Missal,* candles at liturgy are called for, but their material is no longer specified (#269). The Vatican authorities wrote in 1974 only that the material would have to provide a living flame without being smoky or noxious or staining altar cloths. Bishops in each country were free to make further specifications.

Over the two decades since the promulgation of these much more relaxed rules, vendors have been aggressively marketing noncandle products, plastic tubes filled with liquid. In 1984, the secretariat of the Bishops' Committee on the Liturgy warned against such imitations for use at the altar and as paschal candles. Their popularity, though, shows that some sacristans and pastors prefer this version of efficiency over natural and traditional elements. Whether called "candelas" or "liquid wax candles," whether their fuel comes from polyethylene squeeze bottles or sealed tin cartridges, even if called legitimate and worthy by vendors, they do not burn down and change shape. If they are used as paschal candles, they are not new each year. Nor can they mark the year's progress as they burn. They are not candles.

Meanwhile, candles of paraffin, molded stearine, or tallow have been used in liturgy along with beeswax. Sacristans should evaluate all of these options by setting up the various kinds, burning them, checking for smoke and smells. You'll pay more for 100 percent beeswax candles but they continue to come highly recommended because they burn so slowly and fragrantly. Whatever your choice, remember that candles are not merely utilitarian, not merely a way to satisfy a rule. They are a primal element in our interaction in sacred mysteries.

CURRENT USE AND PLACEMENT OF CANDLES: The reformed rites have simplified the numbers and placement of candles. As the reforms take root, the primitive use of candles in the processions of the whole assembly may be restored. Current norms and advice will be found in this book on the pages for the various places where candles are used and stored: in the assembly space (altar, page 51; walls, page 39; pews, page 41), in the baptistry (paschal candle, page 64; baptismal candles, page 66), in the chapel of reservation (page 78), in devotional areas (page 79), and in the sacristy (page 57).

Flowers as Liturgical Art

Flowers can be placed in any part of the edifice. Here are some general notes:

HISTORY: The first uses of flowers at liturgy were in the ancient cemeteries of our earliest ancestors in the faith. Like their neighbors of other religions, they buried their dead in garden settings. Even in those locales where catacombs were dug, the underground corridors and rooms seem to have been painted as gardens, and the land above was almost always a garden. Christians were quite explicit in linking garden settings and their belief in paradise. For example, Perpetua of Carthage, just before her martyrdom in 203, spoke of her paradisal vision,

> a great open space, like a garden, having rose-trees and all kinds of flowers. The height of the trees was like the height of a cypress, whose leaves sang without ceasing. We crossed on foot a place strewn with violets, where we found (those) who were burned alive in the same persecution. *(The Passion of Perpetua and Felicity,* #11)

The document was written soon after Perpetua and Felicity were martyred. It was read with the veneration usually reserved for the Bible itself, especially in the churches of north Africa. With the pervasive link between paradise and the garden, it is not at all surprising that the tombs of martyrs and revered heroes received floral embellishments on their feast days. Many historians note that when the eucharist began to be celebrated at these tombs, then flowers began to be used at rites other than funerals. The use of flowers in the places for liturgy, with or without tombs, may have sprung from a desire to express faith in paradise.

We have no ancient record of flowers being placed on the altar or in a pot before the ambo. On feast days, garlands may have been placed on walls and on columns throughout the building; the decoration of doorways and other architectural surfaces proclaimed the festival of paradise. On some of these same feasts and for certain rites, flowers or herbs were strewn on pathways of special importance. In all of the ancient accounts, we can recognize the appeal to the senses. Like our ancestors, we value the brilliance and visual power of flowers and plants. Unlike them, we tend to forget the power of scent. Venatius Fortunatus, an important hymn composer (sixth century), proclaimed that flowers in the liturgy had more scent than incense itself.

Redolent of paradise, flowers and herbs were used throughout church complexes over the later centuries, but they were never at the altar. Aside from their use around tombs, they were an architectural decoration and scent for the floor, doors, walls and support systems. In keeping with local availability, certain scents and shapes became associated with certain liturgical seasons. These were not codified in law, for the customs of Mediterranean lands were unlike those of England or Poland.

It was only in recent centuries, as Christianity was finding new expressions in the counter-reformation and in the "new world" of America, that flowers were removed from the assembly area and put on the altar. Some said, as they do now, that the presence of flowers called attention to this important place. But the result was usually to trivialize or obscure any sense of life-and-death action at the altar table, while depriving the assembly area of sights and scents that had been welcome.

THE PLACEMENT OF FLOWERS IN THE REFORMED RITES: Two approaches to floral decoration can be seen in most churches. During the centuries and decades before the altars were removed from the walls and the priests faced the people, flowers usually were placed on the shelves behind the altar table. Echoes of this practice are seen when flowers are placed on remaining side altars and when vases are symmetrically placed on the rear wall or on an unused old altar behind the current altar. Especially in renovated churches, where such old altars are removed, another pattern seems to have become almost mandatory. It is the placing of pots of flowers or green plants in one or all of these places: at the foot of the lectern or ambo, on the floor in front of the altar, in free-standing vases on either side of the altar and around the baptismal font. If the font is an immersion pool, the plants there seem be intended to discourage people from sitting on the sides of the font or leaving their coffee cups there. Perched before ambo or altar, flowers and plants usually minimize the strength of the furniture.

We need to pass beyond any current fascination with flowers shoring up the powerful furnishings of public action, any old habits of decorating a high altar that is no longer there. We are not designing a stage set; we are equipping a space for the action of all. As in all other parts of the decorative or iconographic program, we need to have our paradisal forms and scents support the sacred mysteries, the actions that unfold in the church complex. This implies an integrated approach to decorating the walls, the doors, the floors, the devotional shrines, and spaces around representational images.

On occasion, liturgical actions might be facilitated by a free-standing arrangement or tree, an iconographic statement in the entranceway or by the image of the day's saint, a scent-sending call to a particular feast. More often, though, our use of flowers should be integrated into the rite itself. For example, at funerals, a bed of herbs might support a casket on the sanctuary floor; when the assembly will go in procession, the route might be marked by flowers or branches. At all times, the use of plants and cut flowers presumes vessels and forms that connote public action rather than domesticated cuteness.

In addition to facilitating liturgical action, flowers can become sensual signals of seasons. Local traditions can evolve, as they did in early Christianity, from patterns of availability and prevalent expectations. At Christmas, the scent of evergreens is pretty well set and needs little tampering. Lilies may be the scent for early Eastertide, roses for the days of late Easter and Pentecost Sunday (they were used in traditional Jewish Pentecost rites). Just as sacristans need to appreciate the need for integration of the visual program, they also need to coordinate the varied scents of incense and flowers with the liturgical season.

FLOWERS AT WEDDINGS AND FUNERALS: The desire for flowers at these emotional moments is great, but the artistic expressions are seldom attuned to the liturgical action that will unfold. Each and every parish must devise a plan for this problem, a solution that respects the feelings of the participants. These events, as do all liturgical events, belong to the whole church. They are the action of the church, the action of Christ. They are not planned and provisioned as if the church building was rented for a family reunion. Participants book such events at church precisely so that it will be the church acting here, with all its richness of sacraments and seasons. This respect both for the participants' feelings and for the nature of liturgy itself has prompted many parishes to prepare guidelines. Such norms must be communicated at the earliest opportunity to those involved in order to head off any impossible or unreasonable expectations.

Funeral guidelines—about what is brought into the church complex and what is put at the committal site—will have to be communicated at a meeting with funeral directors. New policies for the reformed rites may suggest an annual explanation to the whole congregation of local funeral practices. Many times, during the first house-visit after death, pastoral ministers can suggest that any floral remembrance from the family might take this or that shape conducive to the liturgy.

Marriage guidelines need to be understood by all who lead pre-marital catechesis, and communicated to couples at the same time that they are scheduling the rite. The pastor, the catechists, or a special parishioner who acts as liaison or negotiator can assume this role of communication with couples and area florists. Couples need to know, from the very first moment, that the day they have in mind is this feast or in that season. If it is in the season of Advent, Christmas, Lent or Easter, they need to know how to respect the already-present ambience of austerity or festivity. Parish leaders should not be afraid to issue norms on placement, visual impact, and even the floral containers—for example, banning spray-painted cardboard.

With such once-in-a-lifetime events, some participants are always surprised by this or that longstanding policy of a church. Great tact is needed here, and a diplomacy that knows the liturgical parameters. The sacred mysteries deserve such care.

Inscriptions

Many churches have on their walls tablets inscribed with the names of donors or their beloved. Current liturgical books make no mention of this practice, but the regimen after Trent was quite negative about it. Though they were tolerated in small sizes and quantities, commemorative tablets were generally forbidden. They did (and do) distract us from worship and obfuscate the common ownership of the church building by the church community. New memorial inscriptions should be placed in less obtrusive parts of the church complex (a donor's book in the entranceway or inscriptions along the foundation wall outside). Rarely, if ever, should they be visible in the eucharistic assembly or on liturgical objects.

The one exception is the inscription called for in the rite of dedication (#25). It should state the date of dedication, name (titular) of the church, and the name of the bishop who led the assembly of dedication. This can be on the outside, in the entrance hall, or in an unobtrusive place on the interior walls of the assembly place. Unlike a private donor's memorial, this signals the heritage and holiness of this house for the whole local church.

PART TWO ◆ *Equipping the Church Complex*

5◆ A Place for the Eucharistic Assembly

A Place of Communion

The congregation, the faithful, the parishioners, the gathered people, the assembly—all these terms describe the people who come together for liturgy. Whatever the term used, we must appreciate the unity of everyone present and the action to which they are called.

The word "assembly" is favored by many liturgists, for it connotes a sense of gathering and includes all present—priest and choir and all of the other baptized. The liturgical assembly is quite unlike other assemblies—student assemblies, the national assembly of France, the General Assembly of the United Nations or an "unlawful assembly" in civil law. Because the term can mean just about any gathering for a common purpose, we must understand it in a very specific way when we talk about liturgy. As church, we are a unified assembly, a body of people engaged in particular actions—the liturgical actions, the work of praise that should engage all who are present. Different actions are performed by various ministries, but there should never be a sense of the priest's being the only sacramental agent. All present undertake the sacramental action and share in the saving mysteries.

This place of eucharistic action is not the only part of the church building but part of a complex of interrelated places. Others include the baptistry, reconciliation chapel, reservation of the eucharist chapel, entrance hall and social gathering areas. All these must always relate to the great assembly place for thanksgiving and communion.

History And Current Norms

UNIFIED, ORIENTED PLACES: This action of the entire congregation was at the heart of the earliest Christian liturgies. "Evidence of this is found in their architectural floor plans, which were designed as general gathering spaces, spaces which allowed the whole assembly to be part of the action" *(Environment and Art in Catholic Worship,* #29). For reasons still unknown to us, our early ancestors in faith liked to think of this place as a ship, hence the term "nave" for the assembly-area in church buildings. Whether they were thinking of the ark of Noah, the ship of Saint Peter, or a fine metaphor used by an influential preacher, they meant the nave to be the whole hall, not a room divided into separate places for the active clergy and the attentive laity. Within these unified places, small screens, a few feet high and normally of stone, began appearing at an early date. Their purpose seems to have been to define areas for certain liturgical acts, for example, framing the area where the word was proclaimed.

The places Christians built for the celebration of the eucharist—with a few important exceptions—faced east. They were, literally, "oriented"—that is, laid out to face the Orient. The East is, of course, the source of light. The first Christians lived in the Mediterranean world where people saw this direction of the light as the place where good gods could be found. They interpreted this in Christian and European terms—Christ as the sun of justice or as the East. They looked for paradise in the East, and gazed eastward toward the cross of Christ in Jerusalem, in anticipation of the second coming from the East (Matthew 24:27).

The table that was both sign and source of this communion was sheltered in the eastern end of the church edifice. Often shaped as a half-circle, and vaulted so that it formed a sort of shell or cave, this area (commonly called the apse) was considered the place of divine entry. The churches of the East preferred to use the language of the incarnation to describe the eucharist; it is no wonder that the images on their apse walls there were often of the first coming of Christ, the birth at Bethlehem. In our Western tradition, early Christians focused more on the second coming, with many still-extant apses dressed with images of the new Jerusalem.

MEDIEVAL CONCENTRATION ON THE RETABLE AND TABERNACLE: During the Middle Ages, large screens appeared in church buildings of many regions. Far more than earlier decorative panels had done, these screens divided the place of eucharistic action into two parts: a "sanctuary" and a place for the congregation. The medieval fascination with vertical screens also can be seen in their placement near, or even at, the altar. In most Western churches, the retable or reredos reared up from the altar table. Their size and verticality resulted in most of the iconography being located at or near the altar, too; and it depicted Calvary, not Bethlehem or the second coming. Their shelves were convenient for many appointments. The cross and candles, once carried in procession, became frozen in place. The glorious cross, bejeweled and made of precious metal, was transformed into a "passion cross" with a beaten, lifeless body. Amid these ascending shelves, niches and holes allowed for coffin-type boxes of relics to be enshrined. Later, when churches began reserving the eucharist in public, a center cavity allowed the substitution of a tabernacle for the earlier reliquary.

It is ironic that such constructs, meant to highlight the altar, actually served to miniaturize it. Besides taking to itself all attributes of the altar and all powers of decoration, the retable presided over the demise of the ambo and presider's chair—phased out by the curtailment of ministries (deacons, lectors, cantors) and the absorption of all action to the footpace before the altar-retable.

The post-medieval appearance of the tabernacle in the retable caused the decorative program to shift into throne-oriented details. The preaching and emotions of that time changed this place into the shrine of the lonely prisoner of the tabernacle, hoping for a visit from his pious ones. The eastern end, the place of divine entry, became the place of divine imprisonment.

There were many other plot lines in the devolution of the liturgy into an action done just by the priest for the attending communicants. The end result was that we received church buildings where the assembled people were separated from one another by communion rails and pillars. If the space was somewhat open, as in Baroque churches, the atmosphere was that of a throne room for the reserved sacrament.

CURRENT NORMS: Certain liturgical architects early in the twentieth century saw these problems. With new technologies of structural support available, diminishing the need for pillars, they led the way toward unified places for participation in the rites, not just for devotions before the tabernacle. Their efforts inspired the architectural norms after Vatican II:

> The people of God assembled at Mass possess an organic and hierarchical structure, expressed by the various ministries and actions for each part of the celebration. The general plan of the sacred edifice should be such that in some way it conveys the image of the gathered assembly. It should also allow the participants to take the place most appropriate to them and assist all to carry out their individual functions properly.
>
> The congregation and choir should have a place that facilitates their active participation.
>
> The priest and his ministers have their place in the sanctuary, in the part of the church that brings out their distinctive role, namely, to preside over the prayers, to proclaim the word of God, or to minister at the altar.
>
> Even though these elements must express a hierarchical arrangement and the diversity of offices, they should at the same time form a complete and organic unity, clearly expressive of the unity of the entire holy people. The character and beauty of the place and all its appointments should foster devotion and show the holiness of the mysteries celebrated there. . . .
>
> The places for the faithful should be arranged with care so that the people are able to take their rightful part in the celebration visually and mentally. As a rule, there should be benches or chairs for their use. . . . Chairs or benches should be set up in such a way that the people can easily take the positions required during the various celebrations and have unimpeded access to receive communion. *(General Instruction of the Roman Missal,* #257, 273)

The place for the celebration must convey the image of the gathered people. The sanctuary and the places for the faithful express a diversity of offices and roles, but these zones must form a coherent and organic unity. Communion rails and screens that divide, sanctuaries that are enormously higher than the rest of the floor, and decorative programs that embellish the sanctuary alone—these are all practices that should be left behind.

Active participation is the hallmark recovery made in the reforms. It is for this reason that the assembly hall must do more than gather people. The disposition of places must enable us to act, not just think with the Mass and see it; we must all be able to move in procession, receive the remains of those who have died, greet arriving brides and grooms, pray over the catechumens, interact with and be the redeemed body.

The character and beauty of the place "show the holiness of the mysteries" and stimulate devotion. The mysteries are the ritual actions prepared for by sacristans. The iconographic program should promote higher levels of communal activity and stir the senses to deeper devotion and passion for the reign of God.

Architectural Surfaces

We need to understand the architectural elements that shape this place of action. The walls, ceiling, and floor should be studied, for they either facilitate action and enhance communal identity, or they impede the action and draw individuals into private pieties.

THE OLD SANCTUARY OR APSE: Many old sanctuaries—the early Christian place of divine entry, the medieval place of divine enthronement—tend to look now like the place of divine exit. With tabernacles moved to side altars or separate chapels, with altar tables moved toward the congregation and many retables moved to the dumpster, older sanctuaries often look empty. Some of these works of art should not have been discarded, but reutilized elsewhere in ways more appropriate to the renewed liturgy. Nevertheless, retables had to go. The tabernacle should never have overshadowed the eucharistic action. The table needs to be in the midst of the people. Thus, many cavernous apses, once the place of highest holiness, now look like empty holes.

In the past few decades these zones have often attracted the heaviest furniture possible. In some new constructions, this meant the transfer of the retable from a former building, just "to hold the flowers." In other renovations and new sites, it meant the organ pipes and their casing. Along with spaces for the choir and other ministers of music, this alignment has been touted as a fine replacement for choir lofts. The ministers needed to be part of the community and to be seen, but the use of the heaviest furniture here continues the miniaturization of the altar begun by the medieval retable. Huge cases of organ pipes dwarf the altar now like fancy retables did 30 years ago.

Renovators and decorators in many other places also have sensed the same need to do something with "the old sanctuary back there." Some have, in violation of all the reformed norms, put a new, scaled-down tabernacle "back there," unseen by the priest-presider at the altar, but still visible to almost everyone else. Other renovators and decorators have opened up windows to provide views of the landscaping, or worse yet, the parking lot. But in far greater numbers, these "spaces back there" have become dioramas for "theme-art," festal hangings, or seasonal displays like the Christmas créche or lenten desert.

In all places of eucharistic assembly not laid out as pure circles, these apses and walls are too prominent to the eyes and emotions of the assembly to display old retables, organ pipe cases, tabernacles and dioramas. When we make decisions about the way these kinds of spaces should look, or what they should contain, we need to be attentive to the action of the assembly. We do not need furniture or art dwarfing the altar. We do not need strong paintings or gorgeous trees that draw our eyes and hearts away from the liturgical actions. Often a fine solution is to leave that entire end of the hall empty, with only the architectural surfaces framing the action.

OTHER WALLS: No element in the church complex is neutral. Even the walls themselves hinder or help the liturgical actions. The walls of the eucharistic assembly place most obviously serve to contain the assembly. We should not use them to display diverting expressions of individual pieties. Instead, we should decorate them in ways that maximize the sense of a single expanse—a unified place rather than individual walls enthroning icons here and there. This does not mean the absence of colors and images, but that all images and colors, windows and fixtures should contribute toward unified action.

The principal decoration of the walls should be the 12 crosses, candle holders and candles envisioned by the rite of dedication (#22). (In small chapels, the rite allows for using only four.) They mark the places of the dedicatory anointing of the walls, an action expressive of our unity in the eucharistic assembly. They have a long tradition that can be traced back to an understanding of the assembly place as akin to the new Jerusalem (envisioned in Revelation 21:14 as having 12 foundation stones). Where they were not installed at the time of dedication, later installation is not forbidden.

These markings and candles are far more liturgical in their embrace of the assembly than the latter day stations of the cross. Yet they should not dominate, should never compete with the one cross of this assembly place, the one that is carried in procession and that stands by the altar for the celebration. Such markings and candles should be carved into the walls or made of the same material as the walls. They should serve as emblems, but they should be small images, and they should be accompanied by candle holders that will stand out and up more. The sconces or brackets that hold the 12 candles should be made in a style congruent with the architecture. When the candles are lit on great feasts, this embracing light, these "blazing walls," will illumine and facilitate the act of eucharist. In many of the church buildings passed down to us, however, the only decorations on the walls are the 14 stations of the cross. These should be hung in the eucharistic assembly place only if they are used by the people and if their design does not hinder the visual unity of the place. In most cases, they should be in other parts of the church complex (see page 80).

FLOORS: The most prevalent impediment to the creation of an active space is the use of carpeting. It affects acoustics by absorbing sound, and it impedes the movement of people who use wheelchairs, leg braces, crutches or walkers. More pervasively, it brings the look of home, thereby domesticating a public action. Unfortunately, carpeting is often installed by the altar, or on the processional paths that we call aisles—and sometimes under all the seats of the building.

In ceremonial books that accompanied the rites after Trent, green carpets were suggested for the sanctuary floor. More elaborate carpets were to go on the steps to the altar for high feasts. An old custom of placing oriental rugs on these steps was countenanced, despite warnings against profane symbols. In our own century, it was no accident that full church carpeting appeared first in affluent suburban parishes. They had the funds and they wanted to make their churches into what might be termed the "living rooms of the bourgeoisie."

The appearance of full carpeting and of other domesticating elements (baskets instead of brass vases, windowsills with green plants) was a reflection of the trend in the 1960s toward home Masses. During that period, pastoral workers and theoreticians grasped for some alternative to hurried Masses read in Latin before large congregations. In those first years of the "new Mass," it was a breath of fresh air to have an unhurried Mass with a small congregation in the intimacy of a home. From this it was an easy and natural next step to introduce domestic elements into the church building, and to envision the ideal church as an intimate living room.

Thirty years later, we realize the dangers of domesticating a public event. The parish is not a "family," unless we want to broaden the term to include an unspecific equivalent of community. We do not need or even want the pillows and rugs and couches of our households when we gather in the broader social grouping for funerals, initiation, the prophetic word, and the communion that promises a total transformation of the world. Fortunately, we have come to realize that the places of action cannot be made to look and feel like home.

Stripped of their carpets, floors have great potential to support the assembly's liturgy in more than a literal way. For the great feasts, parishioners can make large chalk drawings on the surface of an outdoor plaza or entranceway, even on the asphalt or concrete of a parking lot. Blossoms strewn on passageways is another way to use floors to celebrate a great feast. At a funeral, instead of a casket being perched on an unattractive collapsible cart, it can be supported by a bed of herbs or flowers on the floor.

Seating and Action Space for the Assembly

For the first 1,300 or more years of Christianity, there was no general seating for the assembly. Provisions were made for those who were too weak to stand, but most people stood (or at times knelt on the floor) throughout the services. The place for the congregation was open. Liturgical commentators described the communities surging toward the ambo for the homily, going to greet the arrival of the bread and wine, streaming with the gift bearers toward the altar, pouring toward the altar for communion. Some small barriers were created in larger churches to allow the movement of ministers through the assemblies, which were described as waves crashing against the sanctuary steps.

During the late Middle Ages, these modest attempts to channel the ebb and flow of the active congregants took a dreadful step. Benches and chairs began to be introduced in various churches; the resulting masses of furniture had the effect of corralling the flowing assembly. The rows of wood came at a time when the eucharist was beginning to be reserved publicly in what had been the action place; they helped begin an era of hushed stillness in the new presence of the "blessed sacrament." Wise commentators of our own century have used various metaphors to describe the effect handed down to all the churches of the Americas. The assembly area became a congested parking lot (James White); bleachers were placed on the basketball court, changing the event into something entirely different (Aidan Kavanagh).

Despite its prevalence, seating has never been (and is still not) required by liturgical law. What counts most is the free space, the open area free of seating and the space between rows. Yet, without major shifts in public habits and expectations, we must continue to cope with the problems posed by seating.

Open space includes the passages or gangways that we commonly refer to as "aisles" (even though that technically means something more architectural), as well as the space around the entrance and font, around the altar and ambo, and the devotional spaces and other chapels. When arranging moveable chairs or otherwise influencing these open spaces, sacristans should recognize the value of processions, the value of people assembling closely around font or altar. In many places, even with pews affixed to the floor, alternative seating arrangements can (and should) be envisioned. Open spaces can be expanded.

Within the seating areas themselves, there should be broad spaces between rows of chairs or benches—for the feeling of enclosure to be minimized, for the ability to stand and face in various directions, for the ability to enter and leave frequently for processions (for example, to communion) and for other interactions. The same approach should be taken with regard to auxiliary equipment like hinged kneelers or kneeling hassocks, hymnal racks or pew-end candles: They should foster as much activity by the assembly as possible.

If pew candles are positioned so as to mark processional passages or to embrace the whole assembly, they can contribute to a program of unified decor. They can be in position for more than Christmas and weddings; they can be used for high festivals like Easter, Pentecost and the dedication anniversary. And for variety, they can be decorated with greens or blossoms. In no case, though, should they be used to divide the assembly.

The Choir's Place in the Assembly

The same quest for unified assemblies and undivided places of sacramental action must direct the position of choirs and leaders of song. The norms for the placement of musical assistants, debated through the decades of the liturgical movement and in the preparatory commissions for Vatican II, are most fully expressed in *Musicam Sacram,* an instruction issued by the Vatican in 1967:

> According to the design of the particular church, the place for the choir is to be such that:
>
> a. its status as a part of the community with a special function is clearly evident;
>
> b. the performance of its liturgical ministry is facilitated;
>
> c. full, that is, sacramental, participation in the Mass remains convenient for each of the members. (#23)

The *General Instruction of the Roman Missal* (#274–275) offers similar notes regarding instrumentalists.

More often that not, these principles have resulted in choirs being moved from the back loft to a position beside or behind the sanctuary. This zone, more or less prominent depending upon its elevation, usually includes seating, a secondary podium for the leader of song, an organ console, music stands, and instruments like the piano.

When considering decorations for a given feast or season, we need to remember that this zone is to be conceived as part of the assembly space. It is not a part of the sanctuary, not a special place for liturgical focus. Therefore, it should not be singled out for highlighting any more than the rest of the assembly space. Those who plan decorations need to maintain sight lines with all ministers of music, avoid obscuring such items as the hymn board, and take into account any existing organ case and its given decoration.

6◆ The Presider's Chair

History

The presider's chair is the most ancient liturgical furnishing, possibly predating even the use of fixed altars. When naming the chair of the bishop, the term *cathedra* is used—an ancient word that has stayed with us in the name of the one building (the cathedral) that houses it in each diocese. The earliest chairs for bishops were shaped and positioned differently in each region, but the styles always were meant to express the role of the occupant as philosopher-teacher or as judge. The fixed placement was in concert with the given region's other liturgical furnishings, so that the bishop would be best able to preside and preach there. Any references to royal or imperial thrones were avoided, because neither the secular rulers nor the bishops would have countenanced such competition. Later, as the ministry of the priests became one of representing the bishop outside of metropolitan centers, places of presiding were designed for them. As ordained presiders took on all of the ministries at liturgy, and as even the scriptural proclamation was moved to the altar, presiders' chairs were radically altered or discarded. The presider came to be seen as a visiting prelate enthroned at the side while the local priest said Mass. On rare occasions priest celebrants sat, taking their ease while something was being done by someone else.

Current Norms

The practices described above are receding from memory. The chair is used not to take one's ease, but as the place of leadership for large parts of the eucharistic action. Now "presider" means more than a visiting dignitary: The priest celebrant is often called the presider, because all of the baptized "celebrate," and the role of leadership is one of coordinating a diversity of ministries. The chair for this role should be strong and simple, with minimum ornamentation. The *General Instruction of the Roman Missal* describes it as follows:

> The priest celebrant's chair ought to stand as a symbol of his office of presiding over the assembly and of directing prayer. Thus the best place for the chair is at the back of the sanctuary and turned toward the congregation, unless the structure or other circumstances are an obstacle (for example, if too great a distance would interfere with communication between the priest and people). Anything resembling a throne is to be avoided. (#271)

Because the chair is normally movable, sacristans and liturgical planners can collaborate with presiders in reviewing various locations for it. It should always face the rest of the assembly, but the warning noted in the *General Instruction* is well taken. Often a position at the back of an old sanctuary is too far from the assembly. Even though audio systems can amplify and carry sound, communication needs to be more than aural. The chair needs to be more physically proximate to the gathered people. In newer churches, where old retables and tabernacles do not occupy the areas behind the altar, distances have been charted properly for the presider to be behind the altar area.

In the exploration of local options, certain trends and criteria should be given close scrutiny. Positioning the chair just in front of the altar minimizes the impact of both chair and altar and makes an empty chair the visual focus during the eucharistic prayer. The zones of our liturgical action need to be kept distinct; the various furnishings each need their own space. Similarly, a position too close to the other side of the altar makes it appear that the presider is sitting at the altar. The presider should be able to see the community, unimpeded by spotlights or by decorations. The position does not have to be at the geometric center, and often a position to the side, but facing all, is best.

In certain buildings, the position will even be outside the traditional sanctuary, but still prominent and distinct. In assembly areas arranged with antiphonal seating—altar at one end of the assembly, ambo at the other—the chair is best placed at the ambo end. During the liturgy of the word, the presider is usually at the chair; for the liturgy of the eucharist the chair is empty. Placing the chair at the ambo end of the assembly area also helps to keep the altar area free of anything but the actions specifically designated for it. In older and larger spaces, the ambo and chair might be close to the seating of the assembly, with a large, open space left around the altar in the old sanctuary. This arrangement allows everyone to move in procession about the altar during the preparation of the altar.

In a cathedral, there are two chairs, the cathedra and the chair for the presider in the absence of the Ordinary. Both should be arranged in distinct zones that meet the criteria.

Seating for Other Ministers

The *General Instruction* puts this simply: "The seats for the ministers should be so placed in the sanctuary that they can readily carry out their appointed functions" (#271). They should be of a simpler design than the presider's chair, and not usually on either side of it (a pattern held over, unfortunately, from former solemn High Masses). Instead, they should be located near their places of action—lectors and cantor by the ambo, servers at the credence table, book-bearer accessible to the presider, eucharistic ministers able to approach the altar. All auxiliary furniture should be removed when not in use, ridding the sanctuary of empty chairs and kneelers.

7◆ The Altar

The Table of the Lord

EARLY CHRISTIANS: There could be only one altar in each early Christian community. The altar was the presence of the one Christ, the center-point of the community's gathering for the sacred mysteries. This centrality was shown in different ways throughout the various regions. In some places, the altar was more like a table, with visible legs or supports. Elsewhere, the altar was an unbroken block of stone. Local traditions sometimes suggested the addition of a roof called the *ciborium*. It rested on four columns outside the altar's corners. In a startling image of the identity of the altar with Christ, some communities began a practice that later became universal—carving five crosses into the table surface to represent Christ's five wounds.

The positioning of the altar was often related to a tomb. Though a city like Rome had both its cathedral complex and its local neighborhood centers for liturgy, other assembly halls were built as covered cemeteries. There, often near the tomb of the most famous of the deceased, the eucharist could be celebrated. Later, when many of these cemeteries were transformed into parish or pilgrimage churches, permanent altars were positioned directly over the tomb of the most important martyr. Homilists reminded their communities that the blood of the martyrs was rooted in the blood of Christ.

MEDIEVAL CHRISTIANS: Eventually Christian communities began to lose their sense of connection to the sacred mysteries and the altar. The table itself moved deeper and deeper into a sanctuary screened from the congregation. A huge retable or reredos reared up from the altar. As the ministries once exercised by deacons and lectors and cantors were absorbed by priests, the altar table itself became longer, so that readings could be done from different ends distinct from the eucharistic action place at the center.

This revolutionary change from a simple table to an altar with numerous and immense accessories did not go unchallenged. Sixteenth-century reformers called for a return to the much simpler practices of early Christianity—an uncluttered table at the center of the community, and once again free of all the trappings of retables.

CURRENT NORMS: The leaders of the twentieth-century liturgical movement knew that the altar had to be freed from the backdrops that people called "the high altar," so that priests could face the community. They also knew that side altars had to go. Though the competing altars have been removed from many churches, two practices still drain energy from the one altar that remains. In those parishes where retables are at the rear of the sanctuary, some sacristans still decorate the retables, investing them with a dignity and prominence that can detract from the altar. Some parishes, especially during the fuel crisis of the 1970s, created weekday Mass chapels to avoid having to heat or cool the main assembly area. Though this practice can lower utility bills, we should, instead, be finding better ways to gather the smaller numbers of weekday worshipers around the one altar.

Today our altars are free-standing, pulled away from rear walls. And now that the proclamation of the scriptures has been moved back to the ambo, our altars also are reserved for the liturgy of the eucharist. These radical reforms have shifted the proportions of the table. It now can be constructed and perceived as an altar table, rather than as a shallow shelf below the retable. After the restoration of concelebration in the 1960s, some thought that the altar should stay long and narrow so that several clerics could offer Mass on one side of the table. Experience quickly proved this notion to be wrong, and altars now tend to be less elongated.

The ancient roofs or *ciboria* that stood on columns about the altar were reintroduced in some reformed rooms. A more widespread introduction of such constructs would make sense only if they were given fresh treatment for the new rites. They seem out of place now because our assembly places are so clogged with furniture. The altar is distinct now because it occupies the only open space that all worshipers face. Where pews and chairs have largely been removed, the altar in the open hall might well benefit from some architectural highlighting.

The *General Instruction of the Roman Missal* collates the reforms:

> At the altar the sacrifice of the cross is made present under sacramental signs. It is also the table of the Lord and the people of God are called together to share in it. The altar is, as well, the center of the thanksgiving that the eucharist accomplishes. (#259)
>
> In every church there should ordinarily be a fixed, dedicated altar, which should be freestanding to allow the ministers to walk around it easily and Mass to be celebrated

> facing the people. It should be so placed as to be a focal point on which the attention of the whole congregation centers naturally. (#262)
>
> According to the church's traditional practice and the altar's symbolism, the table of a fixed altar should be of stone and indeed of natural stone. But at the discretion of the conference of bishops some other solid, becoming, and well-crafted material may be used [in 1969, the U. S. bishops so allowed this extension]. The pedestal or base of the table may be of any sort of material, as long as it is becoming and solid. (#263)
>
> The practice of placing under the altar to be dedicated relics of saints, even of non-martyrs, is to be maintained. Care must be taken to have solid evidence of the authenticity of such relics. (#266)

As these reforms shape consciousness, the altar table will not be treated as just any other table. It will not be a storage place for notes or props to be shoved aside when a choir wants to perform. The ancient practice of bowing before the altar will replace both the genuflections reserved for tabernacles as well as casual approaches that fail to appreciate the beauty of bodily gestures.

Altar Cloths

ORIGINS: The earliest Christians lived in a region where fine linen, especially linen from Egypt, had been highly prized for centuries. Ritual laws, codified in the Book of Exodus, often demanded the use of this Egyptian cloth for screens, tabernacle hangings and vestments. This same linen, or similar fabrics made from flax, were used for burial shrouds. It is no surprise, then, that primitive documents from the Mediterranean basin make note of the use of one fine linen cover for the altar—carrying rich memories of burial shrouds and of vesture for the most significant public rites. It was placed on the altar at the start of the eucharistic rite and removed at its end.

LATER USAGE: By the year 1000, it seems that communities preferred to leave this cloth on the altar at all times. Local customs for such cloths continued to evolve, often multiplying their number on the altar. Eventually, communities allied with the Roman rite followed the same code, using three linen (or hemp) cloths on the altar. Some communities took to dying their cloths various colors, but white was virtually universal. Because the altars had almost always been moved to the wall or had retables reared up behind them, cloths never covered the rear of the altar. For the front of the altar, communities went to great lengths to procure lavish frontals (antependia), often of the color of the liturgical season.

Many sacristies still have cloths from old altars. These typically include white linen top cloths ("fair linens," long enough to hang to the floor on each end); two linen undercloths for each altar (or wider cloths that, when folded, yielded two layers); a chrismale (or "cerecloth," linen waxed on one side and of the exact dimensions of each altar's surface). This last was the cloth that was placed under the other three at the dedication rite and could be used permanently. In addition there were cloths for placement over all the other cloths when candlelabra were used, and for each altar a "vesperale," or dust cover, that was placed over the other cloths between services.

CURRENT NORMS: The regulations have been radically reduced to a single norm *(General Instruction of the Roman Missal, #268)*:

> At least one cloth should be placed on the altar out of reverence for the celebration of the memorial of the Lord and the banquet that gives us his body and blood. The

shape, size, and decoration of the altar cloth should be in keeping with the design of the altar.

Though the directive is general, its application is to be very specific, for each and every cover should be fabricated with a specific altar in mind. A cover designed for a wall-mounted altar should not be used on a free-standing altar. Such a cloth will cover only the top and sides, often producing the look of a large scarf.

Two patterns are rightly favored at this point in the reforms. Often the cloth is of the exact dimensions of the table top. In other places, the cloth will be longer, even to the extent that it might go to the floor on all four sides. This fullest form, termed "Laudean" or "Jacobean" (perhaps related to their usage in England at the time of King James), can create an appearance of great dignity, while also serving to conceal a poorly made altar. On the negative side, it will also conceal a well-made altar, and perhaps diminish the community's sense of the altar as a solid form.

Some communities with strong, well-made altars have been rediscovering the fine practice of covering the altar only for the eucharistic rite. This provides another ritual gesture for the preparation of the altar, and it allows the communal table to be present in all its strength. Other experiments are ongoing, as we strive to find the right covers for our specific tables. Seasonal colors and natural fabrics other than linen can dress the table well, but we are ill-served by polyester.

Several years before Vatican II, the Roman rite dropped the requirement of a frontal or antependium. As altars became free-standing, it became all the more obvious that mandates for decorating only the front should be discontinued. Now *Environment and Art in Catholic Worship* (#95) appropriately calls for festive coverings to avoid covering just the facade and to respect the integrity of the furniture. With the expansion of possibilities for altar cloths and their ability to express the given seasons, we are rightly less inclined to use extra hangings (sometimes called paraments) for festivals.

Another current fashion is trite—having the altar cloth or extra hangings match the season's chasuble, stole, ambo cover, lectionary cover, wall hangings and even book ribbons. When matching becomes so relentlessly pervasive, the priest often appears to be a piece of furniture, or the entire environment resembles a jigsaw puzzle or diorama. Each item in the eucharistic assembly place should be chosen with an eye for its compatibility with the space and with other objects—but each also should have its own vitality and form.

Altar Cross

THE PROCESSIONAL CROSS: In ancient times, this was the basic Christian symbol used at the altar. After leading the community into their gathering place, it was prominently positioned for the rest of the ritual action. The cross has been the subject of mosaics and sculptures, of door-reliefs and illustrations. Communities have depicted the cross as the instrument of death, the tree of life, the archetypal meeting of horizontal and vertical and the symbol of the four directions. Surrounded by so many images of the cross, the earliest Christian communities nonetheless gave the place of honor to the one cross that led them in procession and that provided a focus during every ritual.

THE STATIONARY CROSS: By the Middle Ages, the clergy performed most ritual actions, and processions of the assembly were less frequent. Thus, processional crosses mounted on stands in the sanctuary gave way to crosses positioned at the center of the altar, just above the priest's face. Of the many forms of crosses, with or without various images attached, this one tended to have a crucified corpus of Christ attached. In some sanctuaries, it was enormous, dwarfing the very altar it was meant to embellish.

By the time of the Council of Trent, the style of the crucifix and its position at the center of the altar had become fairly universal. The ritual action associated with it was not the procession, but the mandated glance priests gave to it during the eucharistic prayer. Certainly a processional cross was used from time to time, but it was no longer the principal cross of the liturgy. Though many other styles of crosses were used for devotions and decoration, the Roman church continued to call for the altar cross to have a crucified corpus attached. In the face of the new trends of this past century, Pius XII resisted what he termed "reductions to antiquity" and called for at least some trace of suffering to appear on the altar's crucifix *(Mediator Dei, #62)*.

RETURN TO ONE CROSS: The reforms after Vatican II were just that, reforms that drew on antiquity, but that gave fresh life in a new context. The *General Instruction of the Roman Missal* says: "There is also to be a cross, clearly visible to the congregation, either on the altar or near it" (#270). The U. S. A. appendix to #270 quotes other Vatican instructions to give more specific norms:

> Only a single cross should be carried in a procession in order to give greater dignity and reverence to the cross. It is desireable to place the cross that has been carried in the procession near the altar so that it may serve as the cross of the altar. Otherwise it should be put away during the service.

Almost 20 years later, the final part of the *Roman Ritual* to be reformed, the *Book of Blessings,* was implemented. A directive at the blessing of a cross (#1235) further specifies the official documentation: "The image of the cross should preferably be a crucifix, that is, have the corpus attached, especially in the case of a cross that is erected in a place of honor inside a church." In its use of the term "preferably," the *Roman Ritual* neither ends the artistic exploration of other forms of crosses nor forgets the hundreds of years when communities did become attached to crucified images. And because this directive is more related to stationary crosses than to processional crosses, a variety of forms can be explored. When deciding which form of the cross should be part of the ritual actions, and whether the ideal of a single cross can be implemented, we can relate our review of available forms to a study of the rites where the richness of the cross is unfolded—the texts of Good Friday, the Triumph of the Cross, and the blessing of a cross.

Utilizing the one cross, carried in procession and placed near the altar, has many benefits over the custom of affixing stationary crosses to the walls, suspending them overhead, or placing them on the altar table itself: There can be different placements for various seasons; ritual actions in other areas of the room (especially when all walk in the procession) and those by the altar are linked; the cross is more clearly appreciated as a ritual element than as an item to gaze at; the one cross is able to be touched or venerated by all on Good Friday; the altar is reserved for the bread and wine.

This cross is a standard for processions and a sacred furnishing accompanying the altar; it is the primordial emblem shaping the community. Between services the processional cross can be left in its stand, near the altar yet far enough away to allow for free access to all sides of the table. The altar candles might well be positioned by this cross.

Altar Candles

The *General Instruction of the Roman Missal* (#269, 79) says:

> Candles are to be used at every liturgical service as a sign of reverence and festiveness. The candlesticks are to be placed either on or around the altar in a way suited to the design of the altar and the sanctuary. Everything is to be well balanced and must not interfere with the faithfuls' clear view of what goes on at the altar or is placed on it.
>
> On or near the altar there are to be candlesticks with lighted candles, at least two, but even four, six, or, if the bishop of the diocese celebrates, seven. There is also to be a cross on or near the altar. The candles and cross may be carried in the entrance procession.

Before the reforms, the number of candles to be used was regulated by the then-familiar types of Mass (low, high, solemn high, pontifical). These categories have been abolished, for singing is now normative at all celebrations. Pastoral leaders and sacristans in each parish should review the universal and local calendars and determine which seasons and feasts call for more solemnity and festivity. The greater the solemnity or festivity, the more candles the parish should use. The ritual books suggest that those that are lighted for an event should be part of the opening procession.

The option of placing candles on floor stands away from the table is highly recommended. As in so much of the liturgical reform, this practice draws upon customs from the early church, from a time when the power of an uncluttered altar was recognized. These two or more stands and candles obviously should be selected and arranged in a way that facilitates action, or at the very least so that they don't block sight lines or paths of action. In addition, they should complement the other furnishings of the area and relate well to the overall decor. It is not required that the candles be evenly split on either side of the altar, nor that they nudge right up beside it. Through the various liturgical seasons, we can find ways that make our rooms more conducive to action—for example, by grouping the cross and candles to one side of the area, by arranging flowers and candles away from the altar, by placing a candle at each of the four corners of an altar platform or by adding more candles for festivals.

Credence Table

This table should be as unobtrusive as possible, but large enough to do the job and placed so that it is convenient to use. The table will have to accommodate several communion cups. They remain on the table until needed for communion, and then are returned there after communion to be cleaned by the ministers, all of whom need access to the area more or less simultaneously. The need for many cups may suggest the use of trays that also must fit on the credence table. If the cloth will be placed on the altar during the preparation of the gifts, this might well be set up on the credence table. The credence table should be large enough to be used at the most elaborate rites of the year. Otherwise, credence tables of different sizes should be available.

Depending upon the alignment of the major furnishings and the sacristy, the credence can be off to one side of the sanctuary. There is no longer a universally prescribed side from which acolytes need to approach the presider at the altar. The credence could also be behind the altar on a lower level. If the credence is behind the altar, however, it must not resemble a high altar, nor should it compete with the altar table for attention in any other way. The credence can be a table, a bit higher than a domestic table, or a large shelf mounted by a wall bracket, or a large niche in the wall. Other than the requirement that the credence table be as unobtrusive as possible, there are no set rules governing coverings that might be placed over it. In assembly areas where the presider's chair is quite removed from the altar, another auxiliary table might be near the chair to hold such things as the chair book, water buckets for the sprinkling rite, hymnals and intercession texts. Where the community fully surrounds the table, the credence table should be well away from the central axis, so as not to obstruct the action.

Book Stands

This practical addition also should be as unobtrusive as possible. Some presiders need the several inches of height that the stand provides so they don't have to lean over as they lead the assembly in prayer. For each service, the minimum should be used: no stand at all, a plain-covered cushion, or a higher stand made of metal or wood. Older versions, with fixtures for adjusting the height and unfinished backs, were meant for wall-mounted altars; they are unsuited for today's free-standing altars. If a book stand is used, the acolyte should put it on the altar during the preparation, then remove it after communion. Freed from stands, candles, cross and cloth, the altar can be seen for the sacred table that it is.

8◆ The Ambo: A Place for Proclaiming the Word of God

Every liturgy includes the celebration of the word of God—eucharists, baptisms, ordinations, marriages, even penance. The assembly is more than a mere audience addressed by reader, psalmist, deacon or preacher. Those who listen attentively also are called to act intently: to participate in a full gospel procession (or else to stand and face it), to sing psalms and acclamations, to pray for the catechumens being dismissed, to profess their faith and to offer intercessions. In this interaction with the saving word, they receive fresh life.

Original Places for the Word

Ancient synagogues had a raised area with a reading desk where the word of God was proclaimed. Called a bema, it continues to be used. In some of the old synagogues in America it is located in the middle of the assembly. As Christian communities designated specific buildings for liturgy, they usually continued the custom of using a raised and centered place for the proclamation of scripture. The early Christian bema—or ambo, as it is now often called—was distinct from the altar and cathedra. In Constantinople, it was usually located on axis with the altar, but considerably extended into the open assembly area. In Syria, extant sites show its location on a sort of island or platform in the middle of the nave. In Rome, a second ambo was soon added, and both were located far out into the assembly area.

The Loss of a Specific Place

Through the Middle Ages, the ministries of lector, cantor and deacon were absorbed by the priest, and the priest conducted all the action at a wall-mounted altar. On occasion, rubrics specified the use of smaller lecterns, but these were always in the sanctuary proper. Bemas and ambos were no longer built in the midst of Christian assemblies. In a parallel move, synagogues were designed, especially in recent times, with the bema located near the ark at the end of the assembly place. In designing both churches and synagogues, architects began using many of the same theater-like floor plans, as assemblies simply sat facing the unified stage for all holy actions. The loss of the bema or ambo in both communities has corresponded to the rise of spectator status for the assemblies. Of course, there were exceptions. When sermons were given, and this was not at every liturgy, a pulpit near the assembly often was used. Yet these were often almost aliturgical moments. The "real" action was reserved for the sanctuary.

Current Reforms

The reformers were alert to the way the scriptures were originally proclaimed by lectors, cantors and deacons. So decades ago they called for the use of bemas or ambos. Whether called by one of these ancient terms or called a lectern, it has to be a place that imparts to the word a distinct identity. The Introduction to the *Lectionary for Mass* (1981 edition, #32–34) describes this area of the church complex as follows:

> There must be a place in the church that is somewhat elevated, fixed, and of suitable design and nobility. . . . Great pains must be taken, in keeping with the design of each church, over the harmonious and close relationship of the lectern with the altar. Either permanently or at least on occasions of greater solemnity, the lectern should be decorated simply and in keeping with its design. . . . In order that the lectern may properly serve its liturgical purpose, it is to be rather large, since on occasion several ministers must use it at the same time. Provision must also be made for the readers to have enough light to read the text and, as required, to have sound equipment enabling the congregation to hear them without difficulty.

All too many lecterns or ambos in the United States look as if they were borrowed from a lecture hall. The ambo is not just a shaft with a book-holder. It is a raised and rather large *place,* with a reading desk of dignified proportions normally added. Even a small podium can look and function well if there is a wider space or open platform around it. On solemn occasions, candles and even flowers can be used around this place, demarcating the larger area, but not crowding up against the reading desk.

Just as the early Christian ambos were often located in the midst of the assembly and the medieval pulpits were outside the sanctuary, there is no universal decree confining the place for proclamation to a sanctuary. The location may be determined by values such as visibility, the need for a dignified space distinct from altar and font, the desirability of having the ambo fixed, and the local building style.

Secondary Podium

The reservation of the ambo for the scriptures (including the responsorial psalm) and the Exsultet suggests the use of a very simple podium for the leading of song and the making of any announcements (cf. *Environment and Art in Catholic Worship, #75*). Some presiders use a third podium at the chair. This is not a good practice. The prayer texts are not proclamations, and the use of such a podium further diverts attention from the ambo, and replaces the human act of an assistant holding the book. Once again, all elements of furnishing and decoration have an effect, one way or another, on the liturgical action.

9◆ The Sanctuary

A Distinctive Design

The rooms used for the eucharist in the earliest centuries were remarkable for their unified and open space. We are now returning to that tradition as elements such as communion rails and the total enclosure of sanctuaries by rood screens continue to disappear. As noted in chapter 5, the *General Instruction of the Roman Missal* (#257) states that the sanctuary and the rest of the place "should at the same time form a complete and organic unity, clearly expressive of the unity of the entire holy people." The instruction attempts a careful balance between this unity and the need for a distinct zone: "The sanctuary should be clearly marked off from the body of the church either by being somewhat elevated or by its distinctive design and appointments. It should be large enough to accommodate all the rites." (#258)

Demarcation and distinctive design are no longer intended to keep the laity out. They are intended to allow enough open space for the rites, to give a kind of breathing space around our holiest symbols, those central focal points of holy action. The altar, ambo and chair are reserved for the holy actions and are to be set off from all other interactions—for example, catechesis, socializing with members of the community, or sharing refreshments.

In some buildings, the space is set off and made appropriately visible by risers or platforms. In others—for example, where the ambo and altar occupy different ends of the assembly space—they are distinguished by distinctive design and by floor space free from all other appointments. Decoration plays an important role here. A row of plants where an altar rail used to be may perpetuate division, separating people from their common table. On the other hand, flowers or candles at the foot of the four corners of the altar platform may help provide just the right marking. This balancing of distinct actions against the need for a unified assembly must be the foremost consideration in planning decorations.

The terms used to describe this distinct area of eucharistic action are ambiguous and confusing. At different times in the past and in certain commentaries of our day, it has been called the chancel, the choir, the presbyterium or presbytery, and the sanctuary. None of them is quite right; all carry connotations of "clergy only." Perhaps after we have lived with the reformed rites for a few more decades, new terms will appear.

Space for the Rites

Most of the features needed in these distinct areas were treated above under the main furnishings normally found in the sanctuary—chair, altar and ambo. Yet we must attend to many other rites in this place besides the eucharist—weddings, funerals, anointings and blessings, for example. The use of flowers, candles and decorations for each season must take account of all of these. Perhaps owing to old habits that restricted the sanctuary to the ordained, parishes still do not utilize these open spaces for the holy actions that they are meant to embrace. For example, a couple being married should sit and stand in the sanctuary in positions that allow their participation in word and eucharist. At a funeral Mass, the casket could be placed on the sanctuary floor, perhaps on a bed of flowers, by the paschal candle or other candles. The presentation of gifts should be at the chair or at the altar, not at an old communion rail (nor at an imagined one). Those being blessed or anointed do not need to stay outside of the sanctuary. This is not just "letting the laity in." It is using the ritual center for the holiest of actions.

Space for Few Decorations

The sanctuary should contain very few items other than the altar, ambo, chair, cross and candles. Other things—statues, seasonal "theme" art, banners and their stands—should be in the sanctuary only in the rarest of circumstances—and never impeding sight lines and movement. The emphasis should be on simplicity, on the central furnishings. Chairs, kneelers and candles not utilized for a rite should be stored out of sight. In other words, clutter is out.

National flags—of the U. S. A., the Vatican, or of any country related to members—are never appropriate as sanctuary decorations. This is not a stricture against any one nation, for all flags and all insignia of associations, all banners and posters for causes and fundraising are equally inappropriate. The Order of Christian Funerals (#38, 132) expressly forbids them in the liturgy. *Environment and Art in Catholic Worship* (#101) regrettably allows the use of "identifying symbols of particular cultures, groups, or nations" for particular occasions or holidays. Sacristans faced with a need to use flags on a special occasion should use small poles without finials, and should negotiate the placement of the flags as far from the sanctuary as possible. Because most flags were designed to be carried in parades, they might best be used in opening or closing processions, rather than as additions to the sanctuary.

10◆ A Place for Instrumentalists and Leaders of Music

Liturgy and Music

As an integral part of the liturgy of the hours and of every sacramental event, music should no longer be treated as an audience-pleasing embellishment. The principal musicians for the liturgy are the members of the assembly; through chant and acclamation they exercise their holy right and duty. It is not mere poetry, but the very heart of our belief, that the angels and the redeemed form a heavenly choir, that the church on earth is a full participant in this praise of God. To assist this singing body of Christ, instrumentalists and cantors, choirs and musical directors should be a part of our liturgies. But both the assembly and its assistants need to recover some of these basic beliefs.

The history of music at liturgy is a sad story of divorce. The shifting position of the choir and the installation of grand organs give monumental evidence to the division that has almost irreparably harmed both music and worship. As the participation of the faithful declined in the early Middle Ages, music was increasingly handled by clerics huddled at the side of the altar. Over the later Middle Ages and through the Renaissance and Baroque eras, they moved to positions farther away from and above the sanctuary and assembly. By the time churches were built in the Americas, the choir and organ were in a back loft. Congregations understood their role to be one of listening to the music, which was virtually irrelevant to the sacraments.

Such devolution hurt music; religious compositions were no longer rooted in the liturgy and in the live action of assemblies voicing praise through seasons and feasts. Communal singing in all contexts was impaired as the public lost its principal and most historic forum for feeling itself become a vocalizing body. Liturgy was drastically affected by the transfer of essential acclamations and psalmody to choirs.

We have begun the recovery—the rooting of liturgical music in the texts and action of the rites, the re-emergence of live action and music by assemblies, the touching of communal emotions never approached by mere words, the first awareness of sacraments as actions. In the place for eucharistic assembly, this recovery is evident when choirs and other musical assistants assume positions that facilitate the participation of all (page 41). These reforms also should influence the placement of instrumentalists.

The Pipe Organ and Other Instruments

The Roman rite gives a place of primacy to the pipe organ. This is not the same as the electronic instrument that is often called an organ. *Environment and Art in Catholic Worship* (#83) suggests that organs should be neither grandiose nor dominating. They—or at least their consoles—should be located near the choir.

The norms allow for and encourage the use of other instruments at liturgies. This is particularly helpful when liturgical gatherings form in a part of the church complex far from organ and piano. Examples would include rites of reception in entranceways, baptisms in separate baptistries, outdoor blessings and processions, eucharistic devotions in a chapel of reservation, and committals and other liturgical visits at cemeteries. Singing is normative in all such rites, so leaders of song are necessary, as are portable instruments. The organ cannot provide all of the accompaniment needed for ritual music.

In collaboration with the leaders of music and the instrumentalists themselves, we should see to the safe maintenance and storage of instruments left in the church complex. This includes not only routine security procedures, but attention to environmental factors such as temperature and humidity. Before temperature and humidity controls are set, local experts on the maintenance of the various musical instruments should be consulted.

Auxiliary Spaces

Ministers of music also need a storage place for sheet music, books and other materials. And if choirs or individual ministers such as the cantor regularly vest in choir robes or albs—a highly recommended practice—then they also need a place to vest. Both of these needs might well be satisfied by a common vesting room for all ministers. In large parishes particularly, a separate room might be used, not only for storage and vesting, but for rehearsals as well.

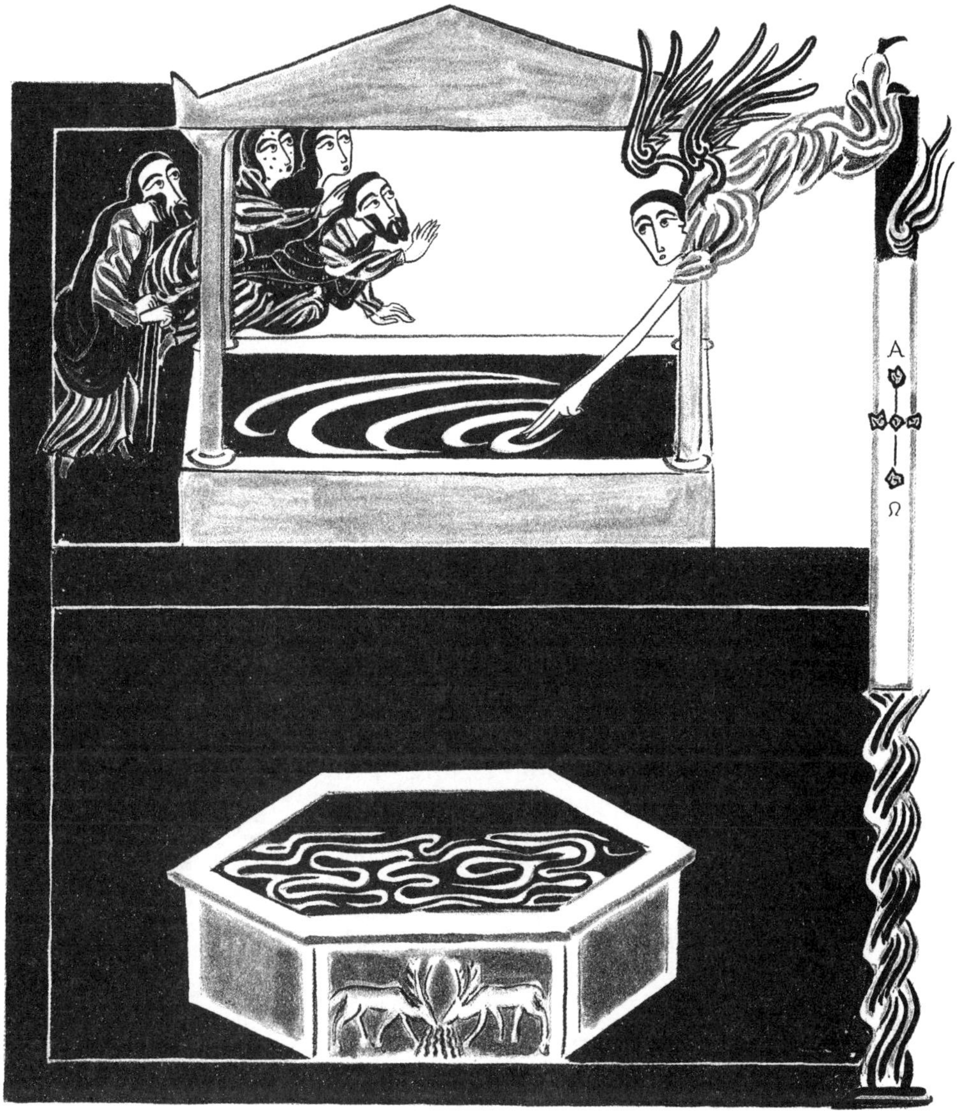

11◆ The Baptistry

A Place Reserved for Baptism

SEPARATE BAPTISTRIES: Early church complexes usually included a special place for baptism. Though some romantics envision catechumens going down to the local river or sea, the event was too closely related to the vigil and eucharist of the community for this to become normative. Besides, our earliest ancestors understood the action to be a dying and rising, or a bathing; the architecture and furnishings of tombs and baths would have expressed their belief better than an open body of water.

As cathedral complexes became public architecture, their urban planning included a special building for baptisms. These buildings often were quite large, and they drew on then-current forms of public baths or tombs. The exact shapes of the baptistries, their placement in relationship to the rest of the city center and cathedral complex, and local meanings differed from region to region, city to city. Many historical reviews of our own day explore some of the various meanings of the architecture of baptistries: the octagon, with the Eighth Day of paradise after our current time of seven days; the hexagon, with its reference to the sixth day (Friday) and death with Christ;

placement by the entranceway—because baptism is entrance into the church; placement north of the eucharistic assembly, the archetypal shadowy or pagan side. So diverse were the local traditions, so complicated were the adaptations of one city's patterns by another, that generalizations about early baptistries are of little use. This is not to minimize the importance of history, but simply to point up its immense variety and richness. The shape, design and location of the place for baptism were matters of great consequence for the early churches. They wanted their baptistries to express certain truths; they wanted the movement between parts of the complex to flow in good ritual order; they reserved the catechumenate and initiation to the cathedrals with definite convictions about the role of the whole urban church.

THE SHRINKING OF BAPTISTRIES: As part of the general devolution of liturgical forms, noted in every aspect of liturgical history, the public catechumenate at the heart of the city died out. Separate baptistries still were built in many conservative regions, but the trend was toward merging a smaller font into a corner of the place of eucharistic assembly. Despite these changes, and the cessation of so much liturgical action on the part of the whole church, communities continued to believe that the shapes of the baptistry-niche and of the font were important. They carried on their local traditions of circles or hexagons, squares or octagons, even though they had sometimes forgotten the original significance of these shapes.

The earliest experiences of baptistries were evidently so strong that the *Roman Ritual* has continued to keep at least minimal rules about conferring the sacrament of baptism in a dignified and reserved area, set apart at least by some railings. Official decrees and commentators always have warned those responsible for liturgical furnishings that the font is not just an object to put in some convenient empty space. It has always needed its own area, and this zone has always been related to the other parts of the church complex. The space certainly shrank over the millennium just past, but the need for a special area was never totally forgotten.

CURRENT NORMS: The *General Introduction to Christian Initiation,* printed before the rites for baptizing adults and the rites for baptizing children younger than catechetical age, reinforces this sense that a reserved place is necessary. It then notes the traditional options that still are operative:

> The baptistry or the area where the baptismal font is located should be reserved for the sacrament of baptism and should be worthy to serve as the place where Christians are reborn in water and the Holy Spirit. The baptistry may be situated in a chapel either inside or outside the church or in some other part of the church easily seen by the faithful; it should be large enough to accommodate a good number of people. (#25)

The *Book of Blessings* (#1083–1084) summarizes these options while calling communities to see how the various parts of the church complex relate:

> In the case both of a baptistry that is erected apart from the main body of the church for the celebration of the entire baptismal rite and of a font that is set up within the church itself, everything must be arranged in such a way as to bring out the connection of baptism with the word of God and with the eucharist, the high point of Christian initiation. A baptistry separated from the body of the church is to be worthy of the sacrament celebrated there and is to be set aside exclusively for baptism, as befits the place where, from the womb of the church, so to speak, Christians are reborn through water and the Holy Spirit.

DECORATING THE BAPTISTRY: The general norms are just that: quite general. We inherit one kind of baptistry or another. On occasion, renovations allow for new perspectives, but our main job is to enhance the vitality of the given space. Whether the baptistry is large or small, separated from the eucharistic assembly area or visible from it, every parish church has one. We should see to its maintenance, provisioning and seasonal decoration.

As in other parts of the church complex, the architectural surfaces should be studied. The colors and textures and materials of the walls, ceiling and floor will help or hinder the action of baptism. For example, the floor should not be covered with a carpet, because it will get wet; tile mosaics or fine patterns of stone are far more fitting. The ceiling, too, can be decorated, and the ancient practice of suspending a canopy over the area will be most helpful for defining the space if it is near the large assembly place. Not every section of the church complex should be decorated at every season, but when the season suggests higher festivity in the baptistry (the Easter Season, especially), the walls, arches, windows, portals and support systems can be fitting fields for decorations. Festooning the entrance portal or overhead canopy with greens or flowers is far more respectful of the font's power and far more visible than putting flower pots up against the font itself.

Font of Life

The font of living water is the heart of both the baptistry and of the community that is born there. One of the more obvious reforms of the late twentieth century was the re-emergence of large fonts. Set in the floor or resting on it, these pool-sized fonts are in many ways similar to the fonts preserved in early Christian complexes. The revived preference for large fonts does not spring from mere antiquarianism, but rather from a deliberate attempt to recover the fullness of the sacramental form by allowing those to be baptized actually to enter into the waters.

The witness of immersion baptism was so strong during the first millennium that the *Roman Ritual* throughout the second millennium maintained the rubrics that allowed for immersion. Even as baptisms were done almost universally by pouring a bit of water, the ritual book maintained the historical record. As parishes have re-experienced this once almost-forgotten action of immersion, norms for larger fonts have been issued. They can help us appreciate this most sacred place.

> The baptismal font . . . should be spotlessly clean and of pleasing design. . . . As for the rite of baptizing, either immersion, which is more suitable as a symbol of participation in the death and resurrection of Christ, or pouring may lawfully be used. (General Introduction to Christian Initiation, #19, 22 [1969])
>
> To speak of symbols and of sacramental signification is to indicate that immersion is the fuller and more appropriate symbolic action in baptism. New baptismal fonts, therefore, should be constructed to allow for the immersion of infants, at least, and to allow for the pouring of water over the entire body of a child or adult. Where fonts are not so constructed, the use of a portable one is recommended. (*Environment and Art in Catholic Worship,* #76 [1978])
>
> Baptism by immersion is the fuller and more expressive sign of the sacrament and, therefore, provision should be made for its more frequent use in the baptism of adults. The provision of the *Rite of Christian Initiation of Adults* for partial immersion, namely, immersion of the candidate's head, should be taken into account. (National Statutes for the Catechumenate, #17, as emended and confirmed by the Congregation for Divine Worship [1988])

Living Water

We need to appreciate these reasons for the recovery of large fonts. We must also participate in the reform by maintaining the strength of these pools of life, by decorating the baptistry's architecture rather than by crowding plants around the font. Most importantly, we need to be zealous in our care for the water itself. Speaking of this primary element, current norms continue the best of Christian tradition:

> The water used in baptism should be true water and, both for the sake of authentic sacramental symbolism and for hygienic reasons, should be pure and clean. If the climate requires, provision should be made for the water to be heated beforehand. (General Introduction to Christian Initiation, #18, 20)
>
> In order to enhance its force as a sign, the font should be designed in such a way that it functions as a fountain of running water. *(Book of Blessings,* #1085)

The maintenance of clean water normally requires a filtered circulation system, but other tools need to be available—for example, nets or strainers on long poles. Similarly detailed plans need to be in place for the warming of water. On a regular schedule when the baptistry is not in use, the font needs to be emptied for a full cleaning.

Mesh guards, added to prevent the drowning of toddlers, drastically alter the clear, clean look of the water. Security provisions always should be a part of the initial design, but, where re-fitting is necessary, these safeguards should be as inconspicuous as possible. The concern for safety actually points to a reason for keeping the font in a more reserved area, away from the traffic of gathering or sharing refreshment.

Running or living water obviously adds sound to the baptistry and to any areas near it. This should not be muffled as if it were intrusive; chutes or splashboards between levels of a font often weaken the design of the font as well as silence the water. Of course, a font too close to ambo or altar or presider's chair will be distracting. This is precisely why our tradition calls for a distinct baptistry area by the entrance or in another separate place.

Easter Candle

THE YEAR'S LIGHT: This is the "pillar of fire that glows to the honor of God." Casting its shifting light, the wax column leads the community into the Vigil. It is at the center of the year whose date is incised on it, at the center of the assembly that bears fire from its flame. It remains lit for all assemblies of the Fifty Days. And then it graces the baptistry and, throughout the rest of the year in many communities, the resting place of the casket.

This always has been the largest candle of the community, made from the finest wax and decorated with great care. This heritage makes a sacristan's work easier. Parish members are often happy to work on its fabrication (Regina Kuehn, "Making the Paschal Candle," *Environment and Art Letter* 4 [February 1992]). If volunteers having the requisite skills and willingness cannot be found, then other options should be explored, such as engaging a professional artist or shopping carefully in church-goods stores and catalogs that have a reputation for quality merchandise.

Despite the availability of "perpetual paschal candles" that are more plastic tube than candle (see pages 28–29), a fresh candle must be used each year. Remaining parts of the former candle can be melted down as part of the preparation of the new one, or else they should be disposed of in a reverent manner. Two traditions suggest ways to recycle the wax and paraffin: Old candles in England used to be melted down and made into smaller tapers for parish use; remains at Rome were used to make wax medallions impressed with the figure of a lamb. These discs were kept through the year as a reminder of Easter.

DECORATIONS: There are equally rich traditions for decorating this pillar, all of them a decided improvement over the sticky decals issued by vendors. The rite suggests incisions in the wax: a cross, the first and last letters of the Greek alphabet (alpha and omega), and the numerals of the year. It also recommends the insertion of five pieces of incense.

The incisions can be made by a presider at the start of the Vigil, but certain preparations are advisable. Well before the Vigil, an artist can mark the lines for the presider. Depending on the depth of the markings, made prior to Holy Saturday, the presider completes or deepens these incisions. If the incisions are to be accented with color, the commercial decals should be bypassed in favor of engaging a professional artist to perform this work, as well as to add any other decorations.

Well in advance of the Vigil, the incense pieces also should be prepared. The wax "nails" that come with most commercially-produced Easter candles should be discarded. Even if they fulfill some old rubric by encasing a fleck of incense, the incense is long lost to the viewer. We are not dealing here with the minimal fulfillment of law, for all of this decoration is optional. Having decided to use incense pieces, we should commission someone to purchase very large pieces of incense and to prepare them for insertion.

In addition to these traditional decorations, local artists can use subtle reliefs or colors to create a pillar of fire that is truly dignified. The decoration might include complements to the alpha, omega, and the year's numerals—images that express the parish's anniversary date, the title of the local church or the specific scripture selections for the year. The rich panoply of Easter images can be reviewed with an eye to choosing one or two (not more) that would best fit the shape of the candle. This form of liturgical art must be kept sublime so that the candle is not lost in the embellishments.

SIZE OF CANDLE AND STAND: Most vendors sell paschal candles that are just under or a little over two inches in diameter, with a height of three or three and a half feet. In some places, this will be a fine size. Within the limits set by the ability of the deacon to carry it steadily, some communities may want a larger candle. In the interests of greater size, however, the ritual actions should not be omitted. This is, after all, a ritual object and not just a decoration. It is self-defeating for a parish to have a paschal candle so large that it cannot be carried in procession or used to spread its flame to other candles.

The size limit of the candle is more often set by the size of its stand, or of the fixture—called a sleeve—at the top of the stand. Existing stands sometimes can be fitted with new sleeves, or new stands might be procured over the years. Though there is only one candle each year, it could be located in different areas and in different stands throughout the year. For example:

- Through Easter to Pentecost, the candle is in the place of eucharistic assembly, either by the ambo or in the middle of the sanctuary. At the Vigil itself, the rite notes its movement from the place of fire to this stand, from the stand to the font and back again. We should see that it is lit long before people arrive for the other assemblies of the season and extinguished only after all leave.

– From Pentecost night through the last baptisms before Lent or the Triduum, it is in a place of honor within the baptistry. Lit for every celebration there, it is the source of light for the candles of infants baptized through the year.

– The *Order of Christian Funerals* allows for the continuation of a custom popular in many regions. Taken from the baptistry or from its Eastertime position, the candle can be placed where the casket will rest during the funeral rites. If the body will be received into the church for prayer vigils on the night before the funeral, the candle also can be in the place of vigil. During Eastertime, the casket can be placed near the candle rather than moving the candle to the customary place for the casket. There is no rubric restricting the casket to a draped trolley in the center aisle.

Baptismal Candles

After his or her baptism, each neophyte receives a baptismal candle as a remembrance. The candle is a symbol of the all-important sacrament of baptism, and it should stay with the baptized person until death, lit perhaps for Easter and on the baptismal anniversary if it falls at a time other than Easter. Even though the annual lighting of the baptismal candle may be rare in most communities, we can encourage its observance by providing the newly-baptized with candles of sufficient size. Tiny candles won't do, nor will decals, pin-on emblems and transfers of goldish dust. Instead, choose large candles and have them decorated with Easter images by local artists. Prior to their use, baptismal candles should be kept in the sacristy or in an unobtrusive storage place within the baptistry.

Holy Oils

The oil of the sick and the oil of the catechumens bear names that denote their usage. The third, and the most important of the holy oils, is chrism. This mixture of oil and perfume is used at the holiest of moments that define Christian life—baptism, confirmation, ordination, and the dedication of churches and altars. In keeping with pre-Christian traditions, chrism also was used at the liturgies for coronations.

According to the rite of blessing for holy oils (#3–4), only olive oil should be used, or where circumstances warrant, other oil derived from plants. The perfume is unspecified, but most dioceses use one of the scents prepared and marketed as chrism fragrance.

On Holy Thursday morning or at another time in late Lent, the bishop presides at a Chrism Mass wherein these oils are blessed for the whole diocese. To show its importance in setting apart persons and buildings, chrism is said to be "consecrated." This setting apart, principally through the sacraments of initiation, is not a setting above or beyond. It is a consecration for service to and for the world and its transformation at the end. Thus, the texts for the consecration rite speak of those marked by chrism as "radiant with the goodness of life," shining God's goodness throughout the world.

With such beautiful texts, the Chrism Mass can be a full celebration of diocesan unity, of the various orders of liturgical service, of the ministries with the sick and with catechumens, of the way of life that makes chrismated persons radiant. Even if the Chrism Mass fails to reach its fullest potential, it can be complemented by a wonderful ritual in each parish at the opening of Evening Mass of the Lord's Supper on Holy Thursday. The oils to be used by the parish through the year, brought from the Chrism Mass by parish representatives—pastor, sacristan and/or others—are carried in the opening procession, incensed, and formally announced after the sign of the cross and greeting. Suggested texts for this ceremony will be published in the next edition of the sacramentary. Until its issuance, they are available from such sources as the diocesan office of liturgy. Thus, each parish can signify at still another level that it is entering the Triduum, the celebration of all the ministries of the church and the premier time to use chrism for initiation into radiance.

Though most oils used during the year will come from this supply, additional oil of catechumens can be blessed by a priest *(Rite of Christian Initiation of Adults,* #101–102). Similarly, oil of the sick can be blessed at that rite *(Pastoral Care of the Sick,* #21–22). As presiders recognize the need to pour oil or to rub goodly amounts of it, instead of just making the faintest smudge, the need for additional oil will become more and more obvious.

VESSELS FOR THE HOLY OILS: There are several kinds of vessels needed in every parish. First of all, every parish has a set of three vessels for the year's supply of holy oils. They are called chrismatories, or a variant of that word, such as chrismals. In our tradition, the history books group them with ampullae. The set of vessels used by the cathedral obviously will be enormous, the size for a given parish much less so, depending on how much oil the parish uses. As described in the *Roman Ritual,* the vessels must be worthy of their function and closed in such a way as to prevent spillage and maintain freshness. Many sacristans seem to prefer glass jars or decanters, but well-crafted ceramic or metal vessels can be recommended as well, and may, in fact, be preferable. It is not always desirable to see the reserved, consecrated elements. That is why glass tabernacles are forbidden. In terms of the reforms, it makes more sense for the assembly to see the oils when they are being used rather than when they are being stored.

Secondly, parishes will need some smaller containers, especially for carrying the oil of the sick. Sometimes called "stocks," the small cylinders of metal, stuffed with cotton, are weak symbols of the oil they bear. Sacristans and the ministers of this rite should search for small vessels and carrying cases that not only will hold the oil, but permit generous pouring or rubbing.

Finally, vessels will sometimes be needed to hold portions of oil poured from the main vessels during liturgical actions. For example, when moving from one sick person to another at a communal anointing, the ministers will need smaller pitchers or bowls for the oil. These might even be the same shells used for baptism when done by pouring.

REPOSITORY FOR THE HOLY OILS: The *Roman Ritual* includes few notes about this place of reservation, but it should be secure, protected by a lock, and located in a public area of the church complex. Its case or door might be translucent, if this will not unduly minimize security. Other materials should be in keeping with the architectural surfaces. Vessels for the three oils may be kept in the same case or they might be reserved in separate repositories. If kept together, the baptistry is the most obvious and popular place for them to reside. If they are not kept together then at least the chrism should be stored in the baptistry; the oil of catechumens might be in the meeting place of the catechumens, the oil of the sick where intentions for the sick can be written nearby.

There is no universal practice here, but it seems quite clear that the oils, even in their smallest vessels, are not to be kept permanently in a priest's jacket, in the rectory, or in a safe or cabinet of the less-frequented sacristy. The most popular custom, before the reforms of this past century, was to reserve the oils near the altar in a case affixed to the wall. The rite of anointing notes that priests should return the small vessel "to the place where it is kept with proper respect" *(Pastoral Care of the Sick,* #22). Reverence for the oils and for the church they serve necessitate the reservation of all of the parish's oils in one common repository or three individual repositories, one for each oil. Thus the oil from the smaller vessels not used on a given visit to the sick is to be poured back into the larger vessel, or the several smaller vessels that are carried to the sick are to be reserved in the same repository.

OTHER OILS: In addition to the holy oils described in the preceding sections, churches may use other oils for quite different purposes. Lamps positioned by the place of eucharistic reservation sometimes use oil as a fuel. In certain shrines, oil is blessed for use in devotions to a particular saint *(Book of Blessings,* chapter 59). These, and the almost infinite kinds of oils used for skin and health care in more secular settings, show that the liturgical oils are not inventions of bishops unrelated to the world. Rather, from the varieties of oils used in every home, certain ones are set aside by the community to touch us with the healing and wholeness that God wants for all.

Other Requisites for the Baptistry

PLACE FOR STORAGE: Unless the vesting room or sacristy is close by, a small, unobtrusive cabinet or credenza might be needed. In the cabinet or nearby sacristy or vesting room the following items should be stored: the ritual for the baptism of infants and any song sheets needed for the assembly, baptismal candles, matches, candle-lighter/extinguisher for the Easter candle and possibly for transferring light from it to baptismal candles, tapers for the lighter, a receptacle for burnt matches, water vessels, towels and perhaps baptismal robes.

WATER VESSELS: Several kinds of vessels and sprinklers will be needed, their size determined by the size of the font and local ceremonial customs. If fonts are large enough to accommodate the pouring of water over an adult standing in it (the traditional method of immersion), then a large pitcher or amphora will be needed. (The method familiar in Baptist communities, the plunging of the candidate into the water, is called submersion to distinguish it from the more traditional immersion form.) If baptism still is celebrated with a smaller pouring into a tiny font, and the baptizing minister prefers not to use a naked hand for this, then a vessel called the shell will be needed. Some seashells work very well. What's more, they come directly from nature, which makes them highly desirable in terms of the value that the liturgy places on natural materials. Metal shells are available from church goods catalogs.

Baptismal water is used regularly for the rite of blessing and sprinkling on Sundays and after the renewal of baptismal promises at the Easter Vigil. It is also a part of many "occasional rites"—marriage, funeral and various orders of blessing. The traditional bucket *(situla)* or a beautiful bowl with a complementary sprinkler are better symbols than the combined-unit sprinklers with reservoirs that look like microphones. The terms *aspersorium* and *aspergillum* in contemporary usage have come to mean either the bucket or the sprinkler, or both. The sprinkler can be metal, or a brush or branches. Traditionally, branches of hyssop, laurel, palm and boxwood were favored. Wisps of straw and the tail of a fox have been used and still can be, although the latter may distract people from the liturgical gesture.

If the laudable practice of bringing baptismal water home continues in the local community, we may want to have additional vessels available (small bottles with twist tops) for those who do not bring their own container. The water for this, as for the other rites described here, should not be drawn from the ugly vats seen in so many sacristies over the first half of the past century. The font should be large enough to provide this water. If it is too small, then the community should use a more dignified tank in which to store baptismal water. This should be near the baptistry, not hidden in the sacristy.

TOWELS: For the baptism of adults by immersion, very large or bath-size towels should be used. They can be held by godparents, then wrapped about the neophytes to catch the dripping water as they step out of the font. Much smaller towels will be needed for the immersion of infants, and still smaller ones for the pouring of water over infants. Ideally, a parish should have plenty of towels in all sizes. The middle sizes also can be used for the washing of the feet on Holy Thursday. The smaller ones can double as hand towels for the washing of hands at the preparation of the altar. All towels should be very absorbent; the traditional material is linen.

ROBES: Local customs will determine what robe (called *chrisom* in some liturgical traditions) is provided for adult neophytes and for children of catechetical age. Parishes should give priority to the alb. It is the basic garment of all liturgical ministers, as well as the traditional baptismal garment. Albs are readily available from many suppliers. See page 127 for a fuller description of them. If the neophytes keep their robes after taking them off at the end of the Vigil, the expense might be borne by special donors.

For the baptism of infants, many communities have experimented with little white items, some looking like bibs, others like stoles, many with insipid decoration. But most parents dress their infants for the occasion in wonderful christening dresses passed on from generation to generation. These are the baptismal garments, not the bibs. If there will be immersion baptism, then the baby can be wrapped "in swaddling clothes" until the baptism, and vested in the gown after. If families are unable to provide white garments like this, then a special group of parish members might be able to provide gowns that carry on the wonderfully full tradition of flowing, white vesture.

PLACE FOR DRYING AND VESTING: With immersion baptism, a side room will be necessary. If none presently exists, it should be a part of any renovation or new construction plans, perhaps with the vesting room and the baptistry near one another and the entranceway. For the immersion of infants, at least a drying table with soft towels is needed.

12◆ Catechumeneon: Gathering Place for Catechesis and Prayer

The Catechumens

The *Rite of Christian Initiation of Adults* presumes that catechumens will be dismissed from the eucharistic assembly near the conclusion of the liturgy of the word, before the intercessions and profession of faith. As noted in #67 of the rite, "After the dismissal formulary, the group of catechumens goes out but does not disperse. With the help of some of the faithful, the catechumens remain together to share their joy and spiritual experiences." Buildings and rooms designed for the gathering of the catechumens and located near eucharist assembly places are by no means a new concept. Archaeological and historical evidence can trace them back to the earliest centuries of Christianity. Scholars have termed this part of the church complex the "catechumeneon."

Today, the place of this sharing most often is called the "center for the catechumenate" (#92). This meeting after the liturgy of the word of the Sunday Mass also may include a minor exorcism, a blessing, or a rite of anointing (footnote to #89).

Whatever term is employed, there needs to be a special place for this Sunday gathering. It also could be used by the catechumens during the week for prayer and catechesis. The celebrations of the word (and exorcisms, blessings or anointings) that may accompany these catechetical sessions also can take place in the same center or room, or in another nearby part of the church complex. The center also should accommodate any uncatechized adults who may be preparing for confirmation and eucharist and who may be participating with the catechumens in catechetical sessions or celebrations of the word (#402, 407). The same should apply to baptized, catechized Christians preparing for entrance into full communion (#478). And the room could be used by "inquirers," as well (#39). If a reception has been planned for inquirers (as envisioned in #39), the room should meet the standards set by the rite of being non-liturgical and fitting for friendly conversation.

In keeping with the history of such spaces and their intimate connection with the sacrament of baptism, they might well be located near the baptistry or entranceway in new church complexes, or in thoroughly renovated older places.

Other Gatherings for Catechesis or Prayer

Depending on the frequency of sessions for inquirers and catechumens, and on the number of catechumens and candidates, a parish community may feel quite comfortable designating an entire room, center, or series of rooms to this purpose. But the catechumeneon or center for the catechumenate can justly and appropriately be used for these other gatherings of a prayerful or catechetical nature:

–Gatherings for the ongoing catechesis of adults, or, if the furniture is appropriate, of children.

–The separate liturgy of the word with children at Sunday Mass envisioned in the *Directory for Masses with Children* (#17). The furniture would have to be appropriate for young children, or all could stand or gather on the floor. If this liturgy is in the same room at the same Mass from which the catechumens are dismissed, then careful timing must be associated with the movement of both groups during the general intercessions of the main eucharistic assembly.

–Infants and toddlers might be cared for in this room at Masses other than the ones from which catechumens are dismissed, and during the liturgy of baptism. They would then be brought in to eucharistic assembly for the concluding rite *(Directory for Masses with Child,* #16), or to the baptismal assembly for the baptisms *(Rite of Baptism for Children,* #43). A location near the baptistry is thus most fitting in this case as well.

–If the community receives the bodies of its deceased on the day before the funeral Mass, then this room might well be fitting for the vigil of prayer and visiting normally associated with this part of the funeral process.

Furnishings and Decoration

This possible combination of occupants—catechumens, those engaged in catechesis, children at their liturgy of the word, infants, and even the bereaved with their beloved's remains—will not work in every parish. It is more a list of possibilities than a recommended combination. But the multiple uses do press us to consider the kinds of furniture and decor that should be in such a room. The catechumeneon, or whatever it is called in the local setting, is neither classroom, corporate conference room, nor group therapy site. Chairs and desks should not be set up as in a parochial school or continuing education center. There will be seating for persons of various ages, there may even be a moveable chalkboard or media center. But the ambience should be that of an ecclesial gathering—with chairs more in a circle than in the straight lines of an auditorium, with decor that speaks of the paschal mysteries, with the seasons expressed in flowers or decorations, with a well-bound lectionary as a focus.

Catechesis always should be enriched by local traditions, stories and art. Because the persons meeting here are either seeking entrance into the church or pursuing ever deeper commitment to the life of the church, then the decor might well include a wall of photographs of parish life, an artistic depiction of local traditions, photographs and job descriptions of local ministers, images of the parish's patron or title, or mounted press clippings about the parish's dedication. If the three holy oils are reserved separately, then this room can contain the repository for the oil of catechumens. If the room or another part of the catechetical center is used for toddlers or children, then their colorful art of the season might grace certain areas.

13◆ Chapel of Reconciliation

Community of Reconciliation

The sacrament of penance has passed through more major transformations than any other rite. The name given to the action has shifted a number of times, and even today remains controversial. Some retain the term confession; others insist that reconciliation is a better term. A few insist on noting that the word penance is the title used on the official ritual book. All of these names have a place in our practice; all of them signify parts of the *Rite of Penance* published in the 1970s.

Through the first centuries, rituals for the reconciliation of penitents were far more demanding and public than in our own age, some of them spread over a lengthy period of time. Scholars still debate the actual forms used then, but it seems clear that the rites took place with the participation of the assembly, in the entranceway and before the cathedra or presider's chair. Through the Middle Ages, churches from region to region adopted new and various ways to shorten the process and allow for private confession and absolution. This individual encounter between priest and penitent took place in the eucharistic assembly space, usually in the sanctuary, at the presider's chair.

The chair of the confessor, situated by the altar and thus expressing his presidential and eucharistic roles, was gradually transformed. The Council of Trent, and the decrees associated with its implementation after 1600, did away with the prominent chair in the sanctuary for the priest. But his chair for the action of reconciliation was still in the eucharistic assembly space, because commentators insisted on the relationship between reconciliation and the eucharist. (Even to our own time, children were taught to pray by the altar after completing confession.) Over the years, the chair became more and more enclosed, with an enclosure later provided for the penitent as well. Through the 1800s, Catholic immigrants arriving in the United States from

Europe discovered that the places for this sacrament had come to be even more enclosed here than in the old country.

During the decades of the liturgical movement prior to Vatican II, opposing trends were at work. Architects and designers of church interiors were perfecting the isolation of penitents in completely sound-proof chambers; liturgists were insisting that the area of confession be related to baptism and the eucharist—for example, by positioning the action off the baptistry. Liturgists began calling for more light and square footage for this action, more ability for the priest and penitent to see each other or at least some outline of human forms, some visibility of the priest making the gesture of reconciliation—a form of the laying on of hands. Some even called for the elimination of all or most of the enclosure, allowing the action to be seen but not heard by those in the church complex, fostering an appreciation of the communal nature of all reconciliation.

Location of the Place

The reformed rites have been quite laconic on this part of the church complex. The U. S. bishops' conference in 1974 asked that:

> . . . small chapels or rooms of reconciliation be provided in which penitents might choose to confess their sins and seek sacramental reconciliation through an informal face-to-face exchange with the priest, with the opportunity for appropriate spiritual counsel. It would also be regarded as desirable that such chapels or rooms be designed to afford the option of the penitent's kneeling at the fixed confessional grill in the usual way, but in every case the freedom of the penitent is to be respected. *(BCL Newsletter* 10 [December 1974])

This type of chapel was further recommended in *Environment and Art in Catholic Worship,* #81 (1978). The new Code of Canon Law a few years later (1983) insisted on the provision of a grill that a penitent could feel free to utilize (#964).

The location of the area reserved for this liturgical action is as important now as during the years preceding the reforms. Then commentators worried about confession seeming too private, unconnected with the liturgical life of the church; they called for its location near the baptistery. Now the new rooms of reconciliation are rarely seen as chapels; they appear more as counseling offices. Thus, they have summoned up the earlier fears that reconciliation is too private, too non-liturgical. We need to address this problem. Renovations should include ways for the reconciliation chapel to be located within the area of the baptistry or accessible to the eucharistic celebration area. When the places of confession are multiplied for penance services, they should be located near the font, altar, ambo, chair, or at least generally within the place of eucharistic assembly.

Furnishings and Decor of the Place

Within the reserved area or room or chapel, the furnishings and decor should be well chosen and austere. They should include seating for priest and penitent, a screen and kneeler for penitents who want to retain a measure of anonymity, cards or books with the order of the ritual for both priest and penitent, and a lectionary or Bible accessible to both. All these should be placed so that the penitent, after entering, can freely choose anonymity or face-to-face sitting before being seen by the priest. The area needn't be enclosed, just removed enough to assure aural privacy. There should be no shag rugs or lounge chairs. The look should not be that of a living room or therapist's office.

The art used in these areas should express the fullness of community, of the eucharistic community that is central to reconciliation. Pictures of a sweet Jesus are less fitting than the images traditional to liturgical art. A cross used to be customary in these spaces, but never has been required. Depending on the size of the area, there may be no space for representational art. A lit candle and open scriptures are quite suitable.

14◆ Chapel for the Reservation of the Eucharist

Serving the Sick and Fostering Adoration

From the earliest times onward, the eucharistic elements, our blessed sacrament, have been reserved after the celebration. The places for that reservation, though, have changed in every era. They have included Christians' homes or priests' residences; side rooms such as the sacristy or the main space for liturgical assembly; a vessel on the altar or suspended over the sanctuary; a castle-like tower away from the altar or a simpler case near the altar. In the years before and after the Council of Trent, the most popular container for the reserved eucharist was the tabernacle case fixed at the center of the altar. In fact, for centuries, right up until Vatican II, this was the normative way of reserving the eucharist.

The *Book of Blessings* (#1192) gives two purposes for the tabernacle:

> The tabernacle for eucharistic reservation is a reminder of Christ's presence that comes about in the sacrifice of the Mass. But it is also a reminder of the brothers and sisters we must cherish in charity, since it was in fulfillment of the sacramental ministry received from Christ that the church first began to reserve the eucharist for the sake of the sick and the dying. In our churches adoration has always been offered to the reserved sacrament, the bread which came down from heaven.

The Reforms after Vatican II

Through the first two-thirds of the twentieth century, liturgists and leaders like Pius XII became more conscious of problems arising from the reservation of the eucharist on the altar. The reception of communion by the assembly became more and more frequent; but the central presence of the tabernacle tempted priests to forget the connection between celebration and communion. The ceremonial of bishops noted that they were not to celebrate the eucharist at an altar that had the reserved eucharist; any tabernacle there was to be emptied before Mass began. Confusion emanated from the difference between the action of the eucharist and the adoration of the consecrated host. The former is an action in Christ addressed to God, the latter is a more static or tranquil adoration focused on Jesus. Participating in the sacramental action—singing, moving in procession, exchanging gestures, acclaiming the Creator, following the course of the scriptures—was in conflict with the behavior appropriate before the tabernacle—silence, kneeling, praying to Jesus, using devotional prayers that are not necessarily scriptural.

Those alert to these problems were encouraged, not surprised, by the changes in eucharistic reservation. In the appendix issued with #128 of the *Constitution on the Sacred Liturgy* (1963) and in the first of the instructions for implementing the constitution *(Inter Oecumenici, #95* [1964]), the centuries-long and problematic link of altar and tabernacle was broken. Thenceforth, the eucharist could be reserved on the main altar (even if turned to face the people), on a side altar, or in "another special and properly adorned part of the church." Within a year, clarifications from the Vatican congregations noted that these were not equal choices. When altars were facing the people, then a place apart from the altar was far better for the reservation.

In 1967, an official instruction *(Eucharisticum Mysterium, #53-55)* repeated the same choices for tabernacle placement, but made an even more forceful case for the preferred option:

> It is recommended that as far as possible the tabernacle be placed in a chapel set apart from the main body of the church, especially in churches where there frequently are marriages and funerals and in places that, because of their artistic or historical treasures, are visited by many people. . . . On the grounds of the sign value, it is more in keeping with the nature of the celebration that, through reservation of the sacrament in the tabernacle, Christ not be present eucharistically from the beginning on the altar where Mass is celebrated. That presence is the effect of the consecration and should appear as such.

All of the reformed liturgical books and our own national documents reinforce this directive, even omitting the qualifier about "frequented" or pilgrimage places. For example, the *General Instruction of the Roman Missal* (#276) notes that "every encouragement should be given to the practice of eucharistic reservation in a chapel suited to the faithful's private adoration and prayer." This is to be separated from "the body of the church" unless it would be impossible due to the building's structure.

Separate chapels are seen in many church complexes today. Other communities still position their tabernacle within the place of eucharistic celebration, either behind the altar in the center line of the architecture or off to one side. Within the given local setting, we need to appreciate the reasons for these reforms and do all in our power to keep the space of action and the space of quiet adoration physically distinct.

Forms of the Reserved Sacrament

EUCHARISTIC BREAD: Whereas in the past it was standard to use the tabernacle as a regular source of communion, the reformed rites stress the central meaning of sharing the eucharist consecrated at the Mass being celebrated (cf. *General Instruction of the Roman Missal,* #56h). Thus, we are to be alert to patterns of participation and plan for the right amount of recently baked bread at each Mass; changes in the amount can be made when all are assembled, up until the presentation of the gifts. If the estimate is found to be incorrect during the communion rite, the eucharistic bread can be further broken by ministers, or else larger portions can be used for individual communicants.

If eucharistic bread remains after communion, it may be consumed at the credence table. In some cases, pyxes will be filled for the special ministers of the eucharist who will be sent from the Mass to take communion to the sick. Remaining eucharistic bread, placed in a ciborium or pyx, should be added to the tabernacle only in preparation for later rites with the sick. The rites envision the reservation of only enough consecrated hosts sufficient for the communion of the sick and others outside Mass. The sole exception to this rule occurs when the eucharist will be placed in a monstrance for a period of adoration. The host used for this purpose will be reserved.

EUCHARISTIC WINE: The restoration of eucharistic cup-sharing has given rise to questions of reservation. The rites and the U. S. national directory on communion under both kinds allow such reservation only in this circumstance:

> Sick people who are unable to receive communion under the form of bread may receive it under the form of wine alone. . . . The blood of the Lord is kept in a properly covered vessel and is placed in the tabernacle after communion. The precious blood should be carried to the sick in a vessel which is closed in such a way as to eliminate all danger of spilling. *(Pastoral Care of the Sick,* #74)

This practice would be more popular, even regular, if those affected (those with an allergy to wheat, those who swallow with difficulty) knew to ask for it. We need to provide proper vessels for this reservation and for transport to the sick.

The Tabernacle

The word tabernacle, with all of its rich religious history, long ago came to designate the locked container or safe in which the eucharist is reserved. There is to be only one in each church complex, preferably located, as noted earlier, in a separate chapel. If local renovations have not yet eliminated extra tabernacles, they should be perpetually empty, unmarked by any decorations or by any traditional indications of eucharistic presence. Decorators should thus remove any sanctuary lamp stands near these unutilized containers, any cloths or veils or lighting.

The various documents of our age describe the tabernacle as solid, unbreakable, made of nontransparent or opaque material, dignified and properly ornamented. It is to be locked and its key is to be kept carefully. None of the current rites gives further specification to the design and materials. Tabernacles in existence before Vatican II were always covered with an opaque veil of white or of the color of the day. The very term tabernacle came to be associated with the tent-like look created. Now such veils are optional, but are recommended where they have come to be taken as a sign of the eucharistic presence.

Once there were several laws and customs regarding interior lining for the tabernacle. Some tabernacles still contain these linen pieces or panels. Where used, they should be removable for periodic cleaning, perhaps during the period when the tabernacle is empty, from the Good Friday communion to the Easter Vigil. Even if such covers are not utilized, and depending on local climate, the box might well benefit from a lining of wood that protects against moisture.

Some sacristans have a special need to consider the lining. Tabernacles with doors that revolve inside on ball-bearings (instead of opening outward) were normally constructed with an asbestos lining between metal plates. Given the justifiable concern about asbestos, the sacristan should consult with local experts if the tabernacle has asbestos lining.

Lamp Before the Tabernacle

As a mark of reverence and as an indication of the presence of the eucharist in the tabernacle, it has long been required to have a lamp burning perpetually before it. While all other liturgical illumination in the church complex is by candles, here there is a choice—a candle (preferably of wax) in a lamp or an oil lamp. (See page 29 regarding strictures against tubes and other inappropriate substitutes for lamps.) There is no set place for the lamp other than near the tabernacle, but local codes for open flames should be respected. A suspended lamp, or multiple suspended lamps, is most traditional, but lamps also can be mounted on floor stands or on wall brackets. Though it may seem pietistic by contemporary standards, the continual vigilance necessary to keep an oil lamp burning is an ancient and biblical symbol of human preparedness for the Lord's coming, and has always been one of the more symbolic acts performed by sacristans.

Other Materials for the Chapel

FURNITURE: The chapel should not be jammed with furniture. Neither chairs nor kneelers are mandated. If present, they should harmonize well with the overall design of the space, and allow for the open space so conducive to meditation. Pastoral ministers may want to provide suitable prayer texts or biblical passages in racks (cf. the readings and responsories in Part IV of *Holy Communion and Worship of the Eucharist outside Mass).*

WATER AND TOWEL: Before the reforms, when tabernacles were regularly used during Mass, the ministers used a small cup of water and a towel to cleanse the thumb and forefinger after communion. These small "ablution cups" are still seen near many tabernacles. They are not necessary, because the ministers and vessels now go to the credence table or sacristy after communion, rarely to the tabernacle. The sacristy or the credence table is where all cleansing occurs. The only vessels brought to the tabernacle should be those that contain the hosts being reserved for the sick.

DECORATIONS: Flowers and decorations, in addition to a finely-made lamp, can grace the chapel. But they should not overwhelm the tabernacle. The reserved sacrament should be a reminder of the sick and dying for whom it is reserved. Thus decorations might include images of this ministry or a book to enter petitions for the sick. This room should be as carefully supervised by sacristans as any other part of the church. Statues should not be placed here haphazardly, nor should the room be used as a storage place.

15◆ Shrines and Other Areas for Private Devotions

Representations of Jesus and of the saints grace our church buildings so that we might interact with them, tracing in our hearts the patterns of their holiness. This activity is not to be equated with liturgical rites, celebrated by the whole local church in communion with other churches. Instead, these devotions, as they have come to be called, involve the exercise of individuals' emotions outside of the set liturgical forms. Over the past decades, commentators and the official rites have pressed for the simplification of the place in which liturgy is done, in order to make it easier for worshipers to focus on the actions of the liturgy. This has been accompanied by designating somewhat distinct areas for devotion or shrines, off of the main axis of sacramental action. Shrines located in somewhat separate and distinct areas are far more conducive to private devotions than they would be if they were located in the sanctuary.

Norms for Shrines

These shrines can be outdoors, off the entranceway, in unused alcoves, or in other corners of the church complex. They should allow the right amount of space for the interaction of people and images, but they should not impede the core actions of liturgy.

According to a long-standing tradition, the church complex should contain no more than one image of any one saint. Exceptions always have been made for images of Jesus and of Mary; one image for any given title can be placed for adoration. Neither does the rule apply to narratives of a given saint played out in windows, mosaics or frescoes.

Not all the images in the parish's collection need be displayed at the same time, particularly if the parish has limited space. If a parish has images of many saints, or many images of the same saint, the images can be moved back and forth between shrine and storage areas according to the seasons of the year or some other logical scheme.

Sacristans, liturgy committees and decorators need to give careful consideration to the practice of veiling images during Lent. If this custom will be revived, then new and old images for devotion need to be removable or fitted for covers.

Image of the Church's Title

Every parish should have an image of its title, either inside or outside the building. The image of this saint or of this aspect of Jesus should be of such a scale, of such dignity, and so positioned that it invites interaction. Examples of interaction include placing flowers and, on occasion, other festal decorations, lighting votive candles, and simple touching. Obviously this will not work for parishes entitled Holy Spirit or Holy Trinity or Transfiguration. Yet even in those parishes, as in all others, consideration should be given to the decorative program related to the title. This might be a permanent change made in a renovation, or it might be something more temporary at the annual solemnity of the local title—for example, collaboration with religious educators to have groups add their art to the shrine.

Stations of the Cross

Despite their optional status, another prevalent work of devotional art is the stations of the cross. The list of 14 has only been codified for a few hundred years, and even at the stations of the cross led by the pope, alternative listings of the 14 have been used. What is important is that the members of the community know the system used and interiorize ways to pray the local stations.

In most cases, these 14 crosses (and the optional images accompanying them) are already in place. They need only cleaning and regular maintenance. Where not yet set, planners can have them placed in any part of the church complex, preferably in a way that permits those making the stations actually to progress along a path. This usually rules out placing the stations in a small devotional chapel or bunching them up in a small area along one wall; rather, the action suggests an installation in the floor. The stone or tile crosses and images could be embedded along a side aisle or in a devotional garden.

Images of Mary and of Other Saints

Most Catholic churches have a Marian shrine or image. As in the case of all shrines, any statue of Mary should be of dignified design. The shrine for Mary might well provide sufficient space for any groups that want to pray the rosary in common. It can be decorated with extra candles and flowers for all of the Marian feasts and memorials.

Seasonal decorations should be set by the liturgical year, and not by civil months like May and October. In Advent, when the great feasts of the Immaculate Conception and Our Lady of Guadalupe occur, when the scriptures describe her preparations for the great coming of the Lord, Mary's shrine might be decorated in keeping with the rest of the complex. Or the Advent wreath might be there. In Lent, the image might well be veiled, along with all other sanctoral images and crosses. To show the unity of the Fifty Days and to honor Mary as *regina caeli,* the shrine might be decorated from the Easter Vigil until Pentecost, days normally including most of May.

After Mary, the most frequently enshrined images are those of the Sacred Heart of Jesus and of St. Joseph. Yet devotional activity surrounding them is nearly nonexistent in some communities. World-wide, the two favorite saints for intercessory prayer seem to be St. Thérèse Lisieux and St. Anthony of Padua. In planning permanent and seasonal images, sacristans need to consider the devotions favored by the specific community they serve.

16◆ Entrance Area

The wondrous vision of the new Jerusalem, described at the end of the Book of Revelation, has inspired every generation: "The city has no need of sun or moon to shine on it, for the glory of God is its light, and its lamp is the Lamb. Its gates will never be shut by day—and there will be no night there" (21: 23, 25). Our medieval ancestors were holding to that same vision when they pictured the entranceway of the church complex to be a sign of paradise. All were welcomed to a place of nightless glory.

The architectural prominence and decor of ancient church entranceways attest to their importance. The communities wanted all who entered to feel the pull of the open doors, to enter into sacramental brilliance. The entrance halls were as large as they were beautiful. They provided both a transition to ecclesial space and shelter for many of the rites. Indeed, the whole congregation often gathered in the entrance hall, so that all could enter the assembly together in solemn procession.

Depending upon the region and upon architectural form, the entrance area might have been called the atrium, narthex, or vestibule. Closer to our own times, terms like lobby, foyer, commons and concourse have been added to the mix. Whatever the term used, there still is a need for an entrance hall distinct from the eucharistic assembly area. As in the past, it provides a transition between the world and the sacraments of the transformed world.

Exterior

Every aspect of the church complex has its importance in revealing the gospel, in drawing the people into liturgical action. The exterior areas associated with parish churches are no exception. Parking areas, walkways, yards and outdoor shrines need to be clean, hospitable, and well suited to their gathering function. They not only draw all into the buildings; they often serve as gathering places for devotions and receptions, blessings and processions.

BELLS: The use of sound to summon an assembly is very ancient. The first reading at Mass on Ash Wednesday contains one of the classic references: "Blow the trumpet in Zion! Proclaim a fast, call an assembly." (Joel 2: 15) The shofar still heralds the new year in Jewish congregations everywhere. Eastern churches from the very first centuries often used a simandron, hanging objects that someone struck with a mallet.

The use of bells for summoning the Christian assembly can be traced to the fourth or fifth century. Many sources indicate that they were introduced by Paulinus of Nola (in Campania), the bishop who said that he really wanted to be a sacristan. Yet this association may have arisen from a similarity between terms like campanile (a free-standing bell tower) and Campania, or from the Latin term *nola* for bells, or from the sacristans' task of pealing bells. Sacristans traditionally have discharged this function.

Over the centuries, bells took on other functions. In addition to calling the assembly, they were used to draw those absent from the assembly into prayerful union—for example, during high moments of the eucharistic prayer or during special hymns of praise. Through the Middle Ages, they also were utilized as civic clocks, as invitations to non-liturgical private prayer (the times of the Angelus prayer), and as heralds of extraordinary events. In its blessing of bells, the *Book of Blessings* (#1305) notes that bells express the sentiments of the people of God "as they rejoice or grieve, offer thanks or petition, gather together." Thus they both signal and enhance the unity of the assembly.

The tradition of silent campaniles from the start of the Triduum (the Gloria on Holy Thursday evening) to the Easter Vigil should be respected. Their stillness is a powerful symbol of the importance of these days. Working with music ministers, sacristans and bell-ringers can establish other customs, with bells especially enhancing outdoor processions.

DECORATIONS: Exterior ornaments should, of course, respect both the local landscape and the architectural forms of the church complex. Perhaps the most obvious item needed by every facility is a sign naming the church and giving pertinent data about services. Sacristans, other decorators, and pastoral staff members should give careful consideration to this simple but powerful element. The wording, the use of lettering that can be read from afar, the updating of festal information and the possibility of seasonal embellishments are all important and should be periodically reviewed.

Other obvious possibilities for the outdoor area flow from this basic sign. If the church's name is that of a saint, there might well be an outdoor statue in his or her honor, specially decorated for the annual feasts of title and dedication. During the great seasons of the year, colorful hangings on the building or arrangements of flowers announce a festive season. At Christmas, it's hard to beat a large evergreen decorated with lights. The manger scene might be outdoors as well, and there are many other possibilities. All should suit the season so well that they don't have to be explained, and be so attractive and durable that parishioners will look forward to seeing them year after year. All decorations need to respect the liturgical seasons, of course—for example, no créche in Advent, no lilies in Lent.

If national, state or territory, city or Vatican flags are to be used at the church complex, their positions should be carefully considered. They should not be in the place of eucharistic assembly (page 57), nor in other areas such as the baptistry. They might well find an appropriate place in a yard or plaza area, or in a memorial area of the parish cemetery. Here assemblies can gather for any civil ceremonies on holidays, keeping the national and the universal distinct for all, and allowing non-Christian neighbors or relatives to feel comfortable.

DOORS: In their materials and surface decorations, their handles and lintels, doors can be a powerful expression of the community. Reviewing the texts associated with their blessing (chapter 34 of the *Book of Blessings),* we should review the liturgical importance of doors. They are the place for receiving bridal couples and infants to be baptized, for welcoming mourners bearing their deceased and for greeting catechumens. They are the passageway for formal processions and for individual entrances. For all of these actions, the doors can provide dignified decoration, invitations to the season and feast.

The possibilities for seasonal decorations are quite diverse. As with other seasonal signals, they should be simple and repeatable on an annual basis. During the Christmas and Easter seasons wreaths might hang from the doors; near the end of Lent, olive branches. At Pentecost, and for the final days of Eastertime leading up to this feast, the door casing could be decorated with greens, much the same as the way the Jewish people traditionally decorate their synagogues. Or one could copy the old European custom of observing all major festivals by framing the main doorway of the church with well-made draperies. Such draperies should be of the utmost dignity, and durable enough to be used year after year at Christmas, Easter, the parish anniversary of dedication and other major feasts.

Entrance Hall

Whether called the narthex, vestibule, commons, foyer or lobby, this area is rightly given careful attention by ushers and sacristans. Here the people make the transition from the outside to the liturgical action, from the world as experienced every day to the transformed world promised in the sacraments. Over the centuries, when congregations understood themselves to be spectators or an audience for the priest's words, the transition was commonly described as one from the hustle and bustle of the street to the reverent silence before the blessed sacrament. Through the twentieth century, from the liturgical movement to the subsequent reforms, parishes came to appreciate a different kind of transition—from private or household preoccupations to action with a broader body of people; from all manner of worthwhile pursuits in the world to a dedicated participation in sacramental action. Thus the entrance hall does not have to be a decompression chamber, but rather a re-focusing place, a place to be equipped for community action, for singing, for the feast.

VESTURE: The old name "vestibule" can remind us that vesture needs are not restricted to the priest and deacon. On any day when members of the assembly enter with coats or umbrellas, special footgear or hats, provisions must be made for their transition to an indoor action that presumes their full participation. The vestibule should have a place to hang coats, and there should be special mats or grates for absorbing moisture from footgear. As Robert Hovda pointed out decades ago:

> Most church buildings seem to have been planned without a thought about cloakrooms, accommodations for coats, hats, overshoes, umbrellas, etc. As a result we get congregations in which people are not only mentally and emotionally isolated from each other, but also physically and materially. If they aren't wearing coats, as if they were taking a breather during a walk in the park, then they are clutching them in their laps, as if determined to make the visit brief. To try to help a congregation in that condition to come to life in liturgy is an exercise in futility. Can you imagine inviting people to a party in your home and failing to take their coats and hats as they come in? (*There Are Different Ministries* [Washington DC: The Liturgical Conference, 1975], 26–27)

For many parishes, coatrooms are a wish that is listed with other renovation needs. In the meantime, perhaps an unused space off the vestibule can be turned into a coatroom (with systems and ministers that assure convenient and secure drop-off and pick-up). Portable coatracks might fit in the vestibule itself—a somewhat ugly, but extraordinarily important, compromise until a new coatroom is built. If no possibilities present themselves at the entranceway, then we should allow enough space for a coat pile in every row of seats.

HOLY WATER STOUPS: Since at least the early medieval period, these vessels or basins with baptismal or holy water have been placed in the entranceway. They are related to earlier precedents (vessels of water in early Christian atria) and to the ritual action of sprinkling that takes place at the start of many liturgical events. In a sense, they are a reminder of the baptismal font that is located elsewhere in the complex. When we enter the building before liturgy begins, dip our fingers in the water and cross ourselves, we are performing the first of a series of liturgical acts that will follow.

In places where the font is at or near the entrance hall, this primordial vessel of blessed water can be the source for signing those entering and for sprinkling caskets being received. In church communities where the font is housed separately from the entrance, one or more fitting stoups or vessels can be positioned for those entering. Sacristans should keep the stoups free of litter and sponges, and filled with water taken from the font after baptisms.

PARTICIPATION MATERIALS: Besides taking off our coats and signing ourselves with baptismal water, we need to receive the hymnals or song sheets, the candles or palm branches that we will use at the given liturgy. These might well be placed in advance on all of the seats, but it is often more efficient and hospitable to distribute them in the entrance hall. Racks or book-carts need to be purchased over the years. These should be simple and unobtrusive, but sizable enough to perform their function. Their position should be a factor in planning any seasonal or permanent decorations.

THE GIFTS: Also called the oblations table in some liturgical traditions, this stand or table should be in the entranceway, not at the front of the first row of seats. The rite that provides for the presentation of bread and wine is meant to be a procession through the assembly, not just a quick passing from front pew to sanctuary. This table can be the place for seasonal decoration or a feast day image that beckons all to the feast.

The close relationship between this presentation of bread and wine and gifts for the poor is expressed in the general norm, printed after the presentation of bread and wine in the *General Instruction of the Roman Missal,* "This is also the time to receive money or other gifts for the church or the poor brought by the faithful or collected at the Mass. These are to be put in a suitable place but not on the altar." (#49)

After the collection, the procession of bread and wine and monetary donations can leave from the gifts table and proceed to the altar area, where the monetary donations are placed off to the side. This ceremonial action is seen most forcefully on Holy Thursday evening, when the directives read, "At the beginning of the liturgy of the eucharist, there may be a procession of the faithful with gifts for the poor." Yet, on regular Sundays and feast days, they might better be collected at a position related to the gifts table in the entranceway—especially when the gifts are of a different sort—canned goods or used clothing. Thus, the bread and wine are visually related to the gifts of the people. In keeping with this relationship, any "poor boxes" or containers for the collection of parish-related funds can be positioned near the gifts table and the reception area for canned goods.

COMMUNICATIONS: These entranceways rightly continue to be the best place to post notices and photographs of parish activities. A board or appropriately covered wall can provide space for all of the posters and sign-up sheets necessitated by an active community. A particularly important facet of this intercommunication is the recruitment of volunteers for all of the parish's ministries. A "wall of opportunity" can be set up with brief job descriptions, requirements, and lines for signing up; this can be done as an annual campaign for volunteers or as an opportunity to promote more involvement before Christmas and Easter. Pamphlet and book racks also can be positioned in relationship to these displays.

Certain displays will occur with regularity each year—biographies of parish pastoral council candidates, background on the group that will receive lenten alms, pictures of those elected for Easter initiation—and these should be remembered in each seasonal plan. When approaching each season, we might consider decorations for this area of the entrance, as well as the areas for the gifts and for the hymnals or song sheets.

OTHER DECORATIONS: The entrance hall might be an appropriate place for certain seasonal decorations such as the Advent wreath or a Jesse tree, for the Christmas manger or tree, for flowers and candles before the statue of the saint of the day.

STORAGE: Most churches have at least a small closet off the entrance hall—and for good reason. Besides the obvious tools necessary for ushers, collection baskets and mops for wet entrance floors, some of the items listed under security and health (page 162) might be stored here. When selecting any of these materials, the sacristan should consult the ministers who are most involved. Their opinions should be weighed along with applicable liturgical principles. For example, when selecting collection baskets or plates, the interaction of the assembly and the dignity of the collection process should be considered. From a liturgical point of view, baskets that can be passed from hand to hand are better in most cases. Here again the selection of an object relates to a style of action.

OTHER FACILITIES: Though rest rooms are best positioned off the entrance hall or "commons," there are many other alignments that are possible or even necessary in older buildings. Both men and woman should have access to changing tables for infants. Halls or rooms for cooking and for other forms of hospitality, offices and conference rooms, all rooms of a less liturgical nature can be related to the liturgical spaces. All of these spaces should be considered in a comprehensive way when decorators, sacristans, educators and pastoral staff meet for joint planning.

17◆ Gathering Place

Socials

The entrance hall or, in a warm climate, an exterior space might well be large enough to allow for many members of the assembly to gather before and after liturgical events. As noted by *Environment and Art in Catholic Worship* (#54), such a space "can encourage introductions, conversations, the sharing of refreshments after a liturgy, the building of the kind of community sense and feeling recognized now to be a prerequisite of good celebration." In many church complexes, this socializing can fit only in cafeterias or basement halls that are considerably out of the way. Yet even in these settings, schedules and programs should be arranged to allow assemblies to develop the habit of visiting these social spaces as often as possible.

Rituals

The Roman rite presumes the existence of another kind of gathering place. These are not just "social halls"; several rituals are set here rather than in the eucharistic assembly hall:

1. Rites of blessing that precede eucharistic gatherings. Each of these is described in the sacramentary as starting in a place that is separate from the church building:

–the blessing of candles on February 2

–the blessing of palms on Passion (Palm) Sunday

–the blessing of fire at the Easter Vigil.

2. Rites of preparation and the gathering of all for solemn processions:

–the penitential procession recommended for the First Sunday of Lent *(Ceremonial of Bishops,* #261; recommended for all parishes in the

Circular Letter Concerning the Preparation and Celebration of the Easter Feasts, issued by the Congregation for Divine Worship in 1988)

–any procession that will later move to the eucharistic assembly place.

3. Rites of reception at the beginning of certain sacramental celebrations:

–receiving children at the start of the baptism of children

–receiving the candidates at the start of the rite of acceptance into the order of catechumens

–the entrance rite of marriage

–the reception of the body at the vigil for the deceased or at the beginning of the funeral Mass.

Location and Decoration

In the *Ceremonial of Bishops* (#54), these rites are envisioned as unfolding in "another church, a suitable hall, a square, or a cloister." The rites of blessing would ideally be at an outdoor gathering place somewhat removed from the entranceway of the eucharistic assembly place. The rites of gathering for processions, indoors or out, should also be somewhat removed to allow for a full movement of the procession. The rites of reception are better held at the doors, just inside or outside the entrance hall that in turn communicates to the eucharistic assembly space.

Local specifications depend so much on the floor plan of the complex and on the climate. It would seem, though, that larger communities should fully utilize the spaces that are already provided. These spaces for liturgical rites of preparation and reception might be found in the entranceways or social halls. Looking at the upcoming rites, planners should evaluate all lawn areas and parish center halls, entrance halls and porticos. The place most fitting for the occasion should be equipped for use. Then local traditions for such preparatory gatherings can be established. There is no need to find a new starting place for Palm Sunday every year, or a new place for the Easter fire. Once a good place is found, it should be used every year. The most fitting place for each of these events may be the same, or varied traditions may be set for different feasts. The blessing of fire, for example, is certainly different from the rite of receiving mourners and their loved one's remains.

In parishes where the movement of whole assemblies presumed in such rites is deemed impossible because of limited space, sacristans and planners should try to review this question on a periodic basis. Sometimes a creative approach becomes clear only after several reviews of options—use of the street out front for one or two annual occasions, a procession arranged with neighboring churches, the removal of rear pews to create space for fitting receptions of infants and bridal couples. Usually it is not space that hinders these full and beautiful rites. It is the hesitation of leaders to use the full rites the way that they were intended.

These preparatory gatherings each will need some equipment from the sacristy: a podium or platform, certain vessels or elements. The gatherings also will benefit from decorations on occasion. These will differ according to the event. Please refer to the descriptions under the lists for February 2 (page 222), First Sunday of Lent (pages 196 and 199), Palm Sunday (page 203), Easter Vigil (page 215), baptism (pages 216 and 237), acceptance of catechumens (page 235), marriage (page 245) and funerals (page 241).

18◆ Cemetery

In various periods of our history, the cemetery was a treasured part of the parish church complex. The bereaved often wanted their loved ones buried near the place of worship or near the graves of important martyrs and saints. Even today, parish cemeteries envelop the church buildings in some dioceses, providing a wonderful context of memory around the holy assembly. Sacristans in parishes with cemeteries on the grounds have received a great gift; they should include the cemetery when decorating for the seasons.

At other times in our history, especially for the first few centuries, Christians were buried away from the places of regular eucharistic gathering. This was generally true in urban communities, where there were strictures against burying the dead within the city walls. The famous catacombs outside Rome are examples of this practice. In the same centuries Christians also used both above-ground cemeteries and covered, hall-like cemeteries. Rites of memorial, perhaps even an occasional eucharist, were celebrated in some of these settings, especially on days of special remembrance for the dead. Even through persecutions, the regular gatherings for liturgy were in the city. Then, as is often the case now, cemeteries were occasional places. Whether distant cemeteries utilized by a parish are owned by the church, the municipality or a private corporation, sacristans and pastoral planners should consider these holy places in their long-term planning.

A Liturgical Space

Whether near or far from the place of the funeral Mass, the cemetery is the hallowed place where the liturgical rites surrounding committal take place. These are not just hurried prayers murmured before the family returns to their automobile. The rite is a public action of the local church involving a range of set texts, music, and the lowering or burial of the body. In the United States, the casket often is not lowered into the grave until all mourners have departed. Despite this truncation of the proper religious action, the rite of committal is always a powerful, even wrenching, event. When it occurs within the church complex cemetery, it flows from the procession of the entire assembly. When it is more detached by time and distance, the assembly, regrettably, will be smaller.

Other actions also occur at the cemetery. Various adults and households visit plots at cemeteries throughout the year. One can always see widowed individuals making their way through the grounds, often on the anniversary of the death of a spouse. On days such as Memorial Day, their numbers increase. Special groups, particularly of military veterans, converge upon the grounds for annual memorial programs.

Pastoral leaders should do everything possible to encourage such interactions. Whether a civic or parish-owned cemetery, they should see that hours are extended and conditions congenial for the regular visitation of the grounds. These efforts can be reinforced by occasional catechetical sessions at the tombs (reading inscriptions or drawing some of the found symbols), or by parish-sponsored memorial picnics. Even when the antiquity of a cemetery decreases the number of personally bereaved, such communal events link all to their local history and provide irreplaceable formation in faith.

In addition to these private and civic prayers, the church has a wonderful Order for Visiting a Cemetery (chapter 57 of the *Book of Blessings).* Meant for use on days like November 2 and Memorial Day, it is a public liturgy for the whole parish, often occurring after a Mass in the church building or at the cemetery.

Decoration

The prayer for blessing a cemetery *(Book of Blessings,* #1432) alerts us to the ambience befitting such a liturgical place. These places of rest and hope are "a comfort to the living, a sign of their hope for unending life." The prayers offered here are "in supplication for those who sleep in Christ and in constant praise of (God's) mercy."

The principal decoration of a church cemetery, whether part of the parish building complex or separated from it, continues to be a large cross erected in a prominent place. Placed under this sign, the cemetery becomes a more powerful place of hope in the resurrection. Where such a central cross exists, it can be decorated for such seasons as Easter, for such festival days as Christmas and November 1–2, and perhaps even for the whole month of November.

When arranging other permanent or temporary decorations, parish ministers should do everything possible to steer clear of the all-too-prominent secular decor of previous ages, such as female figures in theatrical poses weeping over broken urns. Perhaps the parish-sponsored decorations will supplement the cross with improved plantings in common areas of the grounds. Roses and lilies can join the more somber cypress and willow. Obviously the sacristan and any trustees of the cemetery can be joined in this by many parish members with knowledge of local planting cycles.

Besides such care for the garden areas, planners should recall the primitive use of candles in early Christian cemeteries. In cemeteries surrounding church edifices, luminaria might burn by each tomb or along walkways before and after evening Mass on such days as November 2. In those same communities blessed with an on-site cemetery, this might be the gathering place for blessings such as the fire at the Easter Vigil. Candlelight vigils in cemeteries near or detached from churches are an old and still worthy custom, perhaps on the eve of All Saints or of the parish's dedication anniversary. Eternal flames can also be arranged to great benefit.

Whether near or far, cemeteries should be a factor in every season's decorative program. The community will be enormously grateful to every sacristan and planner who allows Advent and Christmas, Lent and Easter to shine in this place of hope and prayer.

PART THREE ◆ *Equipping the Sacristy*

19◆ Sacristy Furnishings

Two Rooms

If there are two sacristies in a given church, they should have a different division of materials than they had before Vatican II, and perhaps new locations. One room, called the "vesting room," can serve all who vest for liturgy, priests as well as all others. If possible, it should be close to the entranceway. The other room, called here the "sacristy," can be closer to the sanctuary, providing preparation areas for all liturgical requisites.

There will be many circumstances in which this newer alignment of spaces and functions is impossible. Yet, even in the older arrangements of small rooms to each side of the sanctuary, we can make certain rearrangements. The reforms of the past 40 years embody many implications for these rooms; their interior arrangements should reflect the liturgy we celebrate today. For example, most vestments are larger now, requiring either more drawer space or larger, sturdier hangers. At the same time, owing to the great reduction in the number of altar cloths needed and the virtual disappearance of antependia, available drawer space may have increased. The extension of eucharistic cup-sharing has increased the number of chalices and purificators, while introducing a need for flagons and trays. Meanwhile the proliferation of texts and the concomitant splitting of the *Roman Ritual* into different volumes have increased the number of liturgical books required.

The vesting room should contain the following items or equivalents:

–cabinets for books and for vesture

–closets with high rods for vestments

–counter tops, perhaps part of the cases, or tables for the laying out of vestments and texts

–sink and materials for washing (unless rest rooms are nearby)

– appointments appropriate to this room's function: clock, bulletin board, full-length mirror, and perhaps a floor-mounted shoe polisher and an umbrella stand

– traditionally, a cross and a sign with local information like the bishop's name were hung here as well.

The sacristy will be most functional if it has these furnishings:

– cases, cabinets, perhaps a metal safe, and/or closets with flexible shelving for vessels, linens, candles and holders, incense materials, floral equipment, decorations and tools

– tables or counter-tops for the preparation of materials

– one or two sinks: one with hot water for the washing of vessels, with a drain board and drying rack (equipped with vertical pegs for holding the cruets, flagons, cups), paper towels or cloth towels and rack

– a janitorial sink if necessary

– other basic appointments: bulletin board, stool or ladder, cart with shelves for moving many vessels at once, dolly for cartons of supplies or larger objects, and hooks for candlelighters.

The Sacrarium

The most unusual sink in the church complex is the sacrarium or *piscina*. It is a basin, usually covered, with a drain pipe having no joints or elbows, that leads directly into the earth. This allows the reverent disposal of baptismal water, water used in ritual purifications, holy oils from a previous year, or ashes made from burning liturgical items for reverent disposal (for example, cottonballs from oil stocks). A sacrarium has been required in Roman rite churches since the early Middle Ages, and few edifices lack one. The usual location for the sacrarium is in the sacristy.

The long history of the sacrarium testifies to the nearly obsessive attention that our medieval and Tridentine ancestors gave to eucharistic particles. Today, however, the sacrarium receives only passing attention in the reformed liturgical books (for the disposing of water used to wipe up spilled eucharistic wine). Perhaps this is why the sacrarium has been omitted from some new sacristies. Yet it is possible to see a role for old and new sacrarium sinks. They still allow for the most reverent disposal of many liturgical elements and for the rinsing of the numerous cups found in many sacristies after Sunday Mass.

Drinking Water

These sinks and their sources of water may be sufficient for drinking water as well. Yet depending upon the quality of local water, and recognizing the proclivity of most Americans to drink very cold water, a separate source of cold drinking water might be necessary or at least hospitable. Small or large, portable or permanent, water coolers and cup dispensers can be installed in both vesting room and sacristy. Better yet, in order to be usable by the whole community, they might be located in more common areas of the complex: near the rest rooms, cloakroom or entrance hall.

The Portable Sacristy

Liturgical events on occasion take place away from the church building—Mass in a nursing home, anointing of the sick and communion, the blessing of homes, for example. The small vessels and packing cases marketed for these functions often contain unnecessary items of trivial size (but not insignificant cost). Though dollhouse-sized items may be easier to transport, today's liturgical requirements persuade us to use larger, more seemly vessels. The need for mobility is better met by packing only those items needed for the rite. In the case of viaticum, those items would be the pyx, oil of the sick, ritual book, song sheets or prayer cards, and vesture. For Mass the list includes cups, purificators, paten, bread and wine, water vessel (and towel), vesture, sacramentary and lectionary, participation materials, table cover, candles and cross. Several of these items may already be at the site. By knowing what's available at the site, we can outfit small or large cases with only those items that are necessary.

20◆ Liturgical Books

Collections of Texts

From the very earliest years, the various texts of Christian liturgies were transcribed and collected. As the centuries unfolded, the sharing of these text collections among churches was determined by their communion with a particular patriarchate or metropolitan see, by trade routes and river valleys, and by theological convictions. The texts themselves have been passed down over the centuries through successive formats, each format related to a liturgical revolution.

For the first several centuries, texts were written on a rotulus, a papyrus roll set on spindles at each end. This first format for liturgical collections still can be seen in many synagogues.

As Christianity spread and was legalized, the second phase began. The codex, folded sheets of animal skin gathered into a book, came into use. It facilitated the fast and broad spread of liturgical and biblical texts. Codices were copied laboriously by hand, but this new format used more durable material, and it allowed random access to a text at any page.

The mechanical printing of codices or books on paper was developed as the prayer texts and lectionary lists were being standardized for all Roman rite churches. This third stage of formats facilitated, and in some respects even brought about, the demise of local variants and the acceptance of conformity to universal models. By this time, the collections came to be grouped as missals (for *missa* or Mass), pontificals (for rites led by bishops), breviaries (the liturgy of the hours) and rituals (for all of the other rites). Current books still use the same titles, but the Roman Missal and especially the *Roman Ritual* have been divided into many different volumes.

The reformed books following upon Vatican II have been issued as the world has been entering into the fourth phase of text retrieval. From now on, computers will have an enormous effect on liturgical text compositions and collections. The conformity of published texts to the mandated "typical editions" has always been a concern of ecclesial authorities. Current technology now can guarantee conformity, even with competing publishers printing from the same official disk. Perhaps computer technology also can be employed to make improvements at the local level, such as distributing liturgical materials to dioceses or parishes on disks. Local planners could then print, in proper sequence, all of the texts including local compositions to be used for a given rite.

Worthy and Beautiful Symbols

In each successive format, the official books of rites have been a significant part of the liturgical environment. Our tradition describes them as signs and symbols of the sacred, expressive of our belief that God speaks through these texts, that the community is shaped by these words. Thus, we should treat them as we do all of the artifacts and works of art in the sacristy: with great care and reverence. When selecting new volumes, we should be guided by the qualities noted in *Environment and Art in Catholic Worship* (#91). The volumes should be large and noble, and exhibit the highest quality of design, typography, paper, printing and binding.

The importance of these books rules out the substitution of missalettes, study text editions, or loose sheets (introduction to the *Lectionary for Mass,* 1981 edition, #37). Visually attractive and impressive books play a formative role in public assembly; flimsy pamphlets convey a disposable or trivial message, as if the texts or the "things" in general do not matter. The forms of our material objects matter a lot. They are at the center of the sacristan's ministry because we believe that communities find holiness in sacramental interaction with material elements.

The Books of the Roman Rite in the U. S. A.

OFFICIAL BOOKS: The books that we use in the liturgy are issued first by the Vatican for the universal church. Then the bishops' conferences of each language grouping and of each nation see to their translation and adaptation. In the official English-language books, many of the texts are translated by the International Commission on English in the Liturgy (ICEL), based in Washington, D. C. Scriptural texts are taken from one of the translations approved for liturgical usage. Publishers of Bibles, ICEL and others maintain copyright ownership to the texts, as delimited on the acknowledgments page of each ritual book. All of these texts and ceremonial adaptations are approved by the bishops' conference and then confirmed by the Vatican before they are published.

In the United States, several publishers provide distinct editions of the liturgical books—all with the same texts, but differing in artistic quality. We should review various editions before selecting one that provides the most worthy symbol.

The following titles are the official English-language books for the Roman rite dioceses of our country. Every sacristy in a parish church should have all of them, with the possible exceptions of the rite of religious profession and the full Pontifical. Chapels where a given rite is never celebrated would not, of course, need the corresponding ritual book. When reviewing this list periodically, we should purchase sufficient copies to cover normal use—several copies of some rites will need to be available for ministers other than the presider. For example, books for funerals include texts used at the same rite by presiders, deacons and lectors.

1. The *Roman Missal,* once a single, very large book, has been published in several parts, mostly to distinguish the various ministries:

a. *Sacramentary:* 1985 (to be revised during the 1990s).

Complementary volumes:

–*The Book of the Chair* (for the presider's chair on Sundays).

–The *Collection of Masses of the Blessed Virgin Mary: Sacramentary:* 1992. (In parishes, this can be used on those Saturdays in Ordinary Time that do not have an obligatory memorial or feast. In Marian shrines, its use can be frequent.)

b. *Lectionary for Mass:* 1970 (to be revised in the mid-1990s).

Complementary volumes:

–The *Lectionary for Masses with Children* (in use beginning Advent 1993).

–A book of the gospels (gospels of the current lectionary also are issued in their own volume). The *Order of Christian Funerals* suggests this as one of the possible symbols to rest on the casket during a funeral.

–The *Collection of Masses of the Blessed Virgin Mary: Lectionary:* 1992 (can be used on those Saturdays in Ordinary Time when the accompanying sacramentary is utilized, but it is always better to waive this option and use the semi-continuous readings of the weekday lectionary).

–An attractively bound edition of the Bible, in the translation used in the local lectionary. This is another of the symbols that possibly would be placed on caskets for funerals.

c. The *Simple Gradual* was published in English in 1968, but it is hard to find as a separate volume. Its collection of psalms has made its way into many available hymnals.

d. *Roman Calendar:* The 1969 universal calendar and the particular calendar of the dioceses of the U. S. A. form our proper calendar. These lists and the "General Norms for the Liturgical Year and the Calendar" are reprinted at the front of every sacramentary. As new saints and the blessed are added to either the universal or national calendars, these lists will continue to evolve and be noted in annual ordos. They always should be complemented by particular feasts of the diocese and parish (diocesan patron, anniversaries of dedication of the cathedral and of the parish church, local church title).

Complementary volume: Dioceses are mandated to issue annual calendars, with local feasts and norms. Many publishers issue annual ordos, often in local editions that incorporate these observances.

2. *The Liturgy of the Hours:* 1975 (4 volumes).

Complementary volumes:

–*Christian Prayer,* a one-volume excerpt.

–*Shorter Christian Prayer,* a simplified edition.

–Supplements with texts for new memorials.

3. The *Roman Ritual,* published in one volume before Vatican II, is now in several volumes, one for each sacrament or rite:

a. *Rite of Christian Initiation of Adults:* 1988. This includes the rite for the Reception of Baptized Christians, formerly published in a separate booklet.

b. *Rite of Baptism for Children:* 1970.

c. *Rite of Marriage:* 1970 (to be revised in the 1990s).

d. *Order of Christian Funerals:* 1989.

Complementary volumes: Various parts of this order, for example, the committal rites, have been published in separate volumes.

e. *Rite of Penance:* 1975.

f. *Pastoral Care of the Sick: Rites of Anointing and Viaticum:* 1983.

g. *Holy Communion and Worship of the Eucharist outside Mass:* 1976.

h. *Rite of Religious Profession:* 1988.

i. *Book of Blessings:* 1989.

Complementary volumes:

–*Catholic Household Blessings and Prayers:* 1988.

–*Shorter Book of Blessings:* 1990.

4. The *Roman Pontifical* includes those rites normally celebrated by a bishop. The rites for confirmation and for a church dedication, at least, should be in every liturgical library:

a. *Roman Pontifical, Part I:* 1978.

Complementary volume: *Confirmation:* 1973 (excerpted from the fuller Pontifical).

b. *Dedication of a Church and an Altar:* 1989 (an important resource for parishes undergoing renovation or construction; useful for parishes preparing for each year's anniversary).

5. Other official books:

a. The *Ceremonial of Bishops:* 1989. (Though not a book of liturgical texts, it is an official compilation of rubrics and of emendations made since the various ritual books were published. The notes are useful for charting parish celebrations.)

b. The *Roman Martyrology:* This is a special kind of calendar, cataloging all the saints according to their date of observance. This includes not only the scores of saints who are on the current universal (Roman) calendar, but the thousands of others who might be part of national, diocesan, or religious community calendars. A new edition taking into account the revisions of the calendar will be published sometime in the 1990s.

OTHER BOOKS: In addition to these books, sacristies should have:

–copies of the hymnal or other materials used by the assembly

–a book or folder with locally prepared intercessions or with copies of the intercessions contained in a particular rite

–a beautiful scroll or book containing the setting of the Easter Proclamation (Exsultet) used in the parish

–special books for presiders and other ministers at complicated or combined rites—using removable tape, copies of varied rites' texts can be collated with local ceremonial directives into a nicely bound book; this might well be more dignified than juggling two or three ritual books during the same event

–official liturgical books in other approved languages of the United States (The list of books in Spanish-language editions for the dioceses of the U. S. A. continues to expand.)

–official liturgical books in other languages, from the respective nations of those tongues when they are unavailable in U. S. A. editions—to be used for multi-lingual rites.

The Care and Storage of Liturgical Books

Past editions, whether pre-dating Vatican II or from one of the phases before the current edition, should not be stored in the sacristy. Every parish, particularly older and larger ones with many of these books, should find a place in its library or parish center to house them. Liturgists, historians and other researchers might utilize them; their block prints are often useful for seasonal or feast day clip art—if the copyrights are expired. Some outdated books, particularly those with leather binding, goldleaf edges and high quality artwork, may be very valuable.

Current books should be in the vesting room. If there is no vesting room, the books should be kept in the sacristy. If individual presiders want any books for their own shelves, these should be separate copies.

In some logical order understood by all, these 30 or more volumes should be available to ministers and planners. The basics of book-shelving should be observed—sturdy bookends, avoidance of horizontal piles that make the bottom books inconvenient to withdraw and the removal of clips and extraneous papers after each use of a particular book.

Preparing Books for Use

COVERS: While reviewing the available editions of a liturgical book, we also can consider the use of special covers. A special cover might be commissioned or purchased, for example, in the case of a book that has beautiful art and typography, but a very plain binding. Certain outfitters can provide covers fitted for the lectionary and the book of gospels (in brass, or in silver or gold plate). Local artists and some suppliers can fashion covers of leather or metal for any book. Fabric covers should probably be avoided. Durable, long-lasting covers convey the sense of "book" better than soft, pliable covers.

SELECTING TEXTS: At a meeting for liturgy preparation, or after such a meeting sets the overall terms for a liturgy, texts of prayers and scriptures can be selected for particular rites. (See notes on page 181.) In many cases, most of the texts are set by the given day. At other times, the selection from options will take place in the vesting room a half hour before the event. On still other occasions, the text-selection process will take place weeks or days before the rite, so that musicians, homilists and other ministers can prepare for the service. In addition to selecting them, the preparation of texts might include some local composition. Sacristans or planners normally arrange for a competent person to draft intercessions, invocations for the penitential rite, and such introductions as are deemed useful.

MARKING TEXTS: As the liturgy nears, the selected texts should be marked in the appropriate books. In the vesting room or sacristy, rather than in the full view of the assembly, the ministers can preview the texts and set the ribbons in the right places. If markers other than ribbons are used, they should be of a kind that will not fall out during the rite. All ribbons or markers should be in place well before the rite begins; no searching should be done during the rite.

For the eucharist on weekdays and many Sundays, the ribbons or other markers need to be set at these pages of the sacramentary:

- the so-called presidential prayers—opening prayer, prayer over the gifts and prayer after communion (On certain weekdays it will be necessary to set two ribbons because the opening prayer is at the day—proper—and the other two are in the general sections—commons.)

- general intercessions, particularly the introduction and concluding prayer texts for the presider (Mark either the samples in the appendix or insert a locally-composed and affix it with removable tape.)

–the profession of faith or the texts for the preparation of the altar if these are not memorized by the presider

–the preface of the eucharistic prayer, unless this is already printed with the selected eucharistic prayer (seasonal, or specific to a day, or related to a type of saint)

–a solemn blessing, if used and if not already positioned with the presidential prayers

–other texts (introductory rite and eucharistic prayers are usually marked with permanent tabs set by the publisher).

In addition, text-marking might include these procedures:

–small, self-stick removable notes (or tiny, removable, colored dot-labels) positioned at the appointed text (e. g., at funerals when there are many options spread on the pages)

–larger notes affixed with removable tape where texts of intercessions or introductions or reminders need to be provided

–similar affixing of copies of texts from other books when rites are combined

–the insertion of hymns (for example, a locally-selected song of farewell at funerals, or a special hymn at evening prayer).

To accomplish these tasks, the vesting room will need an "editorial" or "lay-out" supply drawer by the liturgical books. It should have an ever-replenished supply of removable tape and a dispenser, self-stick removable notes or labels (termed "Post-its" by one manufacturer), loose writing paper of various sizes, scissors, pencils (and pencil sharpener) or pens, and paper clips. This list may appear to be unduly long, but the task of selecting and preparing texts is important, far too important to be left to chance or to be done at the last minute. All these items, trivial as they may appear to be individually, combine to help us reach our goal: equipping our ministers to perform their assigned actions with competence and confidence so that the entire assembly enters into the full action of praise.

21◆ Liturgical Vessels

Sacred and Artistic Containers

REVERENCE THROUGH THE AGES: The vessels used at Christian liturgy always have reflected the importance of sacramental actions. As with our Jewish ancestors and neighbors, and with adherents to most other religions of the world, we set aside vessels for liturgical use that are distinguished by their size, form, nobility and decoration. Reformers and fundamentalists, today as in past epochs, prefer to see an antagonism between art and religion. Jews often are assumed to be anti-art because they are anti-idol. Some say that Christians are at their holiest and most "spiritual" when they have no need of art. Yet both Jewish and Christian history demonstrates that such opinions have never prevailed for long. The artifacts of every century show that liturgical communities have sought to bring their affections to expression with the most beautiful art and materials obtainable.

The sanctuary artisan Bezalel is praised in Exodus (35:30–33) as so filled with divine spirit that he was able to devise artistic designs, to cut stones, to carve wood and to work in gold, silver and bronze. Later, in the 1100 years of the period of the Temples (ending in our apostolic period), all Jews, including the disciples of Jesus, revered their holy place in Jerusalem, a building complex of the finest materials that was filled with precious vessels and artifacts. In later centuries, domestic and synagogue gatherings of Jews utilized wondrous plates and cups, lamp stands and spice boxes. Christians, too, in domestic prayer and in public assemblies of liturgy, always used splendid liturgical vessels made by artists and artisans—their own Bezalels.

By the high Middle Ages, the separation of the liturgical action from the assembly, the clericalization of Christian communities, and numerous cultural forces had led to new understandings of liturgical elements. The presence of Christ in the bread and wine was understood in radically physical ways. At the same time, appreciation of the other modes of presence—in the community and the word—was minimized. Priests were understood to be privileged because they consecrated the elements and could touch them, not because they were pastoral or liturgical presiders in communion. Vessels were cherished and held "sacred" more because they held Jesus, rather than because they shaped the liturgical actions of sacred communities.

The *General Instruction of the Roman Missal* (#289–296) employs the term "sacred" to describe liturgical vessels, especially chalices and patens. Because of their centrality at our most revered and constitutive gatherings, because they "touch the Lord," Christian communities continue to esteem them, continue to hold them sacred. Our respect and our careful handling of chalices and patens, however, should not become so exaggerated or exclusive that we diminish respect for other vessels—for example, those for holy oils or baptismal water. It's only natural that the most central vessels, the chalices and the patens, will continue to be created with more artistry than others. Yet all of our vessels should be considered beautiful and holy and be handled accordingly, for they invite us to divine interaction.

CURRENT MATERIALS AND FORMS: The chalice and paten placed on the altar before the eucharistic prayer should each be large enough to attract the community's attention and to hold all of the bread or wine. The ideal of "one bread and one cup" has once more been enshrined in our liturgical norms (see, for example, *General Instruction of the Roman Missal,* #293; *Environment and Art in Catholic Worship,* #96). Other vessels should be designed and chosen to accommodate today's larger loaves of bread and more plentiful use of wine. These would include flagons to hold any wine that does not fit in the one cup, the many cups and plates into which the eucharistic meal is divided prior to distribution, pyxes, and cruets or pitchers.

The materials used should be solid, with preference given to those that do not break easily. They should be considered noble, "prized" in the locality. And, of course, form should follow function. For example, a chalice should be lined with nonabsorbent material. So long as these vessels function appropriately in the liturgy, they can be made by artists in whatever shapes express the local community's faith. This suggests that local artists—not catalogs of mass-produced items—be consulted when vessels are needed.

Wine and Vessels for Wine

THE MEANINGS OF CUP-SHARING: Eucharistic cup-sharing was so essential to the act of sharing communion that, for early Christians, communion under the form of bread alone was truly rare. Communion from the cup was the sharing that formed ecclesial unity and reconciliation (1 Corinthians 10: 16). It was wine mixed with a little water, like the mixtures shared even today in Mediterranean cultures, but more importantly like the Sabbath cup of the Jews, a beverage of blessing and praising God. It was perceived by communicants as a sharing of life and immortality. To drink of the cup was to express commitment to God's will. Its redness enhanced the sense of sharing blood, its alcoholic content was associated with the stimulation or conversion of human spirits and "spiritual inebriation."

In the Middle Ages, as part of the overall devolution of liturgical forms during that period, the eucharistic wine became reserved to the priest celebrant. Theologians maintained the rich meanings associated with eucharistic wine and the chalice, but the vitality of these meanings was compromised as the practice was curtailed. When reformers pressed for the restoration of cup-sharing to the assembly, Catholic bishops responded with the doctrine of concomitance—the belief that the whole Christ is received under either form of the eucharist, that the sharing of the chalice was not necessary for additional grace.

Through the decades leading to Vatican II, pastoral liturgists recognized the deficiency of this perspective; disallowance of communion under both forms, bread and wine, ignored the integrity of the sacramental sign, even violated the Lord's command to "take and drink." When the reforms came, officials were concerned about explaining how sharing the cup could have been forbidden for so long and now encouraged, and how the doctrine of concomitance was not in question here. So the *Constitution on the Sacred Liturgy* (#55) listed this as a reform fostering full sacramental participation:

> The dogmatic principles laid down by the Council of Trent remain intact. In instances to be specified by the Apostolic See, however, communion under both kinds may be granted both to clerics and religious and to the laity at the discretion of the bishops.

A few years later, the instruction *Eucharisticum Mysterium* (#32) continued the implementation and expounded its rationale:

> Holy communion has a more complete form as a sign when it is received under both kinds. For in this manner of reception (without prejudice to the principles laid down by the Council of Trent, that under each element Christ whole and entire and the true sacrament are received), a fuller light shines on the sign of the eucharistic banquet. Moreover there is a clearer expression of that will by which the new and everlasting covenant is ratified in the blood of the Lord and of the relationship of the eucharistic banquet to the eschatological banquet in the Father's kingdom.

This elaboration of meanings found its way into the *General Instruction of the Roman Missal* (#240). As cup-sharing is practiced by more and more assemblies, as catechists and pastors fearlessly face the doubts about hygiene, these visions of covenant and banquet will more and more become part of common consciousness.

WINE: From time to time, there have been reformers intent on eliminating wine from the eucharist. From the second to the fifth centuries, ascetical groups (termed "Aquarians") refused to acknowledge that the messianic era symbolized by wine had been inaugurated with Jesus. They used water instead of wine, and were fought vigorously by church leaders. Church councils similarly confronted another aberration, the substitution of milk for wine in seventh-century Spain. During the onslaught of experiments of the 1960s, certain groups tried using elements other than bread and wine ("to be relevant"). Even today, certain Baptists and other Protestants use grape juice instead of wine. Despite all this, Catholic liturgical traditions have prevailed. Wine has survived as a vital sacramental sign, proclaiming the covenant, the messianic era and the spiritual inebriation of conversion.

The *General Instruction of the Roman Missal* (#284–85) sets the requirement for wine in brief terms:

> The wine for the eucharist must be from the fruit of the vine (see Luke 22:18), natural, and pure, that is not mixed with any foreign substance. Care must be taken to ensure that the elements are kept in good condition: that the wine does not turn to vinegar.

Sacristans might periodically review their methods of storing and replenishing wine supplies. A good reserve is always appropriate, especially where large funerals can come at a moment's notice. Yet the supply should not be so great that any given bottle is kept for more than six months. For open bottles of wine, a small refrigerator helps preserve its taste.

The wine can be made by parish members (in those few geographic regions where this ideal is possible), donated by members, or purchased from any reputable supplier. Church goods stores and "sacramental wine" distributors can be used, but general wine merchants can provide equally appealing—perhaps better—wine that is natural, pure and without additives. Aside from these canonical requirements, each community should evaluate these characteristics of wine:

- type of grape—some wines are labeled in a more generic way, but the varietal wines are often finer
- color—red fits the symbolic history better
- body—often the lighter-bodied reds taste better in the morning
- sweet or dry—most communities find some middle ground
- price.

When an alcohol-addicted priest has been given permission to substitute grape juice for wine, the sacristan must exercise extra care. A certain chalice and cruet may have to be set aside quietly for this presider. The bottles of grape juice should be kept in a separate location. By following these practices, sacristans should be able to eliminate any confusion, any inadvertent use wine instead of grape juice, or vice versa. Even if a priest uses grape juice, the rest of the assembly shares from the eucharistic wine (placed on the altar in a flagon before the eucharistic prayer).

CHALICES: This term comes from the Latin *calix,* meaning cup. Whether the anglicanization or the translation is used matters little. Some have taken to calling the main vessel used through the eucharistic prayer the "chalice," and the smaller vessels used for communion distribution the "cups." In some designs, the cup vessel rests on a base; the whole object or just the containment cup itself can be signified by either term. Any such distinctions carry only local force. For our purposes, both words are used interchangeably.

In the beginning, Christian ritual cups may well have looked something like the cups of Jewish liturgy. Archeological remains indicate that they were made from a broad range of prized materials. As sharing became more and more restricted to clergy, the size of the cups was reduced. They also came to be seen as emblems and personal possessions of individual clerics, rather than as common cups of the church. By the twentieth century, when mass production succeeded in proliferating certain standard and romantic forms, the rules for these vessels were quite rigid. Every chalice needed a base (with a cross traditionally on it to indicate the place to drink and later purify), a stem with a knob for holding it with thumb and forefinger joined (as in the Tridentine rite), and a containment vessel shaped like a cone. The latter was to be silver or gold, but with gold-plating inside. The other parts could be of certain alternative metals.

Such cups still abound in contemporary sacristies, and can continue to be used if they hold enough wine for the given liturgy. But the rules have been radically simplified. In addition to the general rules for vessels cited above (solid and noble materials, in shapes the local culture can appreciate), the *General Instruction of the Roman Missal* (#291, 294) states:

> Chalices and other vessels that serve as receptacles for the blood of the Lord are to have a cup of nonabsorbent material. The base may be of any other solid and worthy material. . . . Vessels made from metal should ordinarily be gilded on the inside if the metal is one that rusts; gilding is not necessary if the metal is more precious than gold and does not rust.

In selecting old and new chalices for use, we need as many as are necessary for the most crowded assembly of the year. We should evaluate their functionality, their nobility of form, their expressiveness of festivity and messianic fullness, and their congruence with other visible objects at the celebration.

BOTTLES FOR THE EUCHARISTIC ACTION: Wine and a small amount of water are placed in the one chalice during the preparation rite just before the eucharistic prayer. This simple action implies the presence of other vessels or bottles.

1. *Bottles for presenting wine.* The wine must be in a bottle or container when prepared before the celebration until it is presented to the presider and poured into the cup. Few if any examples of these containers exist from the first millennium, and there does not seem to have been a great deal of distinction made between, on the one hand, the bottles of wine brought to the church by members, and on the other hand, the vessels used to pour this wine into the chalice. In the Middle Ages, though, there is evidence of the existence of special bottles for the presentation and pouring of wine. Some of these bottles were, for a brief time, quite large; they quickly gave way to bottles that were quite small (a result of the cup being reserved to the priest). Many confusing names were used for these bottles—ampullae (there were also ampullae of oils), phials or vials, vinaria and aquaria, even the general term "vessel." By the time of the Renaissance, the term cruet was universally used in English-language areas. At roughly the same time, glass became standardized as the preferred material, because it was the easiest to clean and because it was transparent. The latter property made it easy to tell whether the cruet contained wine or water. Stoppers also became normative.

Since Vatican II, the return of eucharistic cup-sharing by entire assemblies has resulted in the use of much larger bottles for the presentation of the wine. These sometimes look like large cruets, but might also appear as carafes, decanters or flagons. All of these terms connote large, ornamental bottles, but the term flagon is most appropriate if the vessel has a handle, spout and cover. Decanters and carafes often appear noble when carried in procession and presented to the presider. Because they usually lack spouts, however, they tend to be less suited for pouring.

Every parish needs a variety of bottles for the presentation and pouring of wine—small cruets for weekday Masses and much larger cruets or flagons for larger assemblies. Though cruets traditionally are made of glass, especially in the smaller sizes, other materials also are acceptable, provided they can be kept clean.

2. *Bottles for the altar table.* In some cases, the one cup will contain sufficient wine for the communion of the assembly. If it cannot, then the rest of the wine should be held in a worthy liturgical vessel and placed with the chalice and paten on the altar for the eucharistic action. The most appropriate bottles for this function are the larger cruets and flagons presented at the preparation rite. Parishes should have as many of these as are needed for the largest eucharistic assembly of the year. In keeping with tradition, these might be glass. They also could be of the same nonabsorbent material as the chalice—precious metal or ceramic. Some writers have suggested that glass is better, for it allows all to see the sacramental sign. This argument, similarly framed in discussing vessels for the holy oils, needs to be balanced with an opposing view. We should not be focusing on seeing the elements; this is what gave us the medieval practices of the elevation and exposition. We should see the elements only in their sharing at communion. Both arguments have strength. The job of the sacristan is to choose vessels that are made of the worthiest materials.

3. *Bottle for the water that will be added.* The mixture of wine with water, rooted in ancient Jewish custom, presumes a vessel of water prepared before Mass and given to the presider at the preparation rite. This was always a small amount of water. For centuries, when the wine vessels were also quite small, water was kept in matching cruets. These small containers, usually made of glass, are still serviceable for this minor action. Except at small gatherings, however, they should no longer match the scale of the wine vessel. It is best if this pouring of the water is kept quite distinct from the washing of the hands, with a separate ewer or pitcher reserved for that later action.

BOTTLES FOR EUCHARISTIC RESERVATION: As described on page 78, eucharistic wine may be reserved in the tabernacle for those sick members who are either allergic to wheat or unable to swallow with ease. This is an admirable practice of our reform era, but seldom utilized, to the detriment of the sick. Bottles or flasks or pyxes (we have no set liturgical term yet) should be found or commissioned. They should exhibit the following characteristics:

–a secure lid

–a worthy design

–a neck or opening that allows the eucharistic wine to be poured from flagon or chalice into it

–a lip or spout that allows pouring into a spoon or cup

–a material that can be cleansed easily.

In addition, they should have cases that will permit them to be carried safely.

OTHER REQUISITES FOR THE WINE: Two other types of functional equipment assist in the dignified use of cups and bottles. They are funnels and trays. Funnels are essential in pouring wine from a bottle or other container into most cruets and into some flagons. They should be large enough at the top so that liquids can be poured into them easily without spilling, and small enough at the bottom to fit into the mouth of the receiving vessel. They should be made of a material that can be easily cleaned. If a funnel also will be used for the pouring of consecrated wine into flasks for reservation, then its dignified appearance is important. Especially in this latter case, but in normal use as well, there might be some sort of saucer or dish on which to place the funnel.

Parishes also should have a variety of dignified-looking trays. In the old days, small trays or casters, often of glass, were used to hold small cruets. They still may be used this way for smaller gatherings, but they should not be used for the washing of hands. Some communities have begun using larger trays for carrying the communion cups from the sacristy to the credence table. If the consecrated wine is poured into these cups at the altar table, the same trays might bear them from credence to altar. They should be of a noble or formal design, and not resemble the trays used in self-serve restaurants.

Bread and Vessels for Bread

THE RESTORATION OF COMMUNION: For many centuries, the priest was the only one eating the eucharistic banquet at many Masses, and he was mandated to do so. Other Catholics waited for special feasts, for a Sunday made special by their group's sharing in communion before a "communion breakfast," or for the mandated reception at Eastertide. Meanwhile, they engaged in "spiritual communion." This act of mental prayer was complemented by other favored practices: silence and devotional prayers at the consecration, participation in eucharistic benediction, and occasional private visits to the blessed sacrament—prayer before the tabernacle.

Though there were admirable aspects to such eucharistic adoration, they eventually became more important than the sacraments themselves, than liturgical actions in general. Spiritual communion and worship of the eucharist outside of Mass were put back into perspective by the many reforms that have unfolded throughout the entire twentieth century. Pius X lowered the age for first communion. Both he and later popes pressed all Catholics to share in eucharistic communion more often. Some parishes were affected by these pleas and by the liturgical movement, and certainly no one could miss the dramatic changes in all of the church's liturgical rites in the 1960s. The return to active participation was most pronounced at the Sunday celebrations of the eucharist.

BREAD: While the bread for eucharist may well have been leavened through large parts of the first millennium, churches of the Roman rite have now been using unleavened bread for many centuries. We in the Roman rite have long been accustomed to round breads, called hosts, and to the frequent imposition of monograms or designs on the shape of these hosts. Current norms are found in the *General Instruction of the Roman Missal:*

> It is most desirable that the faithful receive the Lord's body from hosts consecrated at the same Mass and that, in the instances when it is permitted, they share in the

> chalice. Then even through the signs communion will stand out more clearly as a sharing in the sacrifice actually being offered. (#56h)
>
> The bread must be made only from wheat and must have been baked recently; according to the long-standing tradition of the Latin church, it must be unleavened. (#282)
>
> The nature of the sign demands that the material for the eucharistic celebration truly have the appearance of food. Accordingly, even though unleavened and baked in the traditional shape, the eucharistic bread should be made in such a way that in a Mass with a congregation the priest is able actually to break the host into parts and distribute them to at least some of the faithful. (When, however, the number of communicants is large or other pastoral needs require it, small hosts are in no way ruled out.) The action of the breaking of the bread, the simple term for the eucharist in apostolic times, will more clearly bring out the force and meaning of the sign of the unity of all in the one bread and of their charity, since the one bread is being distributed among the members of one family. (#283)
>
> Care must be taken to ensure that the elements are kept in good condition: that . . . the bread (does not) spoil or become too hard to be broken easily. (#285)

The major change for bread-making is in #283. Breads should be of a much larger size so that all may share from the same loaf or host. These reforms are imbued with an appreciation of sacramental signs, and as that same appreciation permeated local churches, many communities began baking their own bread for the eucharist. There are, of course, any number of ways to moisten wheaten flour, to knead it and to bake it. (Vatican officials strongly criticized those who added ingredients other than wheat flour and water to the bread in order to make it look, taste or smell better.)

Communities that bake their own eucharistic bread might use this recipe from Dennis Krouse:

1. For 70 communicants, use ⅓ cup whole wheat flour to ⅔ cup unbleached white flour. The mixture of flour should be kept in an airtight container in the freezer and used while cold. (The cold flour helps prevent a separate crust from forming.)

2. Use one cup of the flour mixture to approximately ½ cup of naturally effervescent water (Perrier, for example). The water should be refrigerator cold.

3. Quickly mix the flour and water together with a fork until all the flour is moist. Form dough into a smooth ball. Usually more flour needs to be sprinkled on the surface of the dough to prevent stickiness.

4. Gently flatten the ball of dough into a circular loaf about ½- to ¾-inch thick. If necessary, turn any uneven edges underneath.

5. Place unscored loaf on a lightly oiled baking sheet. (Use Pam and wipe off excess.)

6. Place in a preheated oven at 425 degrees.

7. After approximately 12–15 minutes the top crust should have raised slightly. Prick the crust with a toothpick in several places, turn the loaf over and continue to bake about five minutes. (This gives an evenness to the top of the loaf.)

8. Turn the loaf right side up again and continue to bake until the crust is very lightly browned, about 10–15 minutes more for a total of 25–30 minutes. Baking time when using more than 1½ cups of flour needs to be extended.

9. Place the loaf on a rack for cooling. (You may want to slice the bottom crust off to check for any rawness.)

10. Bread is best when made fresh the day of the liturgy. However, after baking, it can be tightly wrapped and frozen for later use.

In parishes where a regular system of baking bread has not been implemented, hosts of various sizes are available from many commercial suppliers and religious communities. Such communities, who sometimes make this bread as their only means of support or to support their social ministries, deserve the patronage of parishes that do not bake their own bread.

No matter where the bread comes from, the sacristan must make sure that it is delivered regularly and on time, and that it is baked in the largest loaves possible. Bread or hosts should be stored in canisters or other containers. Some parishes still have containers from previous decades, including those curious cylindrical ones with interior weights to keep the hosts flat. Large loaves of bread obviously will require other means of storage.

PATENS OR PLATES FOR THE EUCHARISTIC ACTION: In the first millennium, the eucharist was distributed from the same paten or plate that contained the elements on the altar table. These were quite large and circular, holding leavened bread for the entire assembly. With the introduction of wafer-breads, these patens could be much smaller. When communions declined so radically in the Middle Ages, the single paten often held only the one host for the priest. As the paten became smaller, it came to be made of the same material as the chalice and in proportion to it. From this flowed the practice of placing the paten on top of the chalice before and after the eucharist. This continued to be done up until the time that the recent liturgical reforms were enacted.

As with other liturgical artifacts, the norms for patens are quite simple. In addition to the general norms for all vessels (solid and noble materials, in shapes appreciated by the local culture), the *General Instruction of the Roman Missal* says (#292–93):

> Vessels that serve as receptacles for the eucharistic bread, such as the paten, ciborium, pyx, monstrance, etc., may be made of other materials that are prized in the region, for example, ebony or other hard woods, as long as they are suited to sacred use.
>
> For the consecration of hosts one rather large paten may properly be used; on it is placed the bread for the priest as well as for the ministers and the faithful.

This large paten can take one of many different shapes—for example, concave plates, shallow bowls, or larger vessels shaped like pie plates (but of finer materials). As is the case with the one cup and any complementary flagons, additional patens are brought from the credence table during the breaking of the bread. They are filled with pieces as the loaves are broken. These patens may or may not form a matched set with the various chalices. What is more important is adherence to the form and perception of a plate. The eucharistic food should not be contained in anything that resembles a cup, a box or a large bowl. The terms "plate" and "paten" can be used interchangeably, but the latter is a bit more specific for eucharistic functions.

Yet the use of this term should in no way indicate a return to the days of tiny disks of metal perched on chalice tops.

VESSELS FOR EUCHARISTIC RESERVATION: The term "pyx" can signify any one of the many containers that hold eucharistic bread for reservation. They keep the eucharistic banquet fresh and available for the absent, the sick and the dying. In the early centuries, many Christians used these vessels to bring the eucharist to their homes. In the Middle Ages, before tabernacles were regularly installed in sanctuaries, the pyx often was shaped as a dove or veiled with beautiful fabric and then suspended by the altar. On occasion, pyxes were made with base and stem.

In the fourteenth century the term "ciborium" (the plural is "ciboria") came to be used for one variant of the pyx. Earlier this term had been used to describe the architectural canopies or roofs above altars. These new ciboria differed from many other pyxes in that their covers were loose, rather than attached by hinges. They also came to resemble chalices. Like all pyxes, the purpose of the ciborium was to reserve the eucharistic bread for the sick and the dying.

In later centuries, and especially as communities began communicating again regularly in the twentieth century, ciboria began to be used for the consecration and distribution of communion. This modern invention was quite regrettable. Ciboria have little sign value related to bread—they look like drinking cups, not bread plates. "Stackable" ciboria also are inappropriate. They seem to have been designed to take up the least amount of room in the tabernacle, rather than as artistic creations to enhance and dignify the sharing.

Each parish should own as many pyxes as are needed by the communion ministers visiting the sick. They should generally be of a smaller size, owing to the fact that long itineraries of "communion calls" rarely exist outside hospitals. The tabernacle should house whatever portions of eucharistic bread are needed for the sick, and the bread should be placed in one or more of these pyxes. Parishes should use ciboria (no veils required) only when the number of hosts reserved for the sick is quite large and ciboria are the largest forms of pyx available.

The distribution of eucharistic bread at Mass should be performed with the necessary number of patens, not with ciboria. As the *General Instruction* itself notes, all of the consecrated bread should be on the one paten.

VESSELS FOR EUCHARISTIC EXPOSITION: In the twelfth century (and earlier), the eucharist was carried from church buildings in pyxes. Over the next few centuries, as popular devotions excited the desire of the people to see the consecrated host, formal processions and enthronements of hosts in pyxes became common. To accommodate the desire for visibility, some of the new pyxes included glass windows, sometimes with interior devices to prop up a host and sometimes with elaborate architectural forms.

By the fifteenth century, artistic and devotional evolution led to a new kind of pyx—hosts were no longer propped up by some device within the windowed pyx. The new pyx was shrunk to the size of one large host and was totally transparent. Called a lunette, this pyx looked and worked something like a watch case. When not in use, the pyx could be stored in a fitted metal case called the custodia. When utilized for exposition, the lunette could be fitted into any one of a number of large show cases or stands called monstrances or ostensoria. These were often designed in the shape of the sun, with rays extending out on all sides, but other forms were used as well.

The same system of lunette-pyx, custodia case, and monstrance-holder prevails today, but the popularity of exposition has rightly been diminished, as full participation in the eucharistic action has increased. On those occasions when lunettes, custodia and monstrances are used, the sacristan needs to be sure that the lunette fits into the given monstrance, that the host fits into the lunette, that the host is put out before Mass for consecration.

Vessels for Liturgical Washings

The orders for Christian liturgies were first developed and shared between communities that were quite familiar with ceremonial washings. Many civic, religious and domestic settings called for fountains or basins of water. The scriptures and the annals of early churches contain many stories of washing the ceremonial place, the whole body (especially after a cure), the head, hair, feet, hands or fingers. Such ceremonial washings often were done after cures.

FEET: Stories of the Last Supper and traditions that called for foot-washing (on Holy Thursday and at other ritual moments) have provided our current ritual with its only ceremony of washing feet—at the Evening Mass of the Lord's Supper on Holy Thursday. For this we need several towels, at least one large pitcher of warm water and at least one large basin dish. These vessels should be quite a bit larger than those used for washing hands. And even though they are used only once a year, they should be made of materials that are both serviceable and worthy.

HANDS: The Order of Mass continues to include the minor but long-standing tradition of washing the presider's hands before the eucharistic prayer. The first word of the psalm verses (Ps. 26: 6ff.) formerly said during this action, *lavabo* ("I wash"), is still frequently used to describe both the action itself and the equipment used in it. Through the centuries, this washing was considered both a practical and a symbolic act.

Before the reforms, pitchers and basins for this action often were reserved to special and episcopal liturgies (where they often were called "ewer" and "bacile"). At other Masses, the water cruet and even the cruet dish were used not only for their traditional purpose, but for washing, too. The current liturgical books clearly define two containers that are used for very different purposes. One is the cruet that is used in conjunction with the chalice; the other is the container of water used for the washing of hands. All parishes should have pitchers and basins (of metal, glass or other dignified material) that are used only for the washing of hands, and they should not resemble the vessels that are used for wine and water meant for drinking. In deciding the size and number of the vessels needed for the washing of hands, we should consider all of the occasions on which it is done. In some cases, several persons may need to wash their hands at more or less the same time. The most frequent hand-washing is the presider's at the preparation rite of the liturgy of the eucharist. This may seem like a totally symbolic rather than practical moment, but it is in fact both. Symbolic purification and the cleansing of hands after handling various gifts presented by the community are both part of our heritage. All of the other hand-washings in the current rites are more obviously practical. For some washings, the traditional addition of lemon wedge-slices or small bars of soap is helpful. These may rest in the basin itself, or perhaps in a side dish. In general, it is better if ministers stay within the ritual areas (generally at the credence table where the equipment rests) and perform these washings with the assistance of other ministers. This is usually more dignified than disappearing into the sacristy to wash.

Hand-washing supplies usually are most needed:

- for the one who washes feet on Holy Thursday, right after that action (possibly with a small bar of soap)
- for the various ministers who impose ashes, right after that act (with small bars of soap); several vessels can help
- for those performing anointings with oil at liturgies, if the oil is not absorbed, while the songs accompanying the anointings continue and before the rest of the liturgy (communal anointings of the sick, confirmation, rites of the catechumenate).

Lemon wedges are traditionally helpful here. If several ministers are performing the anointings, several basins and pitchers would be helpful. A very important principle is that the one being anointed should not have the oil wiped away after the anointing.

- for newly-ordained priests, who may wash their hands after being anointed. This is an exception to the general rule just noted—the newly ordained cannot handle well the eucharistic elements with oily hands.

FINGERS: Before the reforms, a covered "ablution cup" with water rested beside the tabernacle. Those who had distributed the eucharist dipped their thumbs and forefingers in it after placing the ciboria in the tabernacle. These ablution cups are no longer needed, for two reasons: 1) Sufficient bread and wine should be consecrated for each and every Mass and there should be little traffic to the tabernacle; 2) if crumbs or drops of eucharistic elements remain on ministers' fingers, they can be brushed off into the vessels before purification or the whole hands can be washed. Thumbs and forefingers are no longer specified as the only two fingers for handling the eucharist. For this, a basin and pitcher might be more dignified than a finger bowl.

FLOOR: Older Catholics, and especially former servers, can remember the elaborate measures that were taken if pieces of the eucharistic bread fell to the floor. The *General Instruction* simplifies matters considerably: "If the eucharistic bread or any particle of it should fall, it is to be picked up reverently. If any of the precious blood spills, the area should be washed and the water poured into the sacrarium" (#239). The water can come from the basin at the credence table, and the cloths used with it can be extra purificators from the sacristy. This is a simple matter of wiping up the spillage, and no blame, alarm or drama should be conveyed by sacristans and ministers of communion.

Other Vessels

This chapter has focused on eucharistic vessels. There are many other containers or receptacles used for rites and feasts. Many are described elsewhere in this manual, especially in the chapter on the baptistry. In each case, they are to be both worthy (beautiful in design and in materials) and suited to their particular purpose in the liturgical action. Plates for the rings at marriage should express the importance of this jewelry and the festivity of the rite, but they should be made in such a way that the rings won't slip off easily. Bowls for ashes at the start of Lent should be deep enough to contain the ashes securely, but not so deep and narrow as to complicate the repeated insertion of the minister's fingers. Stands for the reverent display of saints' relics (reliquaries) should be large enough and attractive enough to perform that function efficiently and nobly, but neither relics nor stands should compete for attention with the main liturgical vessels. They should be positioned away from the altar and ambo, then securely stored away after the period of veneration ends.

Care and Storage of Vessels

Not many general rules can be set for such a wide variety of vessels. Each community should establish its own procedures for the regular care of its objects, depending on what kinds of vessels it uses. One general rule is that metal vessels should not be cleaned with paper towels or steel wool pads; they scratch the surface of the metal. Commercially produced polishes and chemicals also may do damage to metal or clay vessels. Periodically, regilding or polishing may need to be done.

Each community also will decide on the best way to store all of these vessels. A metal safe is traditionally useful for the most treasured ones. In any event, every sacristy needs cabinets with flexible shelving and countertops for preparation. A review of the contents of these vessel-cabinets should give an idea of their size to those planning to furnish a new or renovated sacristy:

- the current store of bread and wine
- enough cups for the largest eucharistic event (and at least one quite large cup)
- cruets and flagons for wine
- cruets for water
- funnel and saucer
- trays (especially for multiple cups)
- pyxes for consecrated wine and for consecrated bread (some of these might be ciboria, others might by lunettes)
- enough patens for all communion stations
- a monstrance
- basins and pitchers for water
- any reliquaries
- occasional dishes for symbols like rings and ashes.

22◆ Liturgical Vestments

Vesture of the Liturgical Assembly

Few norms ever have been universally issued for the vesture of the assembly. This manual (page 86) calls for some plan that allows coats to be taken off and storm gear to be stowed—either in coat rooms or elsewhere. The reason is to enable people to engage in communal action.

Other motives—for example, humility or concerns for modesty—also have been seen in rules for the vesture of the assembly. A proper humility before the mystery of salvation fostered the custom (now revived) of taking off shoes before the veneration of the cross. Similarly, a long-standing prohibition against gloves at liturgy, for both men and women, was founded on a conviction that bare hands conveyed the proper humility when receiving a blessed candle or palm, when serving as a godparent and when receiving communion. As cultures have changed, so have liturgical customs designed to express our affections. Yet, to our dismay, we still see people who proffer a gloved hand at the greeting of peace or the sharing of the eucharistic bread or cup.

Catholics of middle age or more will have no trouble remembering other rules that governed the covering—or uncovering—of the head. Through the 1960s, women had to wear hats; men had to take theirs off. The rule requiring hats for women was grounded in hellenistic or Jewish history. The classic articulation by Paul (1 Corinthians 11: 2–16) seems not only culturally bound, but maddeningly sexist. Veils for women, the special sign of consecrated virgins, sprang from similar origins. Interacting with the prevailing cultural trends, local church officials have all too often tried to make up for the scarcity of universal rules. Citing reverence, the avoidance of temptation or the fear of scandal, they have condemned or forbidden this or that vesture. Even today, guards at the Vatican make arbitrary decisions, based on dress, that determine who gets into St. Peter's and who doesn't. Luckily, sacristans are not called upon to enforce admission policies.

We can, instead, have a role in planning for the real liturgical dress of the assembly, the baptismal garment (cf. page 127). We also can prepare the reminder of that garment, the pall, which is placed over the casket at most funerals. We can help ministers with their albs, the baptismal garments that are the common vesture of every minister, every member of the church.

Special Vesture for Certain Ministries

Liturgical commentators often repeat the story that early Christian leaders of liturgy wore no distinctive vesture, just the "Sunday best" of the late antique Mediterranean culture. Images of that culture's vesture and of Christian vestments are too strikingly similar to dismiss their ancient bonds. This does not mean that Christians adopted imperial costume for their events; the vesture communicated more a message of "public act" and of "important act" than of imperial homage.

Once these links are acknowledged, it also must be noted that at a very early date, far earlier than some admit, the robes for presiders and other ministers were distinct from civic dress and from the vesture of others in the assembly. The wearing of special clothes for festivals and to designate special roles is pervasive in every century and in every social grouping. This was not just an abstract, cultural idea or rule. The earliest Christians knew full well that leaders in Jewish prayer, leaders and members of many different assemblies, wore specific vesture. As the centuries have passed, liturgical vesture has evolved slowly, though always revealing its roots in late antique, Mediterranean culture. As one new style of secular dress has replaced another, the gulf between liturgical garments and street dress has widened. This is to be welcomed, not bemoaned. First of all, because of this natural tendency for all groups' leaders to wear distinctive outfits, a diversity of vesture expresses a rich diversity of ministries. Secondly, the beauty of the robes makes a contribution, enhancing the expression of festivity and helping to sharpen visual focus. Two crucial documents articulate these reasons for distinctive vesture:

> The diversity of ministries is shown outwardly in worship by the diversity of vestments. These should therefore symbolize the function proper to each ministry. But at the same time the vestments should also contribute to the beauty of the rite. *(General Instruction of the Roman Missal,* #297)
>
> The color and form of the vestments and their difference from everyday clothing invite an appropriate attention and are part of the ritual experience essential to the festive character of a liturgical celebration. *(Environment and Art in Catholic Worship,* #93)

There is a third reason for our distinctive vesture: These are not just any old "dress up" costumes; they are the robes of our earliest ancestors in the faith. We continue to perform our liturgical actions with ministers dressed more or less like they were in ancient Rome and Gaul and Carthage. Some might miss the point of vesture, dismissing these garments as irrelevant or anachronistic. To do so is to deny the status of vesture as living art and as an historical link between us and all of the Christians who have gone before us.

While maintaining a high level of continuity, the Roman vestments have undergone many modifications over the centuries. There were periods when many attempted to reject the use of vestments altogether, for example sixteenth-century Calvinists. During certain periods, factions for and against vestments were active simultaneously. In the tumultuous 1960s, for example, some of those who were experimenting with home Masses did away with vestments. But during that same decade, the followers of Calvin at Taize adopted the alb. Changes in rites and communal life also have affected vesture, resulting in elements being added and subtracted. For example, the restoration of the permanent diaconate in our own century has given fresh prominence to dalmatics and diaconal stoles. In some quarters, the fuller chasuble has been making a comeback—an alternative to less graceful, minimalistic versions. Available materials and shifting technologies also have played a role, as in the regrettable flooding of markets with mass-produced vestments in recent generations. Finally, reformers have trumpeted austerity and simplicity, a return to basic values and simple lines that speak for themselves.

Whatever garb is worn, it should be evaluated in terms of its ability to serve and enhance the liturgy to the benefit of both the ministers and the people gathered. Any secondary purposes or meanings attached to vesture should be ignored, or at least downplayed. For example, the cincture is considered by some to be a sign of celibacy or chastity. In fact, it is a belt; its purpose is to hold the garment up. When ministers vest for liturgy, they do not need to recall this or that fanciful allegory. They instead should be concentrating on the sacred mysteries about to unfold, the actions that these robes assist.

The Use of Liturgical Colors

For the first millennium, little attention was paid to creating fixed cycles of colors for the vestments that were related to particular seasons and feasts, though white was always central. Through the Middle Ages, most dioceses and local communities of western and central Europe began developing and sharing customs that associated certain days and certain colors. Until 1570, when Roman authorities issued universal rules as part of the Tridentine reforms, these patterns differed from region to region and from parish to parish.

This system, now 400 years old, has been accepted by each generation and was repeated in the recent reforms. It has been an enduring and popular part of the Tridentine heritage because western Christians see it as assisting their progress through the liturgical year, as lending a seasonal unity and as expressing the shifting moods of the assembly.

But there are at least two ways of thinking about these colors that are decidedly unhelpful. The first is to think of the colors as mere decorations, as mobile parts of the environment. Sure, the colors and shapes add to the experience, but ministers should never be treated as props, as part of a "matched set" in a pretty diorama. The second unhelpful way of thinking about colors is to see them as carrying allegorical or mystical meanings. Their value is in providing seasonal contrast and mood, not in imparting didactic messages.

The list of vestment colors for Masses and for all other liturgies is found in the *General Instruction of the Roman Missal* (#308–310).

White:

–festive seasons of Christmas and Easter

–days of the Lord—except days related to the passion

–days of saints—except the anniversary of death of martyrs, apostles, evangelists

–Conversion of Paul, Chair of Peter, Birth of John the Baptist, All Saints, John the Evangelist—days associated with martyrs or apostles, but not anniversaries of martyrdom

Red:

–Passion/Palm Sunday and Good Friday

–Pentecost

–days of the Lord related to the passion

–days of martyrs, apostles, evangelists
(If only a few red vestments are owned by a community, they should not be so specifically decorated for the Passion, for Pentecost, or for martyrs, that they cannot be used on all of these days.)

Green:

–Ordinary Time

Violet:

–Advent

–Lent
(If only a few violet vestments are available, lenten and penitential motifs should not be so prevalent as to disallow their use in Advent.)

Rose:

–The Third Sunday of Advent

–The Fourth Sunday of Lent
(When there are limited resources, this old tradition need not be kept, and violet can be worn.)

Gold or more precious colors and materials:

–solemn occasions

Funerals and liturgies on November 2 can utilize white, violet or even black vesture. The Tridentine rule was black—a very dramatic choice—but many reformers in the 1960s felt that eternal life would be better expressed by white vesture. Others countered that this was too festive and joyous, insensitive to the real mourning and pain. Still others suggested a middle ground: the darker color of violet.

Each community should review its policy on choosing vesture for funerals. In the context of existing pastoral practice and other decorations, a case might be made for one color over another. Perhaps the seasons and colors already in the church complex should be respected. Violet could be used at funerals through Advent and Lent, white during the weeks of Christmas and Easter, black during Ordinary Time. If the community has a truly worthy chasuble in any one of these colors, then this might be the best choice. The chasuble does not need to match the casket pall.

There is no need to memorize any of these lists, to worry about whether to give priority to a season's color or to the color of a particular day. The annual ordo in every sacristy lists the correct colors for each day. When optional memorials are selected for a given parish (see page 180), they determine the color for that day; these, too, are in the ordo. When votive or other special Masses are celebrated, their colors are of the given day (unless there is an obvious association like red with Masses of the Holy Spirit). As we become ever more aware of our local resources, of the emotional power of varied colors, and of visual relationships, we can breath fresh life into this enduring system of linking seasons and affections.

Materials and Design of Vestments

Between the fourteenth and the twentieth centuries, the flowing robes of the late antique Mediterranean, adapted to distinguish liturgical ministries and passed down through the centuries, came upon hard times. In that period, when assemblies were called to look at rather than act with the liturgy, antique simplicity was replaced by complex layers of flamboyant embroidery and lace.

As ornamentation increased, the length and width of most vesture forms were cut back. As in other forms of liturgical art (cf. page 23), private emotions and pieties prevailed. The images and shapes no longer served a public action; instead they bore inspirational messages or dramatic displays. Where once the symbol had been the robe itself, now the attached symbol pictures became the focus.

In 1930, Dom Roulin sounded the alarm over the conditions that then prevailed: "The liturgical vestment has ceased to be a vestment and has become an ornament, and an ornament in a style either of pompous affectation or of stilted ugliness." *(Vestments and Vesture,* reprinted by Newman in 1950, p. 9)

As Roulin called for reform, three trends, somewhat contradictory to each other, were changing these pompous or stilted ornaments. Officials in the Vatican issued warnings against either changing or expanding the forms of vesture. This seemed ludicrous to those local churches that continued to use and treasure the more ample forms of vesture that predated Tridentine minimalism. Meanwhile leaders of the liturgical movement, inspired by the likes of Roulin, insisted that a return to fuller designs with less ornamentation would assist, not harm, the sacred rites. Finally, new technology provided mass-produced vestments. They often reflected a romantic revival of nineteenth-century forms, and were seldom of fine design and materials. They were, however, cheap enough to make them affordable by bereaved Catholics anxious to memorialize their loved ones. As a result, local churches were flooded with unsolicited items of dubious quality, and many pastors felt obligated to accept and wear them. The changes after Vatican II vindicated the stance that prophetic reformers and a few competent vestment makers had taken against entrenched bureaucrats. The *General Instruction of the Roman Missal* (#305-306) collates the advances made regarding materials and design:

> In addition to the traditional materials, natural fabrics proper to the region may be used for making vestments; artificial fabrics that are in keeping with the dignity of the liturgy and the person wearing them may also be used. The conference of bishops will be the judge in this matter.
>
> The beauty of a vestment should derive from its material and design rather than from lavish ornamentation. Representations on vestments should consist only of symbols, images, or pictures portraying the sacred. Anything out of keeping with the sacred is to be avoided.

MATERIALS: The traditional material for albs was linen. For all other vesture, silk and fabrics related to it—satin, damask, or silk interwoven with gold or silver threads—were preferred. Cloth woven from real gold threads was also allowed, but for obvious reasons was rare.

Though the new rules continue to stress the need for dignity in vestments, they also now permit great freedom with regard to the materials used in their manufacture. The traditional materials no longer dominate. New technology has encouraged the nearly universal spread of other materials, often blends of natural and artificial fibers.

Despite the freedom we now enjoy to choose vestments made from a much wider range of materials, we should nevertheless steer clear of materials that are unfit for public wearing and public action. Cheap cotton and polyester that doesn't breathe can be just as distracting and undignified as lace and heavy brocade. Nor should we use leftovers from the bygone era of lavish and distracting adornments on vestments.

DESIGN: Restating the norms of the *General Instruction, Environment and Art in Catholic Worship* (#94) gives a most succinct summary of the designs favorable to liturgy, "The more these vestments fulfill their function by their color, design, and enveloping form, the less they will need the signs, slogans and symbols which an unkind history has fastened on them." The material and design that bring beauty and functionality to liturgical clothes have been understood by all contemporary reformers to presume a pliancy of material, a flowing form and plentiful folds that allow the fabric to hang well. Such fullness is most fitting for the movements and gestures demanded of ministers. Yet it is sometimes resisted by certain ministers, especially presiders, who have become accustomed to cut-back shapes, who see the draped folds as burdens rather than as enhancements to their service of gesturing and presiding. Yet we should invite ministers to try to use more ample vesture. This is not the same as asking a short person to wear a tall person's size: Within each height and girth range there are ways for vesture to be richly draped. We should supply our vesting rooms with robes in a wide range of sizes so that all persons can wear vesture that fits in the desirably ample way.

Ornamentation on the fabric can be justified only if it is well-executed, congruent with the other elements of design and color, and fitting for liturgical action. Any that fails to meet these standards should not be purchased, commissioned, accepted or used. For example, there should be no tassels that will fall in to the vessels. Because albs are to be simple baptismal garments of white, decorations are even less likely to be appropriate here. Some terms associated with the ornamentation of vestments other than the alb, and utilized by many catalogs and artists, are listed below.

–Appliques (often of silk, or of gold metallic threads) are crosses or other small symbols, traditionally applied to the vestment by stitching (with gold metallic cord or with floss of a contrasting color). They are rarely appropriate.

–Cording is a trimming to add detail to other ornamentation.

–Fringes (of varying materials and colors) were often used on the antependia that fit wall-mounted altars. For good reason, they were and are rare on vestments.

–Galloons are colorful and narrow borders, often used along either side of orphreys. They can sometimes highlight the main lines of the vestment.

–Gems and pearls and ornamental glass are sometimes used with restraint (and some success) on miters. They are rarely appropriate elsewhere, but they might be considered because of their allusions to the new Jerusalem in the book of Revelation.

–Inscriptions are rarely appropriate on ministers' clothes.

–Medallions (see vesicas).

–Monograms (see symbols).

–Orphrey bandings are strips of fabric that contrast with the vestment on which they are sewn. They are often multi-colored brocades (tapestries) or are embroidered with symbols. They are often edged with galloon borders. If they are used with restraint and are properly positioned, they can highlight the main shapes and movements of the vesture.

–Protectors, by whatever name their proponents call them, are needless and intrusive strips of linen or other cloth, often edged with lace. They are affixed to stoles in hopes of protecting them from sweat and dirt. This is disrespectful to the design of the stole and to the ministers themselves. It is an exaggerated concern as well, because the stole rarely rides above the alb to the bare neck. They are never appropriate.

–Symbols in this context mean small images of the cross, lamb, dove or other such devices sewn onto vestments. These are often the ugliest renditions of the cherished images; they often repeat Tridentine forms (a wafer-bread suspended over an old chalice). At their worst, they provide sentimental or stylized pictures of saints or other creatures. They were the principal villains in the devolution of vestments from clothing to billboards. They are rarely appropriate.

–Tassels can be used at the bottom of stoles or cope hoods. The extra weight sometimes helps the garment hang correctly, but their positioning, size and color should not be obtrusive.

–Vesicas (often shaped liked medallions) are pieces of colorful fabric (often velvet) that provide background frames for applied symbols. Like the symbols themselves, they are rarely helpful.

Vestment for All Ministers: The Alb and Its Accessories

ROBE OF GLORY: At the Transfiguration, Jesus' clothes became "dazzling white." The angelic herald of the resurrection was arrayed in white. Daniel and Revelation describe the Ancient One in white; the singing multitudes in the new Jerusalem are similarly seen in white robes.

It is no wonder that both early and later Christians wore an equivalent of the basic robe of classical Rome, the *tunica alba,* at baptism and at virtually every other liturgy. In an unbroken tradition, the billowing christening dress of infants, the long white robe of adult neophytes, and the basic vestment of Catholic liturgy all express our baptismal destiny in the new Jerusalem. When first communion was separated from the other initiatory sacraments, it is no mere coincidence that white became the preferred color for the vesture of communicants. This meaning is not some later invention of catechists, for long and flowing white robes are rather archetypal. They have a primal ability to express and enhance the purity of new life.

The unbroken heritage has been periodically diverted, as when a local church or group substituted some supposedly meaningful invention. Some centuries saw the unfortunate addition of ornamentation. Scattered individuals in the Middle Ages and even recently took to wearing colored "albs." Shorter versions of the alb, with wider sleeves, eventually became "surplices" and were worn by various ministers even to our own era. Yet the full, unembellished white robe survives, and once more has been emphasized as the basic vestment for all. The *General Instruction of the Roman Missal* (#298) states:

> The vestment common to ministers of every rank is the alb, tied at the waist with a cincture, unless it is made to fit without a cincture. An amice should be put on first if the alb does not completely cover the street clothing at the neck.

CURRENT ALBS: Over the centuries, from at least Trent to the reforms of the twentieth century, most liturgical ministries were taken by priests who wore additional vesture over the alb. The visible parts attracted some extraneous embellishments and the rest, of a not particularly noble design, came to be treated almost as underwear. Over the cassock—which was the street dress for clerics—the assisting ministers and acolytes wore a drastically abbreviated alb, called a surplice or cotta.

Now many more persons serve in liturgical ministries, and all can wear albs. Surplices and clerical cassocks can be put aside. In some regions, many parish ministers—choir members, lectors, eucharistic ministers and acolytes—all wear the same albs as the presiding pastor. The same motives that have led to the vesting of presiders suggest the vesting of the other liturgical ministers—lectors, eucharistic ministers, acolytes, cantors and choir members. That is the possibility that the *General Instruction* and the reforms have laid before us, a fresh appreciation of the positive roles played by vesture in a liturgical assembly. This possibility, once realized, obviously presents new challenges for sacristans, because sufficient albs in many sizes will need to be acquired and maintained.

For most, the alb is not an undergarment. Many wear it unembellished. Even priests and deacons, who might wear a chasuble or dalmatic over it for certain rites, wear just a stole over it on other, frequent occasions. The design selected by sacristans must reflect this new use and visibility.

For the same reasons that linen was used for altar cloths (cf. page 139), our ancestors usually preferred albs made of linen. This is still a wonderful fabric, though wrinkle-resistent blends requiring less care are more regularly used today. As is the case with all vestments, there should be plenty of albs on hand, all in ample sizes for the wearers, and with nicely hanging folds. This latter quality, so passionately espoused by the pioneers of the liturgical movement, suggests albs designed to hang well without a cincture interrupting the fall of the fabric. The collar should be such that undergarments are covered, making amices unnecessary. The sleeves should be wide enough to accommodate many different-sized arms and to allow for gracious gestures with the amply-vested arm. Also, albs should be long enough to cover the legs. Newly appointed ministers may need a few pointers on how to walk up stairs—for the sake of a dignified liturgy, offering such advice is superior to giving them hiked-up robes.

For a brief period in the 1970s some priests purchased a combination alb-chasuble. Though approved by Rome, this garment, thankfully, has survived only in a very few local churches. It respects neither the integrity of the alb garment, a flowing robe with sleeves, nor the symbolism of all ministers, including the presider, wearing the same kind of alb.

THE CINCTURE: The first embellishment to the alb mentioned in the *General Instruction* is the cincture, to be used only if necessary. Most albs look better without it. When a cincture is used, for example to raise up the hem for a person who is too short for an available robe, then it should be white and as simply made as possible. Colored cinctures and those with elaborate tassels or fringe should be avoided. The alb is what is important, and no ornamental accessory should detract from it.

THE AMICE: The other embellishment is the amice. It is to be worn by all ministers, male and female, young and old, whose albs do not adequately cover their street clothes. If we have acquired the right kind of albs, then amices should seldom be necessary. The old ones existing in most sacristies ought to be sufficient. If, for some reason, new amices must be purchased or made—because there are design flaws in the albs, for example—they should be made or purchased in numbers and sizes adequate for those who will be wearing them.

Amices are square or preferably oblong pieces of white linen, large enough to be stretched around the shoulders and to be tucked inside the neck of the underlying street clothes. From two corners of the fabric, long strings extend for three feet or more—long enough to be crossed on the breast, carried round to the back, crossed there, and brought around again to the front to be tied. Whether the amice originated as a head covering or as a protection around the neck is debated by historians. A minor vestment, it nonetheless gives witness to the first purpose of liturgical vestments—to envelop the minister in distinct garb, to put aside the dress of Main Street and wear the white of the new Jerusalem.

Vestments Proper to the Ordained: Stole, Dalmatic, Chasuble

THE STOLE: This long, scarf-like vestment is the mark of ordination. Deacons wear it over the left shoulder, drawn across the chest and back toward the lower right side. Other ordained ministers wear it around the neck, hanging down in front. On many occasions, deacons, priests and bishops wear just a stole of the day's color over the alb. The dalmatic or chasuble is worn over the alb and stole only for certain liturgies, principally the Mass. When the stole is used with these or with a cope, it usually matches them in material and design.

Many theories have been advanced, none of them conclusive, on the historical origins of the stole, as well as its etymology. Plausible theories hold that it is related to the Jewish prayer mantle, or to a Roman neck-cloth, or to a ceremonial garland, or to another surviving vestment, the pallium (cf. page 135). This last theory is based on the fact that civil and ecclesial officials in late antiquity wore scarfs as badges of office. A bishop's scarf was called a pallium; the scarf worn by priests and deacons was called an orarium. Meanwhile the term *stola* or stole was used in the scriptures to denote a long, flowing robe. Around the ninth century, there was a confusing change of designations, and the orarium scarf began to be called a stole.

Aside from such confusing changes in name, the stole has changed remarkably little throughout its long history. Its shape is much the same; so is the silken material used to make it. As with all vestments, however, it tended to be over-decorated in the period between Trent and Vatican II.

We need to have many stoles in our sacristies: for priests and deacons; in various colors to complement all of the chasubles, dalmatics and copes (usually purchased or commissioned with them); in shapes and colors to be worn independently; for wearers of different heights; sufficient in numbers to accommodate all local rites, including concelebrations. While many ordained ministers have stoles of their own, they may not have them in all colors. In any event, the community should have its own sets, so that the departures of individuals do not strip sacristies of the necessary variety.

There are many variants on the basic shape of the stole, all named differently by individual artists, all to be examined before acquisition. The differences to be reviewed include width, length, finish at the ends (and how well this holds them down evenly), shape at the back of the neck (or over the shoulder of the deacon), and how well the stole rests without riding up onto the neck. Obviously, a lot depends on whether the given stole will be worn alone with an alb, under a chasuble, or over a plain chasuble. With so many variables, those charged with the selection of stoles should inspect and try on as many as possible.

THE DALMATIC: The *General Instruction* has one laconic reference to this ancient robe: "The dalmatic, worn over the alb and stole, is the vestment proper to the deacon"(#300).

The alb began as the *tunica alba,* a long white robe with strips of ornamentation. The dalmatic began perhaps in Dalmatia (later Croatia) as another *tunica alba,* with similar bands of decoration, worn over the first. As both forms of the *tunica alba* passed into strictly liturgical usage, the lower *tunica alba* lost its stripes and became the alb. The upper *tunica alba* was reduced in length, given broader sleeves and slit open at the sides, becoming the dalmatic.

Historians note that the dalmatic suffered less than other vestments during the period of bad decoration before and after Trent. While the dalmatic, too, became more of an ornamentation than a garment, its basic form was preserved—perhaps because true diaconal ministry was such a rarity before the 1970s, reserved to transitional months in seminaries and to priests playing deacons at solemn high Masses.

Dalmatics usually come with matching stoles. They regularly match a chasuble as well, because of the ministerial role that deacons fill beside presiding priests at eucharist. This pairing of proper vestments is never necessary. Indeed, it is sometimes undesirable, owing to the fact that at a number of rites deacons can preside on their own. Even when together, ministers needn't vest themselves as a matched set.

Dalmatics come in all the liturgical colors. Though white always can be worn whenever a community does not have the color for the feast or season, deacons should wear the colors designated whenever possible. In other respects, the materials and design of dalmatics follow the same general rules as other vestments. They should be made of dignified material, and they should envelope the ministers in color, with ample folds and flowing lines.

As with all vestments, we should establish procedures for the ongoing acquisition of dalmatics in sufficient numbers and colors for all the seasons. In deciding how many dalmatics will be needed, keep the following in mind:

–deacons shouldn't be expected to have their own

–multiple deacons all can be vested in dalmatics on festive occasions

–on certain occasions, a bishop can wear a dalmatic between his stole and chasuble.

This latter custom is both ancient and curious. On the few solemn occasions when the extra robe is added, it is the only time that bishops wear different liturgical vestments than priests. At such solemn events, with multiple deacons or a bishop, parishes can borrow dalmatics from neighboring communities, a diocesan liturgy office, or the cathedral.

THE CHASUBLE: The *General Instruction* (#299) is similarly brief about this most visible vestment: "The chasuble, worn over the alb and stole, is the vestment proper to the priest celebrant at Mass and other rites immediately connected with Mass."

The word is related to the terms that other languages use to denote "cottage" or "hut," such as the Spanish *casa* for house, and *casita* for small house. Several ancient sources, indeed, describe it as a "little house" enveloping the presider. Small hut or large robe, the original shape of the vestment was the "paenula" or "planeta" of classical Rome, a sort of poncho or circular garment with an opening in the center for the head. With or without a hood, this eminently practical and ample robe passed into strictly liturgical usage as the proper garb of priests at eucharist. Over time it was considerably cut back until it became a mere shadow of itself—stiff panels of fabric hanging in front and back, all heavily ornamented. Once again, a garment had become an ornament.

Charles Borromeo, the sixteenth-century bishop of Milan who issued many wonderful norms for sacristies, and various councils of his time tried to restore the fuller forms of earlier periods. They failed. Once again, in the nineteenth and twentieth centuries, liturgists who romanticized the medieval period and its fuller forms of vesture formed a strained alliance with forward-thinking colleagues who knew that ornaments had once again to become garments for ministers. Their attempts were resisted by Roman authorities and trivialized by commercial producers who flooded sacristies with shoddy, "gothic" chasubles. Since Vatican II we have had at least four forms of chasubles:

- "Roman" or "Baroque" models that look like heavily ornamented sandwich boards

- reproduction antiques from the gothic period (fuller form, but often of inferior materials or with forced-symbolism appliques); new designs (often with cheap or contrived symbols added on), longer in the front and rear, with sides cut back for presiders who are uncomfortable feeling ample folds of fabric on their arms

- new designs made without mass-production and without applied symbols, striving to recapture in fine materials the fuller form of a circle.

We should supply the sacristy with more than one chasuble in each of the four major liturgical colors—white, red, violet, green. In addition, the sacristy should have as many of the lesser colors—gold, black, rose—as ritual customs and finances will permit. As with other vestments, if the community owns more than one chasuble in a single color, then these should be in different sizes to accommodate the maximum amount of variation in the heights of the presiders. All should be amply cut to hang loosely. As stated before, the beauty of vesture comes from colorful materials and full forms enveloping the ministers and enhancing ministerial gestures, not from form-fitting panels of polyester emblazoned with pretty pictures.

Vestments of Special Festivity: Cope, Humeral Veil

THE COPE: The Roman paenula, which later became the chasuble, was a circular garment extending to the ground. It had a center opening for the head and often a hood. This same poncho-type garment was slit completely up the front and equipped with a clasp (called a morse) to become a great cloak or cape. It was our ancestors' favorite protection against rain. Thus, the word for cope in various modern languages is related either to cape or to rain-cloak *(pluvial* or *piviale).* This raincoat evolved slightly in the early medieval period for use at liturgy: Often orphrey bands or other decorations were added. Some decorative materials, stiffer than silk, made the cape somewhat too heavy for easy wearing. The original hood often was transformed into a decorative, apron-like flap. On occasion, this flap was sometimes attached at a lower point unrelated to the neckline (what Roulin called the "comic hood").

Despite these changes, the cope was passed on to us fairly intact. Old copes often are eloquently full cloaks of splendid material and restrained decoration. They have not been cut back or shortened, and they fulfill most of the standards for full, enveloping vesture.

Given the beauty of copes, it's unfortunate that many communities use them only for priests and then only on rare occasions. This vestment was passed down to us not only with its original form intact, but with its originally broad access unchanged by liturgical law. The cope was never reserved to priests, although in the twelfth century some local churches restricted its use to cantors. Though many cantors were tonsured clerics, rubrics ensured the use of copes by untonsured cantors as well. In other areas before and during the middle ages, monastic communities used such ceremonial cloaks to vest all monks except the presider (who wore a chasuble). Another prevalent and still current custom is for assisting ministers, especially masters of ceremonies and servers (even children) who hold the episcopal insignia (miter, pastoral staff), to wear liturgical capes or copes. These were not aberrations, but fully appreciated ancient customs acknowledged by various liturgical books (especially successive editions of the *Ceremonial of Bishops)*. In keeping with this broad usage, copes were never given allegorical meanings, blessed, or otherwise set aside for the exclusive use of the ordained.

If copes have been an unfamiliar part of our experience in the twentieth century, or were thought to be reserved to priests, it was because they had generally fallen from favor, not because their use was restricted by law. The reformed rites have changed neither their low level of usage nor their great potential. They are hardly mentioned at all.

Most sacristans and priests know that chasubles are reserved to the eucharist, that when other rites are scheduled a cope can be added over the presiding priest's stole and alb. Yet copes also are mentioned in these settings:

- for presiding deacons or priests at liturgies other than Mass (for example, eucharistic benediction, the baptism of infants, orders of blessing)
- for as many priests as are assisting in solemn liturgies other than Mass (for example, celebrations of the liturgy of the hours, eucharistic exposition, public processions)
- for the deacon or cantor at the solemn proclamation of the year's feasts on Epiphany *(Ceremonial of Bishops,* #240).

These occasions provide parishes with extraordinary opportunities. On particularly important occasions, we can provide truly festive vesture for ministers to wear over their albs. The continued use of copes by priests, deacons, monks, cantors, masters of ceremonies, and ministers assisting with episcopal insignia has prevented the use of copes from dying out, as have the brief notes in today's liturgical books. Resistance might come from some who see no point to liturgical vesture of any kind. Others might think that copes are just too good looking! This is not a call to confront those who hold this belief, nor to unduly increase the use of these festive cloaks. Yet, if we agree that the leadership of presiding priests and the aesthetic environment are enhanced by proper robes, then other leaders of our most solemn moments should don copes. In addition to being used by the cantor at the Epiphany proclamation, the cope can be worn by other non-ordained persons on a variety of other occasions, such as by:

–the cantor of the Exsultet

–the psalmist-cantor at the most solemn liturgies

–the leader of a large assembly for an order of blessing

–the presider at the liturgy of the hours.

Such possibilities and current usage can determine how many copes, and of what color, are needed. White or gold, of course, would fit with usage on the most festive occasions. The other colors used on Sundays should be available if copes are regularly used for presiding at evening prayer. Keeping to the standards applicable to good vesture of all kinds, new copes for different ministers do not have to be heavily ornamented. But plain, ample, colorful cloaks for ministerial leadership do have to be available in sizes for all ministers.

HUMERAL VEIL: This is another vestment of high festivity, but it is more restricted to certain occasions and ministers. The term "humeral" comes from the Latin word for shoulder, around which this large, scarf-like veil is worn. It is usually equipped with a chain clasp to hold it on; this is far easier for the minister than strings. The best humeral veils do not display applied symbols; thus, they are better able to continue doing what they have done for centuries: give particular prominence to some of our holiest elements.

In various lands and periods of history, some of them marked by fully participatory liturgies, many liturgical elements were not handled in public by bare human hands, but by hands covered with a vestment. This was a way of showing profound respect in a nonverbal way to such things as lectionaries and other liturgical books, eucharistic vessels and other objects.

Humeral veils are currently worn:

–by deacon or priest at eucharistic exposition, benediction, or in eucharistic processions, while holding the monstrance at the blessing and while carrying the eucharist from (or back to) the chapel of reservation

–by priest or deacon bearing the eucharistic vessel for the transfer at the end of the Evening Mass of the Lord's Supper on Holy Thursday and at the Holy Communion of the Celebration of the Lord's Passion on Good Friday; if there are multiple vessels, more than one minister might be so vested

–by ministers bearing relics in solemn processions

–by ministers assisting with episcopal insignia (in some dioceses, where they are not already wearing copes).

On these occasions all of the humeral veils can be white, although on Good Friday red can be worn. Many communities have humeral veils in all of the liturgical colors but black, owing to the fact that they were once used at all solemn high Masses except funerals. At the present stage of liturgical practice, there is no need for humeral veils in all colors. Yet as the reformed rites evolve, local churches may find new roles for these veils, new ways to balance our touching and seeing with contrasting practices of restraint and veiling.

Final Vestment: The Funeral Pall

Bereaved communities always have honored the remains of their deceased. From the earliest periods of Christian liturgy, cemeteries were an important place for memorial gatherings and for decorations; gardens were the favored setting and lamps were the normal decoration. In later centuries, the caskets or corpses of Christians in many lands were embellished with rich fabric covers or "palls." When these customs spread and became regulated, black became the normative color for covers. These would be large enough to cover the casket, extending down over the bier or trestle as well. The pall could be ornamented with cross, galloons or fringes. White palls were forbidden, except for young children. In the mid-nineteenth century, communities in many areas discontinued the use of palls.

In the late 1960s, during extensive experimentation and preparation for the reformed funeral rite, liturgical leaders in several American dioceses played a strong role in helping communities to rediscover the funeral pall. White was now used to express the paschal nature of the rite, to remember baptism, and to express hope that the deceased be clothed in glory with all in the new Jerusalem. (The pall is the third white robe that Christians wear. The first is the white gown worn at baptism; the second is the alb, worn during any liturgical ministries.)

The pall is not the only symbol that can be placed on the casket as part of the reception of the body before the vigil or Mass. Alternatives include the book of the gospels, the Bible, or a cross. Yet the pall remains as one of the most successful renovations of the late twentieth century. To satisfy the various circumstances encountered over the course of the year, our local places of worship should have a sufficient number of palls on hand. Dimensions of palls depend on the size of caskets for children and adults, the method of carrying the casket after the pall has been positioned, and the resting place of the casket before the altar (bier, funeral-trolley cart, or floor of the sanctuary). The fabric and its lining should hang well and present a dignified appearance. The pall should be white even if the chasuble is black or violet. Decorations should be kept to a minimum. As with all vesture, the material and design are more important. The symbol is a casket enveloped in white, not an appliqued "symbol" on that symbol.

Other Special Clothing in Church Communities

INSIGNIA OF BISHOPS: At any liturgical celebration, the vestments worn by a bishop are the same as those worn by priests—alb (with cincture and amice only if necessary) and stole, with a chasuble or cope if the rite calls for this. At eucharistic celebrations on certain very solemn occasions, bishops may wear a simple dalmatic between the stole and chasuble.

In addition to these liturgical vestments, certain articles of clothing or insignia are often worn by bishops. They are not, strictly speaking, vestments, but they are nonetheless part of the rites and thus part of the sacristy's provisions. Sacristans in cathedrals are often concerned with these items, and periodically they are called upon to care for, procure or store them. For an episcopal visitation or liturgy in other parishes, the bishop normally brings everything he will need, which may include any or all of the following items.

- The ring expresses the bishop's fidelity to the local church; he wears it always.

–The pastoral staff (crosier or crozier), a symbol of pastoral office, is used at many (but not all) liturgies. The bishop decides whether or not to use it, based on such factors as the level of solemnity and whether he is in his own diocese. If it is brought to the sacristy unassembled in a carrying case, the sacristan or the minister who will hold the staff during the liturgy must assemble it and place it by the area where the bishop will vest.

–The miter, a traditional hat and a mark of liturgical presidency, is worn at many (but not all) liturgies—usually at the same liturgies that the staff is carried, and based on similar determinations. There were formerly many regulations about simple and ornate versions—now the bishop is to select the one appropriate to the feast. Sacristans need merely place it on the vesting table. After many stages of development, its current form is two pieces forming a circle at the bottom and rising to two peaks, with two lappets (fannons) extending down off the back. Miters tend to be somewhat shorter and plainer than in recent centuries, more an article of clothing now than the billboards for symbols that they used to be. These very tall hats usually were plastered with romantic art. Now they have become a badge of defiance, worn by some traditionalist bishops in the Anglican communion and by leaders of right-wing movements against Rome. In these cases, the miter is being used to express ideology, as other items of vesture have done in the past.

–The skull cap (zucchetto) is worn at almost all liturgies. It began as a practical covering worn by all tonsured clerics over their bald spot. In most countries, bishops are the only ones who have kept the custom, even though tonsure long ago fell into disuse. Thus, it is perceived by many to be an important episcopal sign. It is not. If the bishop is not already wearing a skull cap when he arrives, the sacristan or an assistant should set it out. An old custom, still in force in some dioceses, is to put a small tray or dish on the credence table before Mass, so the skull cap can be placed there when it is removed during the celebration. But it is much simpler, and more in keeping with the minor import of the skull cap, to have it rest between uses directly on the presider's chair or the cathedra.

–The pectoral cross, which the bishop will be wearing when he arrives, is placed under the liturgical vestments, not over them. It is regrettable when either bishops or any other ministers decide to wear a cross over their vesture. The flowing robes in their proper shapes make enough of a statement. The one and only liturgical cross should be the processional cross.

–The pallium is worn only at eucharistic celebrations of great solemnity and only by residential archbishops, that is, bishops of dioceses designated as the metropolitan centers with certain jurisdiction over neighboring dioceses. The pallium is a narrow band of white wool. It forms a circle around the neck with strips extending down the front and back and is worn over and pinned to the chasuble. Each pallium is given by the pope as a sign of the metropolitan's communion with Rome. This sign is made all the more potent by the traditional manufacture of a pallium. It is made from the wool of sheep blessed in Rome on the feast of St. Agnes, an early Roman martyr (with a name that sounds like *agnus,* the Latin word for lamb). On the night before the feast of St. Peter, the pallium is placed on his tomb, and it remains there until the next day. It is then blessed and presented personally by the pope to the bishop.

CHOIR DRESS: The various items of "choir dress" for bishops include clothing such as colored cassocks that they can wear at a liturgy when they are not wearing liturgical vestments. Choir dress is described in the *Ceremonial of Bishops* (#63–64, 1199–1202, 1205). Few clerics, even those with honorific titles like "monsignor," use choir dress or cassocks and surplices anymore *(Ceremonial,* #66, 1206–1209). When they are not leading a liturgy, they usually wear street clothes and take their places with the rest of the assembly; or they vest as concelebrants. The demise of choir dress, at least for this period of history, seems to show a healthy regard for the power of the whole assembly, a reluctance to introduce special dress on those not serving in actual liturgical ministries, and a trend toward less formal vesture. The substitution of the alb for the cassock and surplice is similarly motivated by respect for the assembly and we should encourage it.

DISTINCTIVE DRESS OF OTHER ORDERS AND SOCIETIES: At certain liturgies, especially pilgrimage gatherings, stational Masses and diocesan convocations, sacristans will see many other special costumes and habits, insignia and symbols. When pontifical knights and ladies, representative of special orders and societies, are scheduled to vest in their respective garb and participate in the procession, we do not have to provide their robes or even know what these items are. We do, however, need to know the amount of space that each group will need for vesting. We also need to provide tables or racks and hangers; ensure the delivery of hymnals, song sheets or orders of service into their hands; and organize vesting areas so that the clusters or groups end up in the right processional order.

At some nonliturgical events in the church complex, bishops or priests might wear special garments. Their traditional ensembles are described in the *Ceremonial* (#1203–1204, bishops; #1205, cardinals; #1207–1209).

Care and Storage of Vestments

PREPARATION FOR USE: Most ministers neither need nor expect their vestments to be laid out. Because closets are used far more than drawers, the various colors and sizes are readily accessible to all. Still, if the preferences and sizes of the ministers are known, their vestments could be laid out as a courtesy. The vestments can be placed on the vesting table, positioned on a garment stand, or hung on racks with ministers' names pinned on.

Before any major liturgy involving many ministers, sacristans should have a list of those who need to be vested. With this information, they can prepare a set-up list.

To assist in vesting, we should always have (in addition to the regular furnishings of the vesting room described on page 97) the following items:

–lint brush or roller

–comb, hair brush

–nail clippers

–a variety of pins (safety, straight, hat)

–shoe horn (many may be needed on Good Friday if all will take off their shoes)

–eye-glass cleaning sheets

–facial tissue

–drawers for the storage of personal items.

Presiding priest ("celebrant") for Mass: chasuble of day's color, complementary stole, cincture (only if necessary), alb, amice (rarely needed). The traditional way to lay these items out is to put them down in that exact order, so that the items to be put on first are found on top. Here, then, is how the items would be arranged, bottom to top:

–chasuble, front-side down, with the bottom of the back folded up a bit so that it can be lifted

–stole splayed out with the middle of the stole resting in the middle

–cincture, unknotted

–alb, front side down, with the bottom of the back folded up a bit, and the bottom opening facing the minister

–amice, opened out and with the strings untangled.

Presiding bishop ("celebrant") for Mass: the same as above; the miter (if used), skull cap (if not already on), pastoral staff (and pallium, if used) placed nearby. On truly rare occasions, a dalmatic may be set between the chasuble and stole.

Presiding priest for liturgies other than Mass: cope of the day's color or rite's color (if used), stole complementing the cope, cincture (if necessary), alb, amice (if necessary).

Presiding bishop for liturgies other than Mass: the same as above; the miter, skull cap, pastoral staff placed nearby.

Presiding deacon for liturgies other than Mass: cope or dalmatic of the day's color (if used), stole complementing the cope or dalmatic, cincture (if necessary), alb, amice (if necessary).

Concelebrating priests at Mass: chasuble of the color of the day or in white if these are worn in local practice, stole in color of the day or white, alb, amice and/or cincture (if necessary).

Other ministers at any liturgy: alb, cincture and/or amice (if necessary). In certain places and for great solemnities, some ministers wear a cope over the alb. In certain regions, some ministers assisting the bishop wear humeral veils.

REGULAR MAINTENANCE: Sacristans obviously need to establish and follow some standard procedures for the regular maintenance of vestments. Thus most vestments will be ready for use at any time. Set procedures are especially necessary when there are multiple volunteers in the sacristy. Procedures should include washing or cleaning instructions for each kind of vestment, whether it is to be washed by hand, washed by machine or dry cleaned. Arrangements may need to be made with a variety of companies and individuals, such as dry cleaning establishments that have the experience and know-how necessary to clean vestments, parishioners with expertise in the cleaning and laundering of vestments, commercial laundry operations that have large washing machines, volunteers who are expert at mending fine textiles, and local tailors.

STORAGE: Vestments can be hung in closets or stretched out in drawers. If the local vesting room is provided with those wide, shallow drawers that were originally designed to store altar cloths and cut-back Roman chasubles, then these certainly should be utilized. Chasubles, dalmatics, copes, stoles, humeral veils and casket palls should be in the drawers if at all possible. Here they are protected from light, dust and the stress of their weight. If this is not convenient, then at least they should be stored in these drawers during the seasons when their particular color is less used. Old drawer linings or acid-free tissue should be used. Folds should be padded with acid-free tissue to avoid creases and damage. The alb's accessories (amices and cinctures) can be kept in smaller drawers, along with the textile items described in the following chapter.

Vestments hanging in closets—those taken out of the drawers for use that week, albs, or all of the vestments if no drawers are at hand—should never be on wire or bendable plastic hangers. They need to be on the widest possible wooden hangers, hung from very high rods. Garment bags of plastic should never be used; natural fibers must breathe. Opaque doors on the closets, or cloth bags, provide better protection against light, and thus reduce fading.

23◆ Linens and Textiles Other Than Vesture

In the rich variety of ritual circumstance and physical movement, many small textiles have become convenient, even necessary, for liturgical communities. Cloth is used not only to make clothes and wall decoration; it is also used to cover tables, clean vessels and absorb moisture. We use textiles, often linen, to cover furniture, to cleanse vessels and to dry people after baptism.

Linen

The plagues upon Egypt included the destruction by hail of its flax (Exodus 9:31), an important part of that country's economy. From the stalks of their flax plants, Egyptians fabricated the most highly prized linen of the ancient world. It was traditionally specified for use in the Temple at Jerusalem. It was used to wrap the dead, and to make clothing, bed sheets, curtains, sails for ships and wrappers for scrolls.

In Christian communities, linen was used for the first altar covers (page 48). It was the premier fabric for public rites and for burial, for vesting the symbols of the body of Christ (altar and people). For two millennia, Christian churches prescribed linen for a wide variety of purposes. It was the fabric of choice for albs and altar cloths, as well as for the smaller textiles at church. These items as a group came to be called "church linens" or "altar linens." Even as communities lost their historical sense of the way linen linked them to the ancient people of Israel and to early Christians, the natural properties of linen continued to make it the fabric of choice.

The use of linen is no longer mandated, and other fabrics are now often used, chiefly cotton or polyester blended with either cotton or linen. Still, the beauty and functionality of linen continue to make it the ideal material for many of the smaller textile items discussed in this chapter. Pure linen may be more expensive, but it probably functions better and lasts much longer than the alternatives. True, it probably wrinkles more readily, but most of these items should be laundered and pressed after every use anyway. Whatever material is chosen, it should launder well. Bear in mind that white fabric without polyester probably will come out cleanest after laundering because higher water temperatures can be used. Whenever it comes time to order new textiles, we should always evaluate all the available fabrics with an eye to their past performance.

As were the vestments, so too were corporals, purificators, palls, veils, gremials and towels often decorated with symbols that duplicated and trivialized the larger and stronger symbols in the place for worship. (Red crosses were either stitched or embroidered on these smaller linens.) Added symbols and decoration are never necessary and usually are distracting. This holds especially true for older items that have been decorated with strips of lace. No matter how praiseworthy or traditional the use of lace may be in certain domestic items such as draperies, its use in liturgy is too frivolous, too linked to this kind of secular ornamentation.

Linens or Other Textiles for Church Furnishings

ALTAR CLOTHS AND CORPORALS AT THE EUCHARIST: Altar cloths are described on page 48. They are closely linked to the piece of linen termed the corporal. Related to the Latin term for "body," the corporal always has been an additional altar cloth spread under the eucharistic vessels. Over the centuries, it has shrunk in size and taken on its own identity, although in a few groups, the Carthusians, for example, it continues to resemble an altar cloth. In most churches the corporal came to be considered as different from altar cloths—different in that it was square and small, spread out just before the eucharistic act, and folded in on itself just after the action, thereby gathering any eucharistic particles. In its late medieval form, it was carried to and from the altar in a fabric-covered case or envelope called a "burse."

Rhetoric and allegories about the corporal in past centuries might remind us of the inordinate attention paid to crumbs and drops, a result of a physical literalism having replaced fuller appreciations of the sacramental presence. Certainly the eucharistic presence of Christ demands a dignified handling of the altar coverings. Yet the scrupulosity of some ministers and commentators demeaned the public action and the other modes of Christ's presence in the assembly. Those other modes include interactions with the word, holy oils, baptismal water, and many other sacramental realities shared by the assembly.

The size for today's corporals should relate to their ritual use and the dimensions of the local altar. Some parishes do not supplement their regular altar cover at all. The *General Instruction of the Roman Missal* continues to indicate that a corporal is spread out as part of the preparation of the altar, as a second altar cover to rest under the eucharistic vessels. Thus the corporal will be measured in feet or yards, not in inches. It will be rolled or folded as befits the size of the altar and the number of eucharistic vessels. The creases once mandated for corporals are no longer required. They related to such now-abrogated rites as resting the host on the corporal and placing the paten under the side of the corporal. The Tridentine understanding of the corporal's purpose was the containment of eucharistic crumbs. Now the corporal also protects the more permanent cover from stains. No burse is mentioned in any of the ritual books; larger corporals usually would not fit in them.

Furthermore, corporals should be seen as altar covers, not as private accessories of the chalice.

OTHER COVERS FOR FURNISHINGS: The credence table, the table holding the bread and wine before a procession of the gifts, and various other occasional tables might benefit from cloth covers. In each case, the need for a cover is to be based on the table's design and placement. If the table is simple, strong and well-designed, it is better left uncovered.

Local planners also can consider the revival of the old custom of covering images and crosses during Lent. Just as we wait in Lent for the water and the light of the Paschal Triduum, so, too, we await the cross. This is why it has long been traditional during Lent either to veil the cross or to store it out of sight. In ancient times, the cross, gilded and bejeweled as a sign of victory, would be veiled during penitential seasons. In medieval times, the entire sanctuary was hidden behind the "lenten veil" or "rood screen." We treat music in similar fashion. We give up the Alleluia during Lent only to sing it with great gusto at Easter. In like manner, the veiling of the cross permits us to restore it joyfully at the Triduum. The often-ignored rubric (printed in the sacramentary after the Mass texts for the Saturday of the Fourth Week of Lent) reminds us of these veils.

Local decisions should be made about the best ways to express austerity. Images can be removed or covered, and the processional cross (or other sanctuary cross) can be veiled from the start of Lent or only for the final, more intense, passion-oriented weeks of the season. If any of these veils have been passed on from earlier generations, they are probably violet. New ones may be made of other colors.

A unified approach to stripping the space may help restore a unity to the room as a sacred space. The stripped-down environment allows us to focus on what is most important: the assembly, the penitents, the catechumens.

Linens or Other Textiles for Use with the Chalice

PURIFICATOR: This cloth functions as a liturgical napkin. It is used to wipe the lip of the chalice after each communicant partakes of the wine; it is used again for drying wine vessels after they have been cleansed. The expansion of eucharistic cup-sharing has necessitated an increase of purificators. Before the current age of reform, the general practice was for a priest to keep his purificator for several Masses, even for a whole week. Now they are more clearly seen as textiles at service to the whole community, one purificator per cup per Mass, to be laundered and pressed after each use. Sacristans should make sure that extra purificators are on hand at Easter and Christmas.

Like the other cloths described in this chapter, purificators should be made of white linen. The absorbent qualities of linen (always unstarched) are particularly important for this textile object. Perhaps some types of cotton will be durable and absorbent, but probably no synthetic fabric will perform very well as a purificator. Its traditional size is still fitting, as is the old way of folding it—twice on itself, giving a triple thickness for enhanced absorbency. If colors other than white are selected, they should not distract communicants. The purpose of the purificator is not the implanting of a whole new symbol, but rather the unobtrusive and effective service of the cup of salvation.

CHALICE PALL: Because pall means cover, this word might appear often in the sacristy, denoting the casket pall, the altar cloth that is a pall, any other covering over ambo or other furniture during Lent or at other times, and a cover for the chalice. The chalice pall is completely optional, but it was formerly seen at every Mass, a stiff square of linen protecting the contents of the chalice from dust and insects. When such a covering is needed today a purificator or corporal might be placed on the cup. This would actually reflect ancient usage, when part of the top altar cloth was folded up over the cup for such protection.

In the years after Trent, this pall actually came to play a different role. The chalice and paten were prepared before Mass in a fascinating construct: empty chalice, purificator straddling its top and falling to either side, small paten resting over this, and then pall over the paten. Over all this went the chalice veil, followed by the burse containing the corporal. To hold this all together, the pall needed to be more than just a bug-deterring cover for the cup. It became quite thick and starched, or a piece of cardboard was added into a linen pocket to provide a firm base and shape to veil and burse. Now that this whole construct is not only unnecessary, but also disadvantageous, the pall need not be as stiff. Older ones still can be used for the few times that bugs might be present, but the ones with excessive ornamentation, especially with fringes of lace, should be retired from service.

CHALICE VEILS: When Catholics looked at the post-Tridentine assemblage of chalice, paten and varied cloths, they mostly saw the chalice veil forming a sort of three-dimensional trapezoid. In some catechetical traditions of a generation or more ago, we were taught that if you came into Mass after the priest took the chalice veil off, then you had come too late to have that Mass "count." Now that we have laid aside such minimalistic attitudes about liturgical participation, now that we know that the vessels should be seen for what they are, many of us are surprised to hear that chalice veils are still described in the current liturgical books. They are seldom seen in many areas, but here's how the documents say they should be used:

- The chalice, resting before Mass on the credence table, not the altar, is covered with a veil. It can always be white, although it could according to tradition be the color of the day (see *General Instruction of the Roman Missal,* #80c). Only at the preparation of the altar is the chalice brought to the altar and filled.

- After communion, the vessels can be purified at the altar or at the credence table. Especially if there are several vessels to be purified after communion (and this is most frequently the case on Sundays in parishes), they can be left "properly covered and on a corporal" either at the altar or (far better) at the credence table. They would then be purified after the assembly has dispersed (see *General Instruction of the Roman Missal,* #120, 138).

The proper cover might be the purificators opened out and spread over the vessels; otherwise, a cloth veil that is large enough to cover all the vessels could be used. If the latter option is followed, this would almost certainly be a larger cover than a chalice veil remaining from a past era. The scale would be more like the humeral veil, although the materials and lining of those stretches of fabric would probably make them too heavy for this function. A larger corporal, perhaps the one taken from the altar, would be more fitting.

Towels

Most liturgical towels of earlier years were of fine linen. They were both properly absorbent and unobtrusive. Only those marred by lace or busy embroidery are unfitting candidates for continued use. New towels can be made either of linen or of the other materials now acceptable for liturgical textiles. As with the purificator, however, we should pay close attention to the absorbency of any material we select. Also, there should be some system to keep purificators separate from any similarly sized towels as they are laundered and are put back into their drawers. We need to have at least the following towels at hand:

–towels of a large size for each of the persons involved in the washing of the feet on Holy Thursday. If towels from rectories or other homes are used, they should be plain and of a subdued color so as not to distract anyone from the ongoing rite.

–towels for washing of the hands at Mass (at the preparation rite or after communion). White is traditional; other colors used should be plain and unobtrusive. The vessels and towels should presume the washing of hands, not fingertips.

–towels for drying neophytes—babies, children, and adults. Obviously the number will vary from year to year, and the size will be determined by the method of baptism. As adults step from an immersion font, they are best enshrouded in a huge towel.

–a liturgical apron ("gremial") is used by a bishop or his delegate at certain rites to protect vestments from drops of chrism. When called for in the rites, this large linen square or rectangle with strings is supplied by the bishop's office. If not, a large amice can be used.

Care and Storage of Linens and Other Textiles

LAUNDRY: The more linens used, the larger the group of laundry-volunteers needed. The setting up of this system, the monitoring of it, and the continuous flow of gratitude need to be high priorities for every sacristan. One or more hampers or laundry bags need to be in every sacristy, often by the sink where the chalices are washed after Mass. The ideal time for washing these linens is Sunday night or first thing Monday, so that stains do not set. There are several traditional procedures for laundry. The simplest is to spray simple stains like lipstick with prewash spray and then wash the item in very hot water (an argument for natural fibers of white). Wine stains can be sprinkled with salt, doused with boiling water, then washed with very hot water containing chlorine bleach. (Once again, white, natural fiber is preferred because hotter water can be used.)

Though the impulse is to remove stains as soon as we see them, candle wax must harden before being removed from textiles. With an instrument that will not cut the fabric, excess wax can be removed after hardening. Then the wax spot should be ironed either with a plain brown paper bag, paper towels or absorbent brown wrapping paper under and on top of the fabric. Once this process has removed the wax, the item should be washed in hot water with bleach added.

Linens that have begun to turn yellow may regain their whiteness by being washed in water and bleach. But some traditionalists insist that fine linens are incompatible with chemical bleaches. The alternative methods they suggest include bleaching the fabric in the sun or boiling it for 30 minutes in water that contains washing soda and mild soap.

IRONING: Starch must never be used. It retards the pliancy and draping ability of veils and altar cloths (including the corporal) and diminishes the absorbency of purificators and towels. The best way to iron a linen item is with a steam iron while the linen is damp, although some insist that linens are best stretched out in the sun for drying (and for whitening). According to many experienced volunteers, both these methods are preferable to using automatic dryers or rolling the wet linens in towels before ironing.

STORAGE: Altar cloths and very large corporals are best rolled on acid-free tubes and stored in sacristy drawers. This eliminates the stress of hanging. Lenten veils probably should be kept with any large textile hangings or in the same place where once-a-year items are kept free of excess humidity and dust. Smaller corporals, purificators, chalice veils, towels, and any remaining chalice palls should all be in readily-accessible drawers near the eucharistic vessels in the sacristy.

24◆ Candles and Their Equipment

Interaction with Light

The candles and oil lamps in our churches are never just pretty decorations or minimal props required by liturgical law. They are symbols of the light of Christ and the light of baptism. Interacting with them can shape and direct our affection. Candles should be natural and beautiful elements within our interactions; to substitute tubes of polyethylene or electric bulbs is an insult to the holy people gathered. (For a fuller description of illumination and natural materials, see page 29.)

CANDLES IN PARTICULAR PLACES: We do not just look at candles in church. We share flames from them, follow their lead in procession, and use them to delimit certain reserved areas. Every parish needs candles for at least these actions:

1. The large Easter candle leads us in procession and continues to share its light with neophytes and the bereaved all year (page 64).

2. Baptismal candles are held by neophytes or by infants' parents and godparents, to be cherished and used for many years afterward (page 66).

3. Altar candles (two, four, six or even seven) should be carried in processions and then positioned in free-standing holders to add festivity to the area near the altar (page 51).

4. Dedication candles (12 or 4) mounted on the walls about the assembly place provide an embracing light on high festivals (page 39).

5. Candles mounted in seating areas can mark processional routes and further embrace the assembly (page 41).

6. The lamp or candle in the chapel of eucharistic reservation is the nonverbal signal of that very reservation (page 79).

7. Votive candles continue to be, as they always were, popular lights that encourage interactions: choosing a candle, transferring light, and pausing in prayer.

These principal candles do not restrict the use of still others, positioned as the community's actions and spaces suggest: defining the open space about the ambo, gracing the catechumeneon, flickering in the chapel of reconciliation, burning before an image of the day's saint, grouped about the casket (especially if the Easter candle is not used), or enlivening a cemetery during communal gatherings.

CANDLES FOR THE ENTIRE ASSEMBLY: At the Easter Vigil, each and every member of the congregation must receive a candle for the service of light and the renewal of baptism. Though these sometimes are called "congregational tapers," they are always more than the wick-sized strings of wax used as candle-lighting tapers. Small shields to protect the hands from dripping wax, called "bobeches," should be distributed as well; these look like paper disks, paper cups, or plastic cups with a hole in the center. The best candles and holders often are marketed by the suppliers to Orthodox and other Eastern churches.

Smaller assemblies on other occasions also will need individual lights. If evening prayer on Sunday includes the opening rite of candle-lighting (lucernarium), then everyone can hold a lighted candle, especially on great feasts. The blessing of candles and procession on February 2 should not be replaced by the minimalistic "solemn entrance." On this one special day of the year, the candles for use throughout the year should be blessed, and everyone—even when February 2 is a weekday—should experience the joy of participating in this wondrous celebration of light and candles. Especially when Candlemas falls on Sunday (1997, 2003, 2014), the entire community should be given candles and invited into the full experience of illumination called for in the Roman Missal.

Candle Stands

The proper stands and auxiliary equipment for all of these candles, as well as for the oil lamp that may be located by the tabernacle, should be determined by the overall decor of the place and by the actual use of the given light. For example, the candles near an altar can be in "pavement candlesticks," "floor candlesticks" or "altar torches" of various dimensions. The right ones are determined by sight lines, congruence with other furnishings in the sanctuary, the way that processional candles will fit in them and the number needed (two, four, six or even seven are possible for Mass, depending on the degree of festivity and the scale of the room).

Stands and candles normally should not be in the view unless they will be lighted and used as part of a rite. In the years before Vatican II, six candles were mandated, three on either side of the tabernacle and cross, whether they were necessitated by a ritual or not. Today, unused candles and stands should be removed. If suitable, they can brought out and used for various special occasions.

Two kinds of candles and stands should remain in the complex even when unlit. When not in use during the Easter Season, the Easter candle remains in the baptistry, bearing the name of our year and waiting for the next celebration of eternal light. In some dioceses, sanctuaries were marked by another traditional illumination—the hanging of three or five lamps, equipped with oil or wax candles. These furnishings often are quite graceful; they do more for visual focus than any floor-mounted candles. When present, they do not need to be removed when unlit. But for all events in their area, they should be lit as fine, architectural-scale indicators of festival.

Advent Wreath

For good reason, this domestic custom made its way into many churches in the twentieth century. It hints at the greens and light of Christmas, the light of Christ, the brilliance of the end time, and the progression of this season of preparation. It is always made from real greens. The natural smell and honesty of form are very important; it would be better to use no wreath at all than one made of artificial branches. The *Book of Blessings* gives the current norms for the wreath. Note the mention of scale if the Advent wreath is to be used in church:

> Customarily the Advent Wreath is constructed of a circle of evergreen branches into which are inserted four candles. According to tradition, three of the candles are violet and the fourth is rose. However, four violet or white candles may also be used. If the Advent wreath is to be used in church, it should be of sufficient size to be visible to the congregation. It may be suspended from the ceiling or placed on a stand. If it is placed in the presbyterium [sanctuary], it should not interfere with the celebration of the liturgy, nor should it obscure the altar, lectern or chair. (#1510, 1512)

Maintenance of Candles and Accessories

LIGHTING: Old manuals had particular indications for the altar candles to be lighted first. Now the rules of common sense apply: When there are several candles nearby, the ones farther away are lit first, extinguished last.

Before any ritual, we should check the wicks, whether in the oil lamp by the tabernacle or on any candles to be lighted. It is far better to extract wicks from dried wax well before the sacristy and the assembly area begin filling up with people. New candles should be lit for a minute in the sacristy before they are set up for a liturgy. In lighting candles, at least four methods are prevalent, each with its own drawbacks and potential:

1. The use of plain matches is thought to be convenient, but disposing several burned matches is awkward when more than one candle must be lit. It is never as graceful looking as the movement with a properly-handled candle-lighting pole. When only matches are used, longer wooden ones work well. Burnt matches should never be left in candle stands.

2. The use of long-reach butane lighters is neater than matches, but again less graceful than the old pole properly used.

3. The use of long wax tapers without holders is very dangerous. The person lighting the candles could lose control of the taper and drop it; wax could drip on the altar or floor. Unless handled by a true veteran who knows how to hold, shield and restrain these wicks, they should never be used without being inserted in a pole.

4. The most traditional method—candle-lighting poles with wax tapers inserted—is also the most graceful way to transfer light to multiple candles. But it should be used only if the minister can follow the proper procedures:

–Use a holder that allows for the bottom of the taper to be inserted in a metal hole, not a wire spring.

–Know how to trim the taper to remove a frayed end.

–Walk slowly and shield flame from drafts.

–Expose only a little taper at a time for burning, obviously watching that just enough is always being pressed up.

–Hold the pole as vertical as possible to keep the flame a manageable size.

–Extinguish the taper after lighting candles by drawing it into the tube and immediately pushing it out again so that it doesn't get clogged.

EXTINGUISHING AND CLEANING: For extinguishing candles, the same candle-lighting poles usually have snuffers on them. They must never be pressed onto the wick; if the wick tips into the molten wax, it should be fished out immediately. Snuffers on poles are far preferable to blowing out a candle (and spraying wax), but they must be cleaned periodically to prevent black soot from accumulating and then dropping out of them onto people, vestments and candleholders.

FOLLOWERS AND BOBECHES: So that candles burn evenly and don't spill wax, especially in places with drafts, caps (followers) and shallow dishes or holders (bobeches) should be used. Many sacristies of older churches have a wide array of these in differing materials. Compared to brass and chrome, followers that are simple glass cylinders are less obtrusive and do not distract from flame and glowing light. Followers should be removed for cleaning while the wax is still warm. Bobeches of clear glass are also better than metal for lining candle sockets and bases. If brass must be used, it should be unlacquered for easier cleaning. Both followers and bobeches (glass or unlacquered metal) should be cleaned by using hot water in a basin, not by scraping and scratching the item. Candle implements should be cleaned in a basin other than the sink, so that wax will not clog the drain.

OTHER EQUIPMENT: In addition to the many candles sized for their respective uses, and their accessories (holders, stands, followers, bobeches), we need at least these items in a sacristy's candle-care section:

–candle-lighting devices (preferably the traditional poles with taper tube and snuffing cup)

–tapers for use in candle-lighting tubes

–a blunt knife

–long matches in a container that retards moisture

–a basin for cleaning accessories

–paper towels

–a receptacle for used matches

–a stylus for the Easter Vigil

–at least one fire extinguisher whose use is understood by all sacristans and ministers (page 163).

All of these materials might best be kept in an area of the sacristy related to the incense materials. Candles, matches and charcoal are best stored in metal cabinets with many adjustable shelves. The traditional cases include useful hooks for candle-lighting poles and thuribles. If possible, the temperature and humidity of the entire sacristy should be carefully controlled, in deference to the many items that can melt, warp, or become useless when damp. The candle and incense areas should be as far as possible from sources of heat and sunshine.

25◆ Incense and Its Implements

History of Incensation

Scent always has been an essential part of human interactions. From time to time, rationalists and puritans may have tried to deny the importance of smells, but the nose still helps to form memory. The frequent use of scents in worship has ancient precedents, and scents still can be used frequently.

Incense was one of the most utilized agents, capable of producing fragrance when heated or burned. In ancient times it was available in its truest, pure form—frankincense. This is the solidified resin from certain trees belonging to a certain species (boswellia or terebinth) found in Arabia and India. Exodus 30:34–38 contains a recipe for mixing frankincense with other elements to make an incense specially blended for fuller aroma and thicker smoke at ritual.

Incense was not given high religious significance in and of itself, but the act of imparting smoke and aroma was. Psalm 141:2 sees the use of incense as an expression of prayer: "Let my prayer be counted as incense before you." Many other literary sources attest to incensations in Jewish prayer through the time of John the Baptist's father, Zechariah (Luke 1:10). The Book of Revelation (8:3–5) attests to the continued power of this fragrance-release in the dream life of early Christians. They envisioned incense as being used by angels.

Despite this history, it seems that early Christians were reluctant to use incense at their liturgies. The writings of many bishops and commentators of the earliest centuries warn of incensation as an action of alien rites and of imperial idolatry. Once introduced into Christian liturgies, in the fourth century or earlier, the practices associated with incensation differed from region to region. Through the centuries, churches united to Rome took on more and more of that city's customs. After the Council of Trent, almost all of these churches followed strict rules governing the use of incense at funerals, Masses and eucharistic benediction.

Current Norms for Incensation

The reforms of the late twentieth century removed both obligations and restrictions governing the use of incense. At all of the points in the eucharistic celebration where incense had to be used for solemn Masses, now it can be used at any Mass *(General Instruction of the Roman Missal,* #235). It also may be a part of other rites, with decisions in this regard usually made at the parish level. Sacristans need to know the services at which incensations will occur, as well as when the lighted charcoal should be ready. The use of incense usually depends upon the solemnity of the event. For example, many parishes use incense at all Sunday Masses, on major feasts such as Christmas and at special rites like funerals. Other parishes restrict the use of incense to funerals and exceptional Masses.

When one or more of these ritual moments will be enhanced by incensations, we need to ascertain the proper times for lighting the charcoal. Quite often this will be about ten minutes before it will be needed. Given the properties of most coals and most incense used these days, the coals lit before Mass will be unable to make additional smoke later in the same liturgy. In most cases, we need to use multiple coals lit at varied times when incensations are spread throughout a celebration. The traditional times when incense can be used at Mass are listed here:

- –at the head of the procession from the vesting room to the altar, with charcoal lit ten minutes before the start.
- –at the altar as the procession ends and the entrance song continues, with the same charcoal that was used in procession. If the charcoal will be used a second time, more of it will be needed in the beginning.
- –at the head of the gospel procession and at the ambo before the proclamation of the gospel, with new charcoal lit after the entrance procession to replace the original. If, however, the gospel will be the first usage of incense, then the charcoal can be lit at the entrance song.
- –during the preparation of the altar and gifts, the altar and assembly can be incensed. Charcoal for this is best lit after the gospel, before or during the homily.

The final time on the traditional lists is during the elevation of the consecrated bread and cup after the institution narrative. This is no longer appropriate, because it suggests that the words of institution are separate from the rest of the eucharistic prayer.

The closing procession or recessional is not listed in the *General Instruction,* but it is often led by incense. Coals can be lighted during communion.

The other rites most enhanced by incensations are communal celebrations of morning prayer and evening prayer (during the gospel canticle), all public processions, eucharistic exposition and benediction, and funerals. When incense will be used as a sign of farewell during the final commendation of a funeral Mass, coals are best lighted at the start of communion.

The same simplification of rules that made incensations possible at any Mass also simplified the rules for the thurifer, the minister who carries the thurible with what the old official books called a "grave and graceful mien." The number of times the thurible should be swung also has been simplified. The details can be found in the *Ceremonial of Bishops,* #91–97.

Benefits of Incensation

Even a cursory review of the history of the public use of incense reveals the benefits envisioned by various communities. From the dawn of recorded history, peoples of the Mediterranean basin and further to the southeast used the burning of incense as an antidote to the lassitude caused by tropical heat. Ancient Hebrews and early Christians burned incense as an intense expression of reverence during prayer. Like their neighbors, they used charcoal pans or other ceremonial braziers to mark important places and shrines. As the use of scent became formalized in medieval Christian rites, and as perfume burners were put on chains, the persons or objects toward whom the smoke was directed were seen as being honored. Chains also facilitated the use of fragrant smoke in leading processions on feastdays.

Contemporary commentators have a more scientific understanding of these and other human emotions and responses. We know, for example, that the release of certain smells and the sight of clouds of incense can create positive or negative associations for the members of the assembly. Some planners may have resisted the use of incense because of fears that it will conjure up only memories of solemn high Masses. Whether incense is used or not, scent continues to be central to all human interactions. And incensation is the action transmitted by our tradition. It expresses adoration and prayer to God, as well as honor and reverence to the holy people and holy elements of our assembly. It is our community's nonverbal way of expressing esteem for the remains placed in the casket, for the table of the Lord, for the assembly gathered in song at evening prayer. The more we recognize the need to engage the whole body and all the senses in common action, the more local communities probably will use incense and other kinds of fragrance.

Charcoal

Lighted charcoal has long been the church's preferred method of burning incense. It is generally available in "self-lighting" briquettes, pieces treated so that only a brief touch of flame is necessary to start the charcoal burning. Since this treatment usually is on the top of the briquette or the edges, it is better to light the tops. Ignition will take longer if the charcoal is chipped or damp. Some charcoal may give off sparks when lighted, so long sleeves should be rolled back. Metal tongs can hold the briquette firmly without cracking it. A candle on a tabletop provides a steady source of flame. Depending upon the size and the burning time of the charcoal, and the size of the censer, more than one piece may be lighted.

The best kinds of briquettes are shaped with a well or depression on one side to cradle incense grains. Obviously, when such a briquette is placed in the brazier, the depression should face up. Foil wrapping or packaging that retards moisture, boxes that prevent crumbling, and as large a size as will fit in the censer are all good qualities.

Incense

This mixture of solidified resin and other sweet-smelling particles is used three ways in the liturgy. Incensation, the principal usage, normally means the swinging of smoke toward someone or something. A secondary use is related but stationary—the insertion of incense grains in a vase or vessel containing many lit coals. This can provide large amounts of smoke and smell before a treasured image or throughout a room. The third use is discussed at page 65—large grains inserted in the paschal candle.

No exact incense mixture or scent is specified for incensation. Even if local churches are quite satisfied with their current scent, sacristans can periodically experiment with other possibilities. The unity of a season—Christmas, for example—may be celebrated by using the same scent throughout the weeks. Having several scents on hand makes it possible to use a different scent for each season, giving each season its own, distinct aroma. One scent can be for Advent, another for Christmas, still others for Lent, Eastertime, and Ordinary Time. Once again, there are no specifications mandated, but certain traditions and the ambience of each season might suggest specific scents. For example, many Orthodox churches could use gardenia (available from Orthodox church supply stores) for the Easter Vigil and Sundays throughout the season. Rose is traditional for the later part of Eastertime and Pentecost Sunday. Commercial products used at liturgy are inappropriate and trite, though—pumpkin incense for All Saints Vigil Masses, or fruitcake for Christmas. Once selected, the seasonal choice can be used in all the incensations of a parish on those days.

Another factor in incense selection is the actual use of the perfumed smoke at a given rite. For opening processions and for the incensation of all persons at Mass or evening prayer, a long period of smoke is desirable. At the gospel procession, or for the incensation just at the one moment of eucharistic benediction, a shorter burst of smoke is better. Powder-like incense often produces aroma immediately and burns only for a brief time; grains usually burn longer after a slower start; very large grains or pellets often take a long time to produce smoke, but they burn for a very long time and with a very rich fragrance.

A word about potential health hazards in smoke: The incense normally used in churches contains nothing harmful, although certain ingredients can affect persons with allergies. Ways of accommodating these persons might include identifying places in the assembly area where they will not be affected by the smoke.

Some studies of cheaper kinds of incense, rarely used in churches, show that its sandalwood sawdust and aromatic oils might give off hazardous substances. Reputable producers should be able to provide documentation on the safety of their ingredients.

Thuribles and Other Burners of Incense

HISTORY: Several forms of charcoal pans and perfume burners have been used in churches over the centuries.

Stationary vessels or pans purified the air, added scent, and honored a particular place or shrine. These were sometimes vases or urns with perforated covers, but without handles. In the old rite at Lyons (France), one urn stood at either side of the altar and grains were added at different points of a service. In other places, vessels were suspended from the ceiling or from wall brackets. Still others resembled braziers on stands.

Portable vessels have been either vessels on chains (our thuribles) or bowls, often shallow and fitted with a long, insulated handle. The bowls allowed the use of many coals, but were more stationary than mobile. As thuribles became more prevalent, the varied movements and swings became set parts of local rites.

CURRENT USE: We should have thuribles that fit the scale of our facilities, as well as the uses made of them in local rites. That could necessitate thuribles much larger than those used in the old solemn high Masses. In those days, incense smoke was "presented" in tight gestures, rather than swung and wafted as it is today. More smoke and larger gestures call for more coals and incense to be spread over the pan. Certain processions call for more than one thurible; for example, two are suggested by the directives for Holy Thursday.

If braziers or other stationary vessels are desired for a particular environment or feast, they are available from church suppliers in insulated ceramics and other materials. In most cases, however, sand added to existing vessels, wide-mouthed vases or pots, can provide a fine burner for charcoal.

Boats and Other Vessels for Incense

The old containers for incense dust or grains were usually metal and equipped with a spoon that was narrow, but long enough not to slide down into the vessel. One of the prevalent shapes led to the odd name "boat." Any square or cylindrical metal box that can be properly handled is acceptable now, but the old ones function quite well in most cases. Some match the thuribles still in use, but this is not necessary. The only ones unacceptable are those too small to contain large grains.

Other Fragrances

Fragrances other than incense can be considered as local churches examine ways to mark each season, to heighten festivity on solemnities, and to foster the involvement of all the senses. There are no specific rules governing these alternatives except common sense, nor is there any obligation to provide a different smell for each day. But on certain days, there are fine traditions for using essential oils and strewing the floor with flowers or fragrant plants.

The practice of using essential oils was restricted to concentrated oils extracted from flowers. If the custom is to be revived, perhaps as a further expression of a season (for example, gardenia at Easter), we must be no less careful to stay with pure fluids from flowers. Under no circumstances would commercial air-fresheners provide the requisite naturalness.

The custom of strewing materials on the floor seems quite odd in contemporary churches with their crowded seating, carpeting and lack of open space. Where there is open space, traditions can be rediscovered. If a casket will rest before the altar on the floor rather than on trestle or trolley, it might rest on a bed of herbs or blossoms spread to accept and embrace it. Wedding processionals can revert to the custom, largely forgotten, of real flowers spread by multiple ministers or real petals thrown by the flower girls or boys.

Processions of sanctoral images or the eucharist can move on pathways strewn with flowers or plants that release their perfume when trod upon. In pre-reformation England, such plants as lavender, hyssop, sage and rue provided materials for this "odorizing." In our country, strewing is considered odd, but it may provide fertile ideas for adaptation, especially at outdoor processions and rites. None of these ideas, however, will work in churches that are carpeted.

The Care and Storage of Materials Related to Incensation

The same metal cabinet used for candles might also house the materials related to incensation. Inside these cases, parishes generally need:

- one or more thuribles, best hanging from hooks after cooling down outside the cabinet
- incense in various powders and grains
- charcoal briquettes, packaged to avoid moisture
- one or more boats and spoons
- tongs
- matches
- candles and a candlestand for igniting charcoal
- fire extinguisher nearby (page 163)
- a good-looking stand to be used in the assembly space for the thurible and boat
- canisters or receptacles for used (and still hot) charcoal.

A further piece of furniture is most useful in every sacristy—a strong table, with a surface of metal or stone, for preparing thuribles and cleaning them soon after each liturgy.

In cleaning thuribles, manufacturers' instructions must be followed. If old thuribles need attention, the traditional method is to dip the vessels in boiling water and then dry them immediately.

26◆ Flowers

The sacristy should have space for the preparation and care of flowers. (Review pages 29–31 on flowers as liturgical art.)

Acquiring Flowers

A parish needs various systems for funding and acquiring these festive additions to the church complex. The best systems free sacristans to perform the many other tasks in liturgical preparation, although some sacristans may enjoy the additional responsibility of handling flowers. Most parishes use one or more of the following approaches:

- Special agreements can be drawn up for a given year with a florist who is sensitive to the scale of the church building and the inherent timing of the seasons of the liturgical year. Such an arrangement often gives the church a priority of attention, fosters accountability, allows for the delivery of material just before it is needed (Christmas just before the eve, Easter on Holy Saturday) and is easier on bookkeepers. The florist could be provided with a key to the sacristy to save the sacristan the trouble of having to go there every time a delivery is made. The florist also could take responsibility for the removal of old flowers and plants. This contract or understanding can be reviewed each year, perhaps even with specifications set down and bids solicited from several vendors.

- Volunteers can be solicited to provide funding or particular arrangements on given days. It might be helpful to post a sign-up sheet in a prominent place. Groups or households also could sign up to assume responsibility for an entire season, including participation in any seasonal planning sessions. This registration also might include the possibility of funds for a day or season being donated in memory of a deceased loved one or in honor of a special anniversary—a process that would be described in a parish mailing. The names of donors or the persons honored could be noted later in the Sunday bulletin.

- For certain festivals, and for special zones in the parish buildings, every member of the parish may be invited to bring flowers of his or her own—sometimes specified by type and sometimes leaving conditions open for a wide variety. These could form a panoply of blossoms and greens before the shrine of the the titular saint on his or her feast. The flowers could be strewn on the path of a Marian or eucharistic procession. Or they might be a grand circle of roses put in vases all around the assembly space on Pentecost.

- Flowers brought to church by families for funerals and weddings can be regulated by local guidelines, so long as these are distributed widely and early.

- After Christmas and Easter, as well as after other major feasts, potted plants can be put in the entrance hall for any gardeners to take. If any are nurtured back to life for the following year, they might be brought back to the assembly.

- Suburban or rural parishes sometimes have their own flower (and vegetable) gardens, tended by volunteers and planted with items appropriate for the liturgy and for the soup kitchen.

- It is not a good idea to buy pots of green plants and leave them around all year. They rarely contribute seasonal expression, scent or color. At this point in the history of interiors, they simply make the worship space look too much like a shopping mall.

- While some silk or metal "flowers" are of exquisite quality and fine materials, they are not flowers. The liturgy needs materials that are honest and natural; floral arrangements should use only real flowers and greens.

The Preparation of Floral Arrangements

The best and most up-to-date advice on floral arranging can be found in local programs of continuing education and in local libraries. There we can learn whatever we need to know about stem preparation, supports, water, forcing or retarding growth, texture and color in arrangements, and the materials best suited for large-scale architecture. These all need to be interpreted in terms of specific sites. In our sacristies, this means that liturgical as well as aesthetic criteria must be met. Those who are qualified to pass on knowledge of large floral displays do not teach abstract principles; they show how the given context of public action must determine the look.

As floral decorations are planned for one day or an entire season, plans must include a specific understanding of who will get the materials, arrange them and place them, water or care for them, and remove them at an agreed upon time. For this work, sacristies usually should have the following equipment on hand: clippers and scissors, tape, florist foam, spikes, watering can, and water dishes to place under all pots. A table or countertop is also important, and there should be a trash receptacle nearby. In many settings, a table with a metal or stone top is needed. The one used for candles and incense should be large enough for the preparation of the flowers, too. Otherwise the sideboard of a sink is often the right size and material.

Most parishes have vases and vessels of their own for flowers, and this is wise if they are congruent with the local architectural style and with the exact placement of the flowers. Some communities also have a good-sized collection of pedestals and bases. These pieces of furniture should never be so large as to seem like tables, nor should they compete with the central furnishings of our sacred actions. For this same reason, they are best used in open places like the entrance hall, rather than in the sanctuary. If the parish has many vessels and pieces of furniture, they must be stored in an accessible cabinet.

27◆ Maintenance and Housekeeping

Maintenance Program

Because many priorities vie for attention, three values related to maintenance should be remembered by all sacristans. As the *Ceremonial of Bishops* (#38) puts it, "The first of all the elements belonging to the beauty of the place where liturgy is celebrated is the spotless cleanliness of the floor and walls and of all the images and articles that will be used or seen during a service." Second, the parish pastoral council, finance council, facilities committee, and pastor all must know that deferred maintenance is dangerously more expensive, and this applies to all worship places, not just to the older ones. Third, the time and money spent to preserve the liturgical facility should never be considered as competing with funding for the poor. Our facilities should be preserved precisely as part of our gift to the poor.

When we apply such serious concerns to the sacristy, we have at least seven levels of activity that should be ongoing:

1. Immediate, emergency repairs. These are understood by all, and due to their unpredictability, mean that everything else must wait for them to be completed. Such "band-aids" are a direct service to the assembly and to ministers who may need the repair completed for the liturgy to proceed.

2. "Once-over" tours of the facility at the start of a weekend or a few hours before a major service. This work is also very important to the liturgical action and includes such things as cleaning any debris from entranceway and assembly seating, making sure that the furnishings are all positioned properly, pulling wilted pieces from plants, and other next-to-the-last-minute details.

3. Planning and preparing for future events. A careful listing (and checking) of all the facilities, furnishings and artifacts needed for a given event may suggest items that need to be fixed somewhat in advance.

4. Regular housekeeping and cleaning. This often is done by custodians or volunteers other than the sacristan, but various persons must collaborate at times. Every community should have a regular system for routine cleaning, and this must be understood by all involved, so it can be done even when the supervisor is away on vacation.

5. Special campaigns or sessions to tackle one job or prepare for one feast. Before Christmas and Easter, and perhaps before some other great days, parishioners are quite willing to volunteer their time for a day or evening of communal cleaning and preparation. Apart from those few holy times, special sessions can be scheduled for volunteers to join the regular sacristy crew in polishing all the vessels, mending textiles (linens, vestments, and decorative hangings), cleaning the sacristy, washing or otherwise cleaning pews. These are not just opportunities to have many hands make light work; they are invaluable times to build community. New members of the parish should be made especially welcome.

6. Periodic inventory of materials in the church complex. Lists can be made in some logical order by categories of items and location, then entered on a computer for easy updating by later inventories. Photographs of all the valuable items should also be filed. Disks and photos should be stored away from the facility. (This is also the time to involve insurance representatives or diocesan agents in updating policies.)

7. Preventive or routine maintenance of facilities. This program will differ from place to place, being determined by the local materials and properties, climate, and other conditions. This suggests the keeping of a central file with all maintenance manuals for products purchased, with records of the building's construction, and with reports from building experts. While this last level is seldom the province of sacristans, we should be a part of the planning, or at least know the schedule of the work to be done.

Maintenance and Miscellaneous Items for the Sacristy

These are lists of additional tools that might facilitate work in the sacristy and vesting room. They do not generally repeat items described in earlier chapters. Local circumstances might expand or abbreviate these lists; they are just starters.

POWER: long electrical extension cords of the proper strength, back-up batteries in all the sizes needed, battery tester, flashlights.

FASTENING: string (various weights), tapes and dispensers (duct, electrical, florist, masking, removable, scotch), tacks, screws and screwdrivers of various types, nails and hammer, glue (regular and wood), paper clips.

SECRETARIAL: paper, index cards, self-stick notes of various sixes, pencils and sharpener, pens, magic markers, correction fluid (the kind for covering pen and ink), paper-scissors, schedules posted for various tasks and ministers.

CLEANING: vacuum cleaner with bags, dust buster with bags, carpet sweeper (if any rugs), dry mop, wet mop and bucket, handbroom, dust pan and brush, rags, dust cloths, brushes of various kinds, wastebaskets and large barrels, garbage bags, basins for washing water, rubber gloves, sponges, knives (butter, paring, Xacto), strainer on pole for font, cleaning fluids (for brass, for floor, furniture polish, tile cleaner, window cleaner).

VESTMENTS AND LINENS: steam iron and ironing board, steamer, sewing kit, scissors, lint rollers or brushes, spot remover, pins (hat, safety, straight).

28◆ Security and Health

We need a range of materials to assist in health, hygiene and security for the parish, as well as security for the liturgical objects that serve the community. Not every sacristy or vesting room will have all of these materials. Many will need fewer; some will need more. Here are some ideas to stimulate list makers.

Inclement Weather

The clearing of ice, snow or other hazards from public ways, including sidewalks, is, like other matters of public safety, a grave concern of the local church. This concern must be translated into systems that commission volunteers or contractors to clear public and parish-owned surfaces for walking soon after any storm. If certain areas of a parking lot are prone to quick flooding during showers, then the drainage should be improved and visitors need to be alerted to not park there until such improvements are made. We need to collaborate on these matters with members of the pastoral staff or facilities committee. Hospitality begins before people get to the door.

Health and Hygiene

We should know if any members of the assembly, especially ministers and members who are regular participants, are trained in current methods of CPR and of the Heimlich maneuver. Then these materials, or some equivalent, should be in every vesting room or entrance hall:

- –a large, complete first aid kit, freshly stocked, especially with Band-aids of every size
- –paper cups and a bottle of water for taking medications, if sinks and water coolers are far removed
- –material to cover and absorb vomit and other liquid spills—sawdust is traditional, but suppliers have newer mixtures available

–latex gloves of various types and sizes, to be worn when using certain cleaning liquids, or picking up refuse.

Security

The key to the tabernacle was once surrounded by many strictures and warnings about custody and disposition. Now the ritual books are much simpler and more sensible: The key must be kept safely, entrusted only to sacristans and those who need to get communion for the sick. Other keys should be kept in a secure place as well, preferably on a key panel where the numerous keys are hung and labeled in logical order.

If there are many valuable vessels, the sacristy might be equipped with a metal safe. This may be too expensive an item for new sacristies, but many older places already have one. The safe should be utilized for all valuables, including the collection funds if this is the most secure spot on the property.

Fire extinguishers need to be positioned for easy access, especially near sources of open fire or candlelight (baptistry, eucharistic assembly place, sacristy). If new extinguishers are being purchased, the best models often are the ones that are simplest to operate. With ushers or greeters, and with members of the pastoral staff, we may need to review (at least annually) local procedures for the evacuation of the assembly. All concerned need to know the locations of fire extinguishers, fire alarms, and telephones for summoning emergency assistance. Exit signs, extinguishers and emergency lights need to be maintained on a regular schedule. (See page 166 for alarm and sprinkler systems.)

In the coat room, vesting room or some other logical place, there needs to be a "lost and found," where found objects can be kept for later retrieval. If unidentified items are not claimed after a long time, they can be given to local shelters or charities. Larger objects might be turned in to the police, or at least reported to them by phone.

In places subject to civil disorder or disruptive protests, we need to do everything possible to be hospitable despite security restrictions, to ensure a liturgy as unimpeded by barriers as possible. The right of the community to assemble for liturgy must be upheld, even though demonstrators might disagree. Such concerns must be translated into very clear policies when parish leaders, ushers and sacristans meet with police about access, disruptions of the assembly, suspicious parcels, security for the collection, or the presence of the homeless. The worst problems are caused by local ministers who are unfamiliar with policies or who interpret them differently.

Telephone Contacts

Current directories for area telephones and for the diocese should be available. A bulletin board in the vesting room or sacristy should have a list of these numbers:

–at the head of the list: emergency services (common number if used in area; otherwise ambulance, fire, poison center, police)

–civic officials (fire marshall, parade permits, police offices, transportation and parking departments, trash collection)

–contractors (audio system, electrician, heating, ventilation, air conditioning, plumber, trash collection if not handled by municipality)

–diocesan offices (bishop, building commission, liturgy office)

–parish leaders, liturgical ministers and regular volunteers (with residences listed only by permission of the party)

–shelters and dining facilities for the homeless

–suppliers of liturgical elements like bread, wine and candles

–time of day

–transportation (bus or transit schedules, taxi)

–utilities, especially the numbers they provide in case of outages (electricity, gas, oil, telephone, water)

–weather forecast.

29◆ Mechanical Systems

The mechanical systems that serve liturgical buildings differ widely from place to place. The basic liturgical criteria are quality and appropriateness. In appearance and function, all systems must be appropriate to the liturgy. They must be the best systems obtainable in terms of the economy of natural resources and parish funds. The parts that are seen by the assembly should contribute to the overall decor, not neutralize it or detract from it.

Light

Under no conditions can the altar candles, Easter candle, lamp before the tabernacle, or other liturgical elements be replaced by electricity. The artificial lights that we have come to expect in all our buildings serve different functions. They can highlight certain architectural forms or features. More importantly, they can provide brightness for the assembly in places and directions that unify and facilitate its action. For example, the seats should not be dark while the sanctuary is bright like an opera stage. Spotlights should not blind preachers from seeing listeners. (Spotlights as well as colored lamps were long resisted by liturgists as electricity was introduced. Sensible leaders decried lights that were "theatrical and puerile.")

In addition to these general principles of liturgical appropriateness, other specific requirements need to be set in each local church. Exterior lights should provide sufficient security for all services and meetings held after dark, yet there should be a way to have the Easter fire and all outdoor candlelight processions in darkness. Indoors, the configuration of rooms and rites should indicate the many places that electrical receptacles might be useful. All switches on the light panel should be clearly labeled.

Sound

Audibility in an active assembly involves much more than installing a sound system. First we need to maximize the inherent acoustics of the building.

That means studying the acoustics with other planners, helping lectors and presiders learn the art of proclamation, having people gather more closely to each other, and avoiding the use of carpeting. In many small church buildings and in many rooms such as the baptistry or chapel of reservation, no microphones should be used at all. The absence of microphones can be a blessing; too often they force people to focus on just one speaker, to hear the rite as a transmitted message. And they rarely allow communities to hear themselves sing. When newscasters report on a feastday Mass, it is no accident that they use phrases like "Bishop Murphy delivered the Mass." That is what it sounds (and looks) like.

Where communities elect to use amplification systems, any harm to liturgical action should be minimized. The amplified sound should be as clear and natural as possible. Wireless mikes should be used, or there should be sufficient cable and cable receptacles so that movement is unimpeded. The source of the sound should somehow be related to the direction from which people are hearing it. For example, when the assembly faces the door, as at a funeral when the body is received, they can become disoriented if the sounds come from behind them.

Air

The air in any place of assembly needs to be fresh and uncontaminated. When air is heated, it should be comfortable for gathering without coats and gloves, with humidity regulated for the preservation of the building's fabric and contents. When air is circulated by fans, these devices should be neither visually nor aurally obtrusive. When air is cooled, the controls should be accessible. An extra-large crowd may require a lower setting; an extra long liturgy may require a manual override of the automatic shut-off.

Security

The mechanical systems for security should be similarly unobtrusive and conducive to liturgical gatherings. (For notes on other security arrangements, see page 163.) Systems related to fire—smoke detectors, heat detectors, alarms, sprinklers—should allow for the use of full incense and congregational candles. Security alarms should be set up to minimize accidental soundings, and then monitored so that those inside and neighbors are not subjected to unnecessary noise. Emergency lights and signs should be placed according to code, but as unobtrusively as possible.

Visual Displays

Environment and Art in Catholic Worship said in 1978 that "it is too early to predict the effect of contemporary audiovisual media—films, video tape, records, tapes—on the public worship of Christians"(#104). That stance allowed the document's framers to call for screens or projection walls. They termed the neglect of audiovisual possibilities "a serious fault" (#105). Almost a generation later, it is not too early. Some of the vocabulary has changed and technology has pressed forward. But we've plenty of time since 1978 to learn that "cool" media are almost always interruptions of "hot" communal activity. Too many congregations at large-scale liturgies are subjected to inept projections of visual images.

The optimism about media in that 1978 document was balanced by correct warnings against reducing the congregation to audience, against replacing action with passivity. Though well- suited to some educational events in the church complex, video projections of the live event sap the live action. Looking at a projected blow-up of the presider's fingers holding the host is simply medieval fundamentalism reborn. Even if a large assembly cannot see all of the ministers, the community still should remain an organic group looking at each other—not glued to television sets and colossal projections.

30◆ Liturgical Items No Longer in General Use

When we look at liturgical artifacts that are no longer in general use, any humor about their oddity must be balanced by an understanding of their role in particular centuries, in rites now changed. The list in this section of the manual is an invitation to further reading about the history of liturgy. Each set of historical forces shaped an ever-evolving church, and occasioned the rise of new artifacts as well as the demise of others.

The same process continues today. The many old items listed here are balanced by the many new items described in other chapters. A sacristy always serves the current set of rites. We must judge the appropriateness of our implements by the quality of their service to the current rites.

When a decision is made to discard any liturgical artifact, great care should be taken in this disposition. Some items can be used in other liturgical traditions of Christianity; some would be welcomed in archives or museums. They should never be turned into frivolous, or worse, scandalous uses. The traditional method of disposing of many of these objects was by burning, followed by pouring the ashes down the sacrarium. Or the items would be buried. These methods of disposal respected the sacred role once played by the items, and prevented them from being used for trivial purposes. Other methods are open to us, but whatever method is used, it must be respectful, sensitive and discreet.

The list of obsolete items that follows contains the principal items that one can find stored in today's older sacristies or in museums. A tour of medieval or early Christian treasuries and museums would produce a much longer list.

Decorations and Furniture

1. Altar Canopy: Some older churches still have some form of architectural canopy over the altar area; the most famous is at the main altar at St. Peter's in the Vatican. Canopies usually took one of two forms:

a. A civory, or ciborium (the original meaning of that word), is a roof held up over the altar area by four or more columns. The one designed by Bernini at the Vatican still accomplishes its task of calling the attention of the assembly to this place and giving it some shape and force.

b. A baldaquin or tester is a smaller roof of metal or wood that is hung over the altar. It is either suspended by cables from the ceiling or fixed to a rear wall.

With free-standing altars now the rule, only the civory form is still possible in new constructions. These often seem too heavy when the church space already is clogged with seats or pews; they work better in large, open spaces. In existing churches, an old canopy over a still extant but unused "high altar" to the rear of the current altar serves no good liturgical purpose. A decision to remove this whole construct, or to move it out to be at the new altar for the reformed rites, rests more on emotional and artistic preservation questions. If neither removal nor reutilization is possible, then such existing monuments should be diminished in importance by being stripped of anything that would call attention to them: cloths, lights, flowers and any other adornments.

2. COMMUNION RAILING: Sometimes called a sanctuary rail or altar rail, these low fence-like structures are still seen in some older churches. Reasons for their introduction included the protection of the altar from profanity and the reservation of the sanctuary for certain persons and rites. Later rails were of a height and width to serve as leaning places for those kneeling to receive communion. Their removal was often a deliberate attempt to emphasize the unity, as opposed to the separateness, of all those at liturgy. The removal also accompanied the transition to standing for communion—the ancient posture of praise and one that is certainly more fitting for the actions of procession and communal sharing. When removed, communion rails often have provided wood or stone for the creation of new furnishings congruent with other interior finishes.

See page 56 for more on the unity of the eucharistic assembly space—nave and sanctuary—and the usefulness of keeping some artistic demarcation or distinction for the sanctuary. This distinction, however, should not be created by fences or guard rails. The catechumens are dismissed before the act of eucharist. All present are a priestly people of praise.

3. ROOD SCREEN: These architectural barriers or veils often closed off the entire sanctuary and choir area from the rest of the assembly place. The name for them is related to the cross erected at the summit of the partition. Most of these screens were rightly dismantled decades ago. Where rood screens remain, planners need to treat each side as a separate room in the church complex. Some rites can be in one room with the whole assembly present on that side (eucharist for all in the choir area). Other rites can take place in the other room, with all participating there (at the rite of reception of catechumens, for example). If the two rooms are used consecutively, then all move in procession from one side of the wall to the other as one rite moves into the next.

4. CATAFALQUE: In liturgical lexicons, this was a piece of wood shaped like a casket, set on a stand and covered with a pall as if it were a casket. They were used for memorial services or funerals without a body present. Due to their (literally) empty symbolism, they were discontinued. The dead body is what

should be honored with signs of farewell—the actual flesh, not a picture or representation of the deceased. In some dictionaries, the word catafalque is defined as a platform, not for an empty casket, but for the actual casket or corpse.

5. STATUES AND IMAGES: Many sculptures and other representational images have been removed from their original positions. No less a document than the Constitution on the Liturgy of Vatican II (#124) called for the removal of artistic works that are "repugnant to faith and morals and to Christian devotion," works "that offend true religious sense either by their grotesqueness or by the deficiency, mediocrity, or sham in their artistic quality." Not all the works that were removed were repugnant or offensive in these ways. Some were of great artistic quality, evidencing fidelity to revered Christian traditions of iconography. Motives behind the removal of artistic works varied all the way from pastoral whim to a sincere attempt to follow the tradition that only one image of a given saint should be on display, to a faithful clearing of the main liturgical spaces of all that does not pertain to the rite itself.

See pages 20–32 for descriptions of the legitimate role of images in the reformed liturgy. Works of quality still remaining in storage can be used within these standards, perhaps during specified seasons or on related feasts.

Sound-Makers

6. SANCTUS BELLS: One of the functions assigned to exterior bells in the medieval period was to signal that certain important actions were taking place in the church building. Through the centuries, this came to be imitated by the ringing of a hand-held bell in the sanctuary. The Tridentine Missal called for this to be a small bell, and the best commentators interpreted this to mean simply one tongue in a small metal cup. Yet the sanctus or "sacring" bells passed on to us in many older churches are triple bells with many tongues, chimes or gongs. They were the source of much consternation in synods and liturgical conferences through the decades before Vatican II. Now they can all be passed to the music ministers for use in settings that call for them. They have no ritual use otherwise. The only church bells to be rung during the Gloria on Holy Thursday and at the Easter Vigil are the exterior bells.

7. CLAPPERS: In the centuries when small bells were rung in sanctuaries during Mass, hinged pieces of wood were substituted on Holy Thursday and Good Friday. Again, some music groups may be able to use these instruments.

8. SACRISTY BELL: Many sacristies had a bell hung by the door to the sanctuary, rung to signal the start of a service. We have other cues now. One is the ancient and beautiful tradition of ringing the tower bells.

Texts

9. ALTAR CARDS: In the Tridentine order of Mass, a large card was used at the center of the altar, in front of the tabernacle, with some standard texts to assist the priest's memory. In the seventeenth century, two smaller cards were added, one on each side of the altar. These were sometimes very elaborate decorations, but they were more of a necessary evil than a liturgical symbol. Depending on their ornateness, they may be museum or archival material. The same impetus that produced them has led in recent decades to a

proliferation of notes placed on altars and ambos. These should be taped into the appropriate ritual book.

Vessels

10. Communion Plates: In the Tridentine rite, a white linen cloth was spread on the communion rail for the distribution of the eucharist. Its purpose was to catch any falling particles, as well as to carry over the appearance of the covered altar (cf. #23 in this chapter). In the late nineteenth century, the Vatican "tolerated" the substitution of a metal plate, a paten with side handles, passed from communicant to communicant and held under one's own chin. In 1929 this was formally adopted for all churches, but not as a substitute for the cloth. Both were needed as precautions for particles. Except at solemn Masses when the actual chalice paten was held under chins by the deacon, communicants themselves passed along this communion paten. It was to be kept dust-free in a cloth bag (burse) when not in use. This came to be a significant bit of bodily action on the part of communicants who now had to do more than just open their mouths. The fostering of passivity and a lack of trust in communicants soon caused this action to be curtailed. In most places, a long handle was added and servers moved from chin to chin in tandem with the communion minister. These are given brief mention in the current rite, but have been largely discontinued following the authorization of communion in the hand.

11. Repository Tabernacle: During the Easter Triduum, ancient customs required the eucharist to be reserved away from the altar of celebration. If the only tabernacle was on the main altar, then this large vessel was used at a side altar or shrine decorated with many candles and flowers. The purpose was not to create a shrine distinct to the Triduum; it was to have a place of reservation away from the altar. Now that the eucharist is always reserved in a separate place, the regular tabernacle is used on Holy Thursday evening as well. In some renovations, a new chapel of reservation uses the old repository as the new year-round tabernacle. In other settings, it might be re-fit as a repository for the holy oils.

12. Throne of Eucharistic Exposition: This is a small stand or elevated platform equipped with a back that supports a canopy over the monstrance. Communities with perpetual exposition had permanent thrones over the altar. All others were to use moveable ones so that an empty throne would not distract from the celebration of the eucharist (the same logic that later motivated the transfer of the tabernacle from the altar). The preferred form suggested in the current rite of exposition is for the monstrance to rest directly on the altar. Old thrones are really portable niches and might, depending on their design, hold statues, relics or holy oils in a different part of the church complex.

13. Eucharistic Tube or Straw: The *General Instruction of the Roman Missal* (#243-252) and ancient traditions suggest four possible methods of eucharistic cup-sharing: directly from the chalice, through a tube or straw, in a spoon, or by intinction—dipping the bread in the wine. Only the first form is recommended in the large assemblies of our country.

14. Eucharistic Spoon. This, too, is an artifact used in one of the alternative means of sharing the cup. The minister would pour wine from the spoon directly into the communicant's mouth, taking care not to let the spoon touch the communicant's lips or tongue. This method was rightly perceived as too awkward.

15. INTINCTORIUM: This was the name coined for the odd vessels invented to give communion by dipping eucharistic bread into a small cup fixed in the middle of a paten (like a platter with a dipping bowl). These are generally not used, and such patens can have the cups removed to resume service as regular patens. This form of communion is to be avoided in almost all settings because it removes the communicant's legitimate options: to receive the eucharistic bread in the hand or to omit the reception of eucharistic wine. Further, it does violence to the anonymous commitment of many recovering alcoholics.

16. WATER SPOON: These tiny spoons, with long handles, were used by a few priests (often those given to scrupulosity), who wanted to be sure that only a drop or two went into the chalice. The spoon-bowl is often attached at a right angle to the spoon-handle for dipping into narrow-necked cruets.

17. HOLY WATER SPRINKLERS: The bucket with separate sprinkler is far preferable to the one-piece sprinkler with a reservoir that looks like a laundry-sprinkler. The four- or five-inch-long tube of plated metal, stored in a leatherette case or clipped in a shirt pocket, looks like a fountain pen. Neither form bears any visual or traditional relationship to the font of life. If holy water is worth carrying outside of church, then it should at least be in a bottle.

18. SMALL VIAL OR VESSEL WITH SAND: The current *Order of Christian Funerals* states that the act of committal—lowering the body into the vault or earth and burying it—should take place either in the middle of the rite of committal or at the conclusion of the rite (#209). Though a deeply religious and communal act, it is too often left for cemetery workers and bulldozers. If a committal is not possible with the gathered community, the "gesture of final leave-taking" envisioned in the rite could be "the placing of soil on the coffin" (#210). The earth should not come from a vial or flask carried by the mortician or presider. It should be taken from the site and tossed into the grave by hand or with a shovel or something similar. If the coffin is in a cemetery chapel, the gesture of leave-taking could consist of placing flowers on the coffin.

Vestments and Other Textiles

19. BIRETTA AND VARIOUS HATS: See page 135 regarding the miter and skull cap for bishops at liturgy. In the Tridentine rite, there were many rules on the wearing and handling of hats for the ordained, generally the biretta. None of these was carried over in the reforms. The red cardinalatial hat (galero) was abolished in 1969. The custom of hanging it in the cathedral when the cardinal dies will itself die out upon the death of the last cardinal named before 1969.

20. TUNIC OR TUNICLE: This was the *tunica alba* of ancient days, modified and worn by subdeacons until that order was suppressed in 1972. See page 127 regarding the evolution of the same *tunica alba* into both the alb and the dalmatic. Because the dalmatic and tunic were the same in origin and virtually the same until 1972, remaining tunics with lines and decor appropriate to modern vesture can be renamed dalmatics and used by deacons.

21. MANIPLE: These were vestments about three inches wide and three feet long, looped over the left wrist and fastened there by one method or another. They began their existence in antiquity as linen rectangles, handkerchiefs carried or worn. By the Middle Ages, clerics used other cloths to wipe vessels, noses and hands; the maniple became an ornament of rank. They are no longer part of the Roman rite. In a few cases, narrow maniples of the right design can be fashioned into wide ribbons for the largest liturgical books.

22. LITURGICAL GLOVES, HOSIERY, FOOTWEAR OF BISHOPS: The decorated gloves with large cuffs, the *caligae* or stockings of the day's liturgical color, and various forms of decorated sandals (also called soleae, campagi, calcei or sandalia) were used for a thousand years as signs of office, dignity and tradition. Their use is no longer legislated since Vatican II.

23. COMMUNION CLOTH: In the Tridentine rite, a white linen cloth had to be draped over the communion rail during the distribution of communion. It often made a visual link between the covered altar and the reception of communion. It was also one more of the many extra precautions taken to save particles of the consecrated host. Along with corporals, communion plates, the first rinsing of linens in the sacrarium by an ordained person, and so much more, it attests to an admirable but often excessive respect for eucharistic particles. Still, the absence of communion cloths should not signal a swing to excessive casualness over the elements of our communal meal. Old cloths often can be cut and made into purificators.

24. ALTAR CLOTHS ON SIDE ALTARS OR FORMER MAIN ALTARS: There is only one altar in a church building, and only it should be covered with an altar cloth. Decorative or side altars should no longer be constructed; existing ones should never be given the mark of respect reserved for an altar: a cloth, candles or a cross. Cloths on these other surfaces, especially when they hang down the front (antependia) or sides, draw undue attention and confuse the notion of one altar per church.

25. PILLOW(S) FOR GOOD FRIDAY: These are no longer required for the act of prostration that should begin the celebration of the Lord's Passion. Depending upon their design, they can be used as part of other decorations. Otherwise, they should be retired.

Candles

26. BUGIA: This was a candle, normally with a small base and long handle, that was held near the bishop by an assisting minister for the reading of certain texts. It obviously had a practical purpose before electricity, but it was abolished in 1968 ("unless needed"). Something similar is often needed near the text of the Exsultet while it is being sung. Assisting ministers should not hesitate to give such help when needed.

27. CANDELABRA: These were often used for eucharistic exposition, and they were obviously a practical necessity a hundred years ago. Now the rite of exposition calls for four or six candles, as at Mass; candelabra can be used for festal decor at saints' shrines, seasonal illumination in the entrance hall or other appropriate uses. The special stand of candles for Tenebrae can still be used at that combined liturgy of the Office of Readings and Morning Prayer on Good Friday and Holy Saturday.

28. CANDLES FOR THE EUCHARISTIC PRAYER: A single candle used to be mounted on a wall bracket of the sanctuary or on the credence table. This "sanctus candle" remained lit from sanctus to the end of the communion rite. Its lighting is no longer a part of the rite, nor is the procession of assisting ministers bearing tall candles or torches during the eucharistic prayer. Any wall-mounted candle can be lit throughout the services on feasts as part of the overall decorative program. Old torches still can be used for other processions. There can be up to six or even seven candles for the opening procession of Mass, for example.

PART FOUR ◆ *Checklists*

31◆ The Liturgical Year and the Sacristy

Calendars

Our lives are deeply influenced by many calendars. They organize and comfort us. Sometimes they compete with one another for our attention, as when the Christmas lights twinkle in the malls before the violet of Advent is donned. Calendars invite us toward treats. How we longed as children for October 31! They make us dread the turn of a month's or week's page, say to April 15. They always provide ways to understand the flow of time, frames for interpreting events. They shape us as communities and as individuals.

The seven-day week is the basic structure for dividing time in our world. For Christians, Sunday is the source and summit of the week, the first day on which God began the creation, the day on which Christ rose from the dead, the day on which the Spirit rushed upon the church, and the symbol of the eighth day—that day of eternity in which we will enjoy life in the new Jerusalem.

For us Christians, the year of Sundays is arranged in another calendar besides the January-to-December one—the liturgical calendar.

The liturgical year calls communities to remember the life of Jesus. It also invites us into our own identity as holy ones of God. It is a way to organize time that can inspire and enliven all other schedules, forming us as a people of Christian affections and integrity. In each season, we are put in touch with another aspect of life in faith. For example, we hope in the future always, but Advent lets us sense our hope more tangibly. In Lent and Easter we experience and express more intensely the penitence and joy that our baptism brings us year-round. These intense experiences are facilitated by the communal symbols and actions proper to each season.

The liturgical year, in its delineation of seasons and days, structures our work as sacristans. We do not prepare artifacts for an ethical society gathered just to hear about abstract concepts, about hope, flesh, commitment, new life and good spirits. No, we prepare the place for a church gathered to embrace Advent's hope, to become flesh for the world at Christmas, to change hearts in Lent, to experience new life over the Triduum, and to be enflamed by the Holy Spirit through Eastertime. Each season has a distinct ambience of texts and colors, artifacts and songs. We need to know the liturgical year so that our work and all of the requisites we prepare can enhance our community's experience of the season.

Our appreciation for the liturgical year must quickly take on very practical forms. As we do more and more sacristy work, living through each year's progression of days, we must learn to think about the season long before its opening day. This is a discipline central to all ministers serving the community through preparatory work. We must read the scriptures, review the prayer texts, and most importantly list the necessary artifacts in advance. As local traditions form and careful files are kept, this will be easier. Seasons and individual feasts are not invented. We pass on notes from year to year to let our discipline of preparation be more and more expressive of local traditions and cherished patterns of action.

System for the Liturgical Year

Though Sunday is the building block of all Christian calendars, various churches and liturgical traditions structure their respective liturgical years in slightly dissimilar ways, with different demarcations of seasons and particular lists of saints. This manual is written with a special emphasis on the Roman rite parishes of the United States. We follow the calendric system described in the *General Norms for the Liturgical Year and the Calendar* (in the front of every sacramentary).

Our system includes five seasons that equal about 140 days and an Ordinary Time of about 225 days. The seasons are Advent, Christmas, Lent, Triduum and Easter; Ordinary Time is the time between these. Various days within the 365 have more or less importance in our tradition. For example, Christmas is more important than Wednesday of the Fourteenth Week in Ordinary Time. Texts for all of these days appear in the "proper of seasons" section of the sacramentary, lectionary and liturgy of the hours. Other requisites appropriate to days of a season are listed in the various rites. The decorative program for a season is rarely set by universal norms, but traditions are shared by many local churches. Some lists of texts, requisites and decorations follow in this manual, as examples or guidelines.

Since the earliest days of Christianity, communities have marked the seasons with local color. Energy and variety were brought by schedules paralleling the seasons—days remembering church dedications and the anniversaries of the death of holy ancestors. These local lists were shared among urban areas, with reverence shown to another city in the adoption of feasts for its honored saints. Through the centuries, some aspects of Jesus' life (for example, the Presentation) were added to these calendars. These lists came to be called the "proper of saints."

The general calendar issued by Rome has a few hundred saints on it; it is printed at the front of every sacramentary. In our tradition, this basic list is meant to be supplemented with local lists drawn from the thousands of other saints and blessed. The bishops' conference of the United States has added about 20 other days, generally of saints and blessed with particular connections to the United States. They also are listed at the front of every sacramentary. Some dioceses have added a few more. In each parish, the anniversary of dedication and the day celebrating the parish name also are to be added. The general list plus the local supplements form the proper of saints.

The interaction of the two lists, the proper of seasons and proper of saints, gives a distinctive quality to each year. Seasons and days all have various levels of importance, with set orders of precedence. For example, the seasonal Sundays always take precedence over saints' days; weeks like holy week and Easter week are similarly important. Because Sundays and Easter are on different dates each year, each year some saints' feasts are eclipsed. There are also discoveries and relationships for each year—a certain saint's day falling on Thanksgiving, or Memorial Day falling on the day after Pentecost, for example.

To ensure the observance of the most important feasts and to show the lesser status of other days, all observances are ranked:

- solemnities (They are always celebrated—for example, if March 25 is Good Friday, the Annunciation is moved to the first available day, right after Easter week.)
- feasts (Feasts of the Lord take precedence over Sundays in Ordinary Time; all other feasts are eclipsed only by Sunday or the weeks surrounding Easter.)
- obligatory memorials (These are kept on weekdays by all parishes, except in the two weeks surrounding Easter.)
- optional memorials (Communities decide which to keep.)

Using an Ordo

A liturgical almanac—called an ordo, Latin for "order"—is issued annually by several dioceses and publishers. (The "order" referred to is the order of rites and actions to be used throughout the year.) Even when an ordo is published by a national company, it often comes in regional or diocesan editions, with the particular observances of the diocese (for example, diocesan patron) listed at the appropriate date. These are very informative and convenient, but they are by no means magical. Anyone with a clear understanding of the seasons, the table of precedence, and calendar lists could interpolate the liturgical observances onto a civil calendar. Ordos are not meant to mystify, but to save a lot of work and list-making.

The line-up of feasts in a week and weeks in a season should always be considered in liturgical planning and in the scheduling of nonliturgical parish events. Ordos regularly give even more than the basic name or observance for each day. The following information in found in any good ordo. If one is unavailable, the information must be secured from another source. All of these elements provide direction for work in the sacristy.

1. *The season.* The seasons' boundaries are clearly listed. This helps us plan ahead for seasonal decorations: when they go up, when they come down, and how long they must last. Advent can be anywhere from 22 to 28 days.

Christmas is 15 to 20 days. Other seasons run for fixed numbers of days: Lent (43), the Triduum (3) and Easter (50). It is important to respect these parameters, for the decorations should not transmit a message or create an attitude that is at odds with the texts and music of the liturgy. For example, any decision to let the Christmas decor go up early, in mid-Advent, betrays a seriously wrong attitude: Either we think that Advent is not important, or we think that decorations are just trivial dressings without power. A decision to change the decorations between Easter and Pentecost shows a denial of the great reform that has unified the Fifty Days and shown the place of texts related to the Holy Spirit in the Easter Season.

2. *The day.* Before the recent reforms, observances falling on the same day might have been merged into one liturgy, with prayer texts for both. Now there is one observance each day. This happens in one of three ways:

a. In many cases, one day is set for everyone to observe—a day from the "proper of seasons" or a day ranked as a mandatory memorial or higher from the "proper of saints."

b. At the start of each year, local planners need to chart those days that are particular to the diocese and to the parish. The diocesan dates are in regional editions of the ordo or on diocesan mailings. The particular parish feasts are not in the ordo, but are significant days. The most important are:

–the anniversary of dedication—a solemnity (generally on the Sunday nearest the dedication date if in Ordinary Time, or on the Sunday before All Saints)

–the day celebrating the local title—a solemnity (often this is a patron saint, but it might also be a title of Jesus or of Mary; generally celebrated on the preceding Sunday in Ordinary Time or on the actual date)

–solemnities or feasts related to religious orders staffing the parish.

c. On other days, several choices are offered, and the local community must choose which one will be observed on that date. This happens only on some weekdays, when one or another optional memorial might be chosen instead of the ordinary weekday. If an optional memorial is chosen, it is then *the* memorial for that place and time. If all of the optional memorials are bypassed in favor of the ordinary weekday, then they are no longer factors in planning for that day. This choice should be made in advance by some planning group, perhaps while previewing the year as a whole, not just by the presider a few minutes before Mass. Those in the community who use the liturgy of hours for daily prayer and those who prepare ahead for weekday liturgies would benefit from knowing in advance what day it is, what option is being followed locally. When such options are offered, they are always listed as optional in the ordo.

3. *The scripture texts for Mass.* Ordos and most liturgical desk calendars cite references for these. The semi-continuous lectionary of the proper of seasons (Sunday or weekday) is followed on most days, even on a majority of the memorials of saints. On a few days—on solemnities and feasts and a rare few of the memorials—readings come from those days in the proper of

saints. When the continuous pattern is interrupted by such a day, presiders and planners can interpolate the lost passages into an adjoining day. This is particularly important when the surrounding days have first readings with dramatic narratives and the skipped passage contains an important element. We should always be in communication with those who decide such matters to see how the lectionary should be set.

For some days and rites, a choice of readings is given for the observance. When selected, they might be marked in the lectionary with a self-sticking note, especially if a whole series of first readings appears on a page.

4. *The prayer texts for Mass.* Once the day is ascertained (#2, above), many texts are selected for their seasonal or topical connections, sometimes in prior planning, at other times in the sacristy before Mass—the preface of the eucharistic prayer, the main body of the eucharistic prayer, the form of blessing. Other texts are prepared locally—for example, the general intercessions. See page 105 for information on setting ribbons and notes in the sacramentary. The presidential prayers (opening prayer, prayer over the gifts, prayer after communion) for the given day are determined according to this pattern:

a. Most days have a set of prayers assigned to them and positioned with that title in the "proper of seasons" or "proper of saints."

b. Some days in the "proper of seasons" have only an opening prayer that is assigned ("proper"); a few have no assigned prayers. A reference always is made under their title in the sacramentary (and in ordos) to the sections of general texts (commons) from which prayers can be drawn. When a couple of possible commons (for example, pastor or doctor) or several texts in a commons are available, selections should be made according to both the needs of the community and the merits of the texts.

c. Weekdays in Ordinary Time with no saint's observance (or with an optional memorial passed by) offer texts under their names only in the liturgy of the hours. For the celebration of the eucharist, those who choose texts usually adopt one or more of the traditional systems for this selection:

- Use prayers from the prior Sunday in Ordinary Time (not from a feast falling on Sunday).

- Use votive Masses (printed after the "commons").

- Use "Masses and Prayers for Various Needs and Occasions" (printed after the "commons").

5. *Choices for the liturgy of hours.* Many ordos contain notes on special choices for the various hours. As with Mass texts, texts for the hours should flow from the day being observed. This is usually not a question, but when optional memorials are offered in the calendar, those praying should know the option selected.

6. *Color of vestments.* These are usually listed in ordos. The logic informing the assignments is outlined on page 122. If the day's color differs from the seasonal color, it is neither necessary nor advisable to change the whole decor for one day. Instead, the contrast can indicate, for example, that St. Joseph is being celebrated in Lent.

The Lists in This Manual

The pages that follow describe the physical requisites for some of the most important or unusual days in our liturgical year. The first list is a basic list for celebrating the eucharist at any time. Then follow lists for the specific seasons and feasts. These are all meant as general examples; local plans and customs will always call for adaptations. All lists should be prepared and reviewed with presiders and planners long before the day of celebration.

32◆ Basic Checklist for Celebration of the Eucharist

PLACE FOR EUCHARISTIC ACTION

Seating:
hymnals

Open space:
solemnities outside of Lent: dedication candles, pew candles lit

Altar:
covered with one cloth, unless this comes at preparation rite
gospel book with text marked, if used and not carried in procession
nearby: any candles, candlestands not carried in procession
nearby: stand for processional cross

Credence table:
Sunday: vessel of water and sprinkler, if rite of sprinkling will be performed
large cup (can be covered by pall and/or white veil)
purificator
corporal
book stand, if needed
water in small cruet, if not in procession of gifts
basin, pitcher of water, towel
any bread, wine not in procession of gifts
additional cups and purificators for the assembly (on tray)
additional patens for the assembly
pyx or ciborium, if extra bread consecrated for the sick

Presider's chair:
sacramentary (after review in vesting room)
hymnal, if not carried in procession

Ministers' seats:
texts for concelebrants, if any
hymnals, if not carried in procession

Ambo:
lectionary with texts marked, if not carried in procession
psalm setting for cantor (unless carried there for this action)
general intercessions, if done here

Music stand (or secondary podium):
general intercessions, if done here

SACRISTY

charcoal lit in thurible, then put in vesting room
extra charcoal (and tongs, matches) for adding during Mass
controls set for air, sound and lights
microphones put in place and turned on

VESTING ROOM

vesture (see page 120); chasuble, dalmatic of day's color
lavaliere microphones, if any
lectionary or gospel book with texts marked, if carried in procession
local texts (dismissal of catechumens, intercessions) inserted and other texts marked in sacramentary for review before placement by chair
thuribile, with lit charcoal
vessel of incense, seasonal scent
processional cross
two or more processional candlesticks with lighted candles

ENTRANCE

Table with gifts:
bread for all on one paten, more if needed, if in procession
wine for all in one vessel, more if needed, if in procession
water in small cruet, if in procession

Other:
collection baskets ready
booklets, bulletins or other handouts

CATECHUMENEON

opened and prepared, if catechumens present

CHAPEL OF EUCHARISTIC RESERVATION

lamp lit
key at tabernacle if eucharist for the sick will be added

33◆ Checklists for Liturgical Seasons and Feasts

Advent

THE SEASON: The season is described in our official books:

> Advent has a twofold character: as a season to prepare for Christmas when Christ's first coming to us is remembered; as a season when that remembrance directs the mind and heart to await Christ's Second Coming at the end of time. Advent is thus a period for devout and joyful expectation. . . . The weekdays from 17 December to 24 December inclusive serve to prepare more directly for the Lord's birth. *(General Norms for the Liturgical Year and the Calendar,* #39, 42)

> During Advent, the playing of the organ and other musical instruments as well as the floral decoration of the altar should be marked by a moderation that reflects the character of this season, but does not anticipate the full joy of Christmas itself. *(Ceremonial of Bishop,* #236)

VESTURE: In former centuries, Advent was a penitential season. Though violet has been maintained as the color, Advent should not be marked by decorations of Lent, of Christ's passion, of penance. The retention of rose as an optional color for the Third Sunday of Advent is another reminder of penitential heritage—when an infusion of joy and a softening to rose in mid-season were welcomed.

DECORATIONS: Decorations should reflect our anticipation, not the fullness of Christmas lights, evergreens, and splendor. What is translated as "the floral decoration of the altar" in the *Ceremonial of Bishops* should be applied to the entire decor. Despite the full-throated carols of praise sounding through malls, the churches holding to Advent require of their sacristans (and musicians) a certain discipline. We must hold back from Christmas decorations until after the Fourth Sunday of Advent, and let our communities savor Advent longing for weeks before we jump into the full-throated praise of the incarnation.

The Advent wreath is highly recommended as the one item to add to the year-round furnishings of liturgy. This wreath hints at the greens and light of Christmas, the light of Christ, the brilliance of the end time, and the progress of this season of preparation. It must be fashioned from real greens, even if these are replaced with fresh ones halfway through the season. True smell and honesty of form are important enough that, if artificial branches were to be proposed, it would be better to have no wreath. The *Book of Blessings* (#1510, 1512) describes it:

> Customarily the Advent Wreath is constructed of a circle of evergreen branches into which are inserted four candles. According to tradition, three of the candles are violet and the fourth is rose. However, four violet or white candles may also be used. If the Advent wreath is to be used in church, it should be of sufficient size to be visible to the congregation. It may be suspended from the ceiling or placed on a stand. If it is placed in the presbyterium (sanctuary), it should not interfere with the celebration of the liturgy, nor should it obscure the altar, lectern or chair.

If the local wreath is the proper scale, then few other flowers, if any at all, are needed. Other customs include:

- a Jesse tree (in the entrance hall, decorated with representations of the ancestors and prophets, not arcane symbols of virtues)

–highlighting statues or windows of John the Baptist, images of Isaiah or of the other prophets

–candles by the Marian shrine, especially if the image there follows one of the eschatological images so central to Advent (Immaculate Conception, Our Lady of Guadalupe)

–a whole wall in the entrance hall dedicated to signing up volunteers for the various tasks of Christmas

–outdoor decor that announces Advent (violet strips of cloth, an outdoor tree with "Jesse" figures).

Christmas Season

THE SEASON: This season provides us each year with two or three weeks for high festivity. We should do all within our power to have the physical requisites and decorations encourage and sustain the expressions of joy called for in the liturgy. The intensity of the celebrations rises from the birth of Jesus, from the first manifestations of Christ described on all the later days of the season, and from our share in divinity. God took human flesh to raise this very flesh to divine dignity.

A devout and fully Christian observance of these days thus calls for more than pious emotions before the manger scene. We must also thrill to the retellings of the manifestations, sing in wonder of our new dignity. These aspects will be seen more fully if Christmas is more than a day, if the decorations and other artifacts give external cohesion to the inner unity of the days from Christmas to the Baptism of the Lord. Festal decorations must be held back until just before Christmas Eve. Then their ability to last until the end of the season must be a factor in their selection. The feast of the Baptism of the Lord, the final day of the season, is somewhat over two weeks after Christmas day—on the Sunday after Epiphany Sunday (unless Epiphany Sunday is as late as January 7 or 8, with the Baptism feast on the very next day, Monday the 8th or 9th).

VESTURE: White is assigned for this season. As always, gold or "more precious vestments" can be worn on solemn occasions such as Christmas and Epiphany. Red is often associated with Christmas in today's culture, and can be a part of the decor. But in vesture for this season it is used only for the martyrs' days.

DECORATIONS: The decor should show the unity of these 15 to 20 days, facilitate the joyful experience of the sacred mysteries, and draw the assembly into a sense that the manifestations continue. From the shepherds and the magi to our day, we see the Lord. The traditional decorations often are best:

1. *Manger.* The manger scene can be a reminder of Bethlehem, but also, with a touch of glorious decoration, a signal of the paradise promised and brought on that holy night. The *Book of Blessings* (#1544) sensibly notes that the manger must not be placed in the sanctuary. It can be outdoors or in an easily accessible part of the interior that is conducive to "visits." When figures and accessories are replaced or added, the paradisal quality of the mystery can be expressed by angels, bright colors and representations that are more glorious, more manifestly redeemed than the overly-sentimental faces too often seen.

2. *Christmas tree.* Whether an evergreen tree is outside the church complex or one is brought indoors, the lit tree is a marvelous symbol of the tree of paradise, the tree of life and light. It is perhaps the best non-verbal invitation to hope and brilliant rejoicing. It certainly does more than turn us back in nostalgia; it draws us forward to the kingdom of fullness and light. It is also a strong signal of the season's dates when lit from Christmas Eve to Epiphany or the Baptism of the Lord. Of course, an indoor tree should neither interfere with liturgical actions nor violate fire and egress codes.

3. *Flowers.* Where poinsettias are traditional, they certainly should be used. Traditions are hard to invent and should be respected and enjoyed when found. Creativity would better be spent in arranging them for color throughout the assembly space, not crowded up against the altar.

4. *Exterior decorations.* When planning the decor for any season, the exterior should always be included. Possibilities for Christmas include: a weatherproof banner, lights on a large evergreen tree, an outdoor manger, garlands or fabric over the entries, *luminarias* along the parish walkways (lit at night on Christmas and Epiphany), or one huge wreath on the tower.

Christmas Eve: Vigil Service and Mass Late at Night

Midnight Mass is often preceded by a vigil service—the Office of Readings ("vigils") or some form of lessons and carols before Mass. Here is a checklist for items other than decorations, which were discussed above:

PLACE FOR EUCHARISTIC ACTION

Seating:
hymnals or booklets

Open space:
dedication candles, pew candles, Advent wreath lit (if kept)
créche outside the sanctuary

Altar:
covered with one cloth, unless this comes at preparation rite
gospel book with text marked, if used and not carried in procession
nearby: any candles, candlestands not carried in procession
nearby: stand for processional cross

Credence table:
large cup (can be covered by pall and/or white veil)
purificator
corporal
book stand, if needed
water in small cruet, if not in procession of gifts
basin, pitcher of water, towel
any bread, wine, not in procession of gifts
additional cups and purificators for the assembly (on tray)
additional patens for the assembly
pyx or ciborium, if extra bread consecrated for the sick

Presider's chair:
sacramentary (after review in vesting room)
hymnal or booklet, if not carried in procession
candle, bobeche (if light service is done)

Ministers' seats:
texts for concelebrants, if any
hymnals or booklets, if not carried in procession
candles, bobeches for all (if light service is done)

Ambo:
lectionary with texts marked, if not carried in procession
psalm setting for cantor (unless carried there for that action)
general intercessions, if done here

Music stand (or secondary podium):
general intercessions, if done here
additional texts (the proclamation of Christmas, if sung)

Sacristy

charcoal lit in thurible, then put in vesting room
extra charcoal (and tongs, matches) for adding during Mass
controls set for air, sound, lights
microphones put in places and turned on

Vesting Room

vesture (see page 120); chasuble, dalmatic of white or gold
lavaliere microphones, if any
lectionary or gospel book with texts marked, if carried in procession
local texts inserted (dismissal of catechumens, intercessions) and other texts marked in sacramentary, for review prior to placement by chair
thurible, with lit charcoal
vessel of incense, Christmas scent
processional cross
two or more candlesticks with lighted candles

Entrance

Table with gifts:
bread for all on one paten, more if needed, if in procession
wine for all in one vessel, more if needed, if in procession
water in small cruet, if in procession

Other:
collection baskets ready
booklets, bulletins or other hand-outs
candles, bobeches for all, if service of light at vigil

Catechumeneon

opened and prepared, if catechumens present

Chapel of Eucharistic Reservation

lamp lit
key at tabernacle if eucharist for the sick will be added

Epiphany Sunday: Celebration of the Eucharist

The liturgical books suggest these additional elements: extra candles in the room, a proclamation of the year's movable feasts and a special presentation of gifts.

PLACE FOR EUCHARISTIC ACTION

Seating:
hymnals

Open space:
as many candles lit as possible (dedication candles, pew candles, too)
creche outside the sanctuary; magi added now

Altar:
covered with one cloth, unless this comes at preparation rite
gospel book with text marked, if used and not carried in procession
nearby: any candles, candlestands not carried in procession
nearby: stand for processional cross

Credence table:
vessel of water, if rite of sprinkling occurs
large cup (can be covered by pall and/or white veil)
purificator
corporal
book stand, if needed
water in small cruet, if not in procession of gifts
basin, pitcher of water, towel
any bread, wine, not in procession of gifts
additional cups and purificators for the assembly (on tray)
additional patens for the assembly
pyx or ciborium, if extra bread consecrated for the sick

Presider's chair:
sacramentary (after review in vesting room)
hymnal, if not carried in procession

Ministers' seats:
texts for concelebrants, if any
hymnals, if not carried in procession

Ambo:
lectionary with texts marked, if not carried in procession
psalm setting for cantor (unless carried there for that action)
general intercessions, if done here
additional texts (proclamation of movable feasts, if sung)

Music stand (or secondary podium):
general intercessions, if done here

SACRISTY

charcoal lit in thurible, then put in vesting room
extra charcoal (and tongs, matches) for adding during Mass
controls set for air, sound, lights
microphones put in places and turned on

VESTING ROOM

vesture (see page 120); chasuble, dalmatic of white or gold
lavaliere microphones, if any
lectionary or gospel book with texts marked, if carried in procession
local texts inserted (dismissal of catechumens, intercessions) and other texts marked in the sacramentary, for review prior to placement by chair
thurible, with lit charcoal
vessel of incense, Christmas scent
processional cross
two or more lighted candles; more suggested for this day

ENTRANCE

Table with gifts:
bread for all on one paten, more if needed, if in procession
wine for all in one vessel, more if needed, if in procession
water in small cruet, if in procession

Other:
collection baskets ready
booklets, bulletins, parish calendars for the new year

CATECHUMENEON
opened and prepared, if catechumens present

CHAPEL OF EUCHARISTIC RESERVATION
lamp lit
key at tabernacle if eucharist for the sick will be added

Lent

THE SEASON: Lent is the season of paschal preparation, from Ash Wednesday to the start of the Easter Triduum on Holy Thursday. The community prays over the catechumens with heightened intensity and frequency. All who truly keep Lent prepare themselves, through a spirit of repentance, to renew baptism at Easter. The baptismal and penitential aspects of Lent have given rise to many customs and practices related to our work in the sacristy. The best ones assist the whole community to look beyond just private discipline (giving up this or that) to communal actions of renewal.

Just as Advent—the other preparatory season—shifts to a more intense mode on December 17, Lent has an internal structure of building fervor. Ash Wednesday and the next three days form a solemn prelude. Later, the first four weeks give way to the final two weeks, when attention to the passion of Christ inspires our renewal. Holy Week is the last days of Lent and then the Easter Triduum arrives. Its most intense air of remembrance does more than point us back to a cross two millennia ago. It brings us to a living reality, a cross and resurrection that shapes us and all who will ever live. This internal movement of the season does not have to be reflected in decorations, and in most cases probably should not. It is far more important, at this stage of reform, for us all to appreciate the fundamental unity and purpose of this entire 43-day period.

EQUIPMENT FOR ASHES AND PALMS: To prepare the vessels and equipment needed, we should think through the life cycle of our palm branches. For Palm Sunday, we need great receptacles to hold palms that are not stripped into smithereens. It is better to buy whole fronds and have volunteers break them into sizable pieces—the emotional attachment of Catholics to this sacramental is marvelous, and we should do all that we can to involve volunteers and to encourage physical contact with the symbols of our prayer. After Palm Sunday, we need containers or bags in which to save remaining palms for the following winter.

Then, over the weeks of winter, we can invite parishioners to bring their used palms to church by the Sunday before Ash Wednesday. Thus, we need baskets for collecting them back. Either on that Sunday after Mass, with parish members gathered around and singing, or more quietly over the next two days, all of these palms must be burned in a large brazier or clean, outdoor grill. After the fire has burned down, we need a large, fine-mesh strainer (to sift the collected remains from the fire), a large vessel to catch the sifted ashes, and a covered jar to store them safely until Wednesday. For the services on Ash Wednesday, we need a large bowl for the ashes, smaller ones for ministers, and a large spoon. In such practical ways, we allow this eloquent dirt to tell of death, penitence, and start of a new season.

VESTURE: The violet vesture might well be different from that used in Advent. Appliqued symbols of the passion are to be avoided—austerity is important everywhere in this season, and Lent is not a six-week passiontide. The white vesture used on the few solemnities should be as plain as possible. The red for Passion (Palm) Sunday should not have Pentecost symbols.

DECORATIONS: Emptiness speaks as forcefully as any of the floral arrangements used over the rest of the year. By customs firmly restated in the liturgical books, this is the season for bare buildings, for avoiding all manner of flowers, and for veiling cross and images. In the midst of this austerity, three elements at the core of Lent can be highlighted: the collection place for alms, posted information on those whom the community will be welcoming at Easter, and exterior signs with clearly-worded invitations to the pending paschal feast.

Ash Wednesday: Celebration of the Eucharist

If ashes are distributed apart from Mass, at a liturgy of the word following the order found in chapter 52 of the *Book of Blessings,* use this checklist except for those items particular for Mass.

Place for Eucharistic Action

Seating:
hymnals

Open space:
spaces designated for ministers to distribute ashes
stand or pedestal with bowl of ashes in prominent position

Altar:
covered with one cloth, unless this comes at preparation rite
gospel book with text marked, if used and not carried in procession
nearby: any candles, candlestands not carried in procession
nearby: stand for processional cross

Credence table:
vessel of water with sprinkler (for ashes)
empty bowls for ashes
large spoon, to transfer ashes from large bowl to small bowls
basins with small bars of soap, pitchers of water, towels (as many as needed—all ministers distributing ashes wash hands)
large cup (can be covered by pall and/or white veil)
purificator
corporal
book stand, if needed
water in small cruet, if not in procession of gifts
any bread, wine, not in procession of gifts
additional cups and purificators for the assembly (on tray)
additional patens for the assembly
pyx or ciborium, if extra bread consecrated for the sick

Presider's chair:
sacramentary (after review in vesting room)
hymnal, if not carried in procession

Ministers' seats:
texts for concelebrants, if any
hymnals, if not carried in procession

Ambo:
lectionary with texts marked, if not carried in procession
psalm setting for cantor (unless carried there for this action)
general intercessions, if done here

Music stand (or secondary podium):
general intercessions, if done here

SACRISTY

charcoal lit in thurible, then put in vesting room
extra charcoal (and tongs, matches) for adding during Mass
controls set for air, sound, lights
microphones put in place and turned on

VESTING ROOM

vesture (see page 120); chasuble, dalmatic of violet
lavaliere microphones, if any
lectionary or gospel book with texts marked, if carried in procession
local texts inserted (dismissal of catechumens, intercessions) and other texts marked in the sacramentary, for review prior to placement by chair (the *Book of Blessings* instead of the sacramentary, when the celebration is not Mass)
thurible, with lit charcoal
vessel of incense, Lenten scent
processional cross
two or more candlesticks with lighted candles

ENTRANCE

Table with gifts:
bread for all on one paten, more if needed, if in procession
wine for all in one vessel, more if needed, if in procession
water in small cruet, if in procession

Other:
booklets, bulletins or other hand-outs

CATECHUMENEON

opened and prepared, if catechumens present

CHAPEL OF EUCHARISTIC RESERVATION

lamp lit
key at tabernacle if eucharist for the sick will be added

First Sunday of Lent, with Penitential Procession

This outline provides for a procession of the entire assembly to begin Mass and signal the start of Lent. As called for in official documents (1988 *Circular Letter Concerning the Preparation and Celebration of the Easter Feasts*, #23; *Ceremonial of Bishops*, #261), all gather in a separate place for a hymn, an introduction to Lent, and prayer. Then a solemn procession of all is accompanied by the litany of the saints. At Masses with catechumens present, a rite of sending for election is provided for this day in the *Rite of Christian Initiation of Adults*.

PLACE FOR EUCHARISTIC ACTION

Seating:
special seats for catechumens after the procession, if reserved hymnals or booklets, unless these are in other gathering place

Open space:
area set for catechumens and sponsors, when called forward

Altar:
covered with one cloth, unless this comes at preparation rite
gospel book with text marked, if used and not carried in procession
nearby: any candles, candlestands not carried in procession
nearby: stand for processional cross

Credence table:
large cup (can be covered by pall and/or white veil)
purificator
corporal
book stand, if needed
water in small cruet, if not in procession of gifts
basin, pitcher of water, towel
any bread, wine, not in procession of gifts
additional cups and purificators for the assembly (on tray)
additional patens for the assembly
pyx or ciborium, if extra bread consecrated for the sick

Presider's chair:
nearby (on robe stand?): violet chasuble if cope worn in procession
hymnal, if not carried in procession

Ministers' seats:
texts for concelebrants, if any
hymnals, if not carried in procession

Ambo:
lectionary with texts marked, if not carried in procession
psalm setting for cantor (unless carried there for this action)
intercessions for the catechumens and candidates, if rite of sending is celebrated, and if done here

general intercessions, if done here

Music stand (or secondary podium):
intercessions for the catechumens and candidates, if rite of sending is celebrated, and if done here
general intercessions, if done here

SACRISTY

charcoal lit in thurible, then put in vesting room
extra charcoal (and tongs, matches) for adding during Mass
controls set for air, sound, lights
microphones put in places and turned on

VESTING ROOM

vesture (see page 120); cope or chasuble, dalmatic of violet
lavaliere microphones, if any
lectionary or gospel book with texts marked, if carried in procession
local texts (introduction to Lent, rite of sending for election, intercessions) inserted in sacramentary, for review prior to placement in gathering area
thurible, with lit charcoal
vessel of incense, Lent scent
processional cross
two or more candlesticks with lighted candles

ENTRANCE

Exterior:
signs directing assembly to special gathering place

Table with gifts:
bread for all on one paten, more if needed, if in procession
wine for all in one vessel, more if needed, if in procession
water in small cruet, if in procession

Other:
collection baskets ready
booklets, bulletins, Triduum schedule or other handouts

CATECHUMENEON

opened and prepared, if catechumens present

CHAPEL OF EUCHARISTIC RESERVATION

lamp lit
key at tabernacle if eucharist for the sick will be added

OTHER GATHERING PLACE

place arranged for entire assembly
space reserved for instrumentalists and other leaders of music

place reserved for the presider and other ministers
sacramentary (carried there by assistant?)
hymnals or booklets for all

First Sunday of Lent: The Rite of Election

This rite normally takes place in the cathedral on the First Sunday of Lent. It can be combined with the Call to Continuing Conversion of candidates (for confirmation, eucharist, reception into full communion) previously baptized. The list here presumes a diocesan-wide gathering, where the liturgy of the eucharist normally does not follow (*Rite of Christian Initiation of Adults,* #561).

Place of Assembly

Seating:
- hymnals or booklets
- signs indicating positions if parish-by-parish seating plan
- reserved seats for chief catechists or others as needed

Open space:
- area arranged for those to be called forward
- requisites to meet local procedures related to book of elect, for example, fairly high table or stand with book of elect and pens
- place determined for the person or persons presenting the catechumens (and other candidates) by name

Altar:
- altar cloth may be removed
- gospel book with text marked, if used and not carried in procession
- nearby: any candles, candlestands not carried in procession
- nearby: stand for processional cross

Cathedra:
- hymnal or booklet
- places nearby for ministers assisting with miter, pastoral staff, and ritual book

Other ministers' seats:
- hymnals or booklets (if not carried in procession)

Ambo:
- lectionary with texts marked, if not carried in procession
- psalm setting for cantor (unless carried there for this action)
- text of intercessions, if done here

Music stand (or secondary podium):
- text of intercessions, if done here

Sacristy

- charcoal lit in thurible, then placed in vesting room
- controls set for air, sound, lights
- microphones put in place and turned on

Vesting Room

cope, dalmatics of violet
lavaliere microphones, if any
lectionary or gospel book with texts marked, if carried in procession
texts marked in ritual book, for review prior to assistant carrying it
texts, lists of names for person(s) presenting catechumens
thurible, with lit charcoal
vessel of incense, Lent scent
processional cross
two or more candlesticks with lighted candles

Entrance

booklets, bulletins or other handouts
table(s) for registration or for diocesan information
clear charts posted if parish-by-parish seating plan followed

Chapel of Reservation

lamp lit

Scrutinies and Mass on the Third, Fourth, Fifth Sundays of Lent

Exorcism still brings to mind some fantastic ideas of demons and several bizarre movies. Yet exorcisms remain in the liturgy, most especially in these public rites of the assembly and those elected for Easter initiation. Neither fantastic nor bizarre, they are public statements of the power of Christ over the evil in our lives. Through self-searching and repentance, but chiefly through a shared reliance on God, our communities prepare for Easter. The list here presumes that the optional rite of sprinkling is omitted during Lent.

PLACE FOR EUCHARISTIC ACTION

Seating:
hymnals
designated seats for catechumens and elect, if reserved

Open space:
space designated for the elect and their sponsors to stand (and kneel) after coming forward; this does not need to be near the altar but might be closer to assembly in center aisle

Altar:
covered with one cloth, unless this comes at preparation rite
gospel book with text marked, if used and not carried in procession
nearby: any candles, candlestands not carried in procession
nearby: stand for processional cross

Credence table:
large cup (can be covered by pall and/or white veil)
purificator
corporal
book stand, if needed
water in small cruet, if not in procession of gifts
basin, pitcher of water, towel
any bread, wine, not in procession of gifts
additional cups and purificators for the assembly (on tray)
additional patens for the assembly
pyx or ciborium, if extra bread consecrated for the sick

Presider's chair:
sacramentary (after review in vesting room)
hymnal, if not carried in procession

Ministers' seats:
texts for concelebrants, if any
hymnals, if not carried in procession

Ambo:
lectionary with texts marked, if not carried in procession
psalm setting for cantor (unless carried there for this action)

intercessions for the elect, if done here
general intercessions, if done here

Music stand (or secondary podium):
intercessions for the elect, if done here
general intercessions, if done here

SACRISTY

charcoal lit in thurible, then put in vesting room
extra charcoal (and tongs, matches) for adding during Mass
controls set for air, sound, lights
microphones put in place and turned on

VESTING ROOM

vesture (see page 120); chasuble, dalmatic of violet (rose optional on Fourth Sunday of Lent)
lavaliere microphones, if any
lectionary or gospel book with texts marked, if carried in procession
local texts (scrutiny rite, general intercessions) inserted and other texts marked (ritual Mass, "Christian Initiation: The Scrutinies") in sacramentary, for review prior to placement by chair
thurible, with lit charcoal
vessel of incense, Lent scent
processional cross
two or more candlesticks with lighted candles

ENTRANCE

Table with gifts:
bread for all on one paten, more if needed, if in procession
wine for all in one vessel, more if needed, if in procession
water in small cruet, if in procession

Other:
collection baskets ready
booklets, bulletins, Triduum schedules or other handouts

CATECHUMENEON

opened and prepared for sharing after dismissal of catechumens

CHAPEL OF EUCHARISTIC RESERVATION

lamp lit
key at tabernacle if eucharist for the sick will be added

Passion Sunday (Palm Sunday), with Procession

The first form of the Commemoration of the Lord's Entrance into Jerusalem is by far the best. According to the sacramentary, it should begin "in a secondary church or chapel or in some other suitable place distinct from the church to which the procession will move."

Place for Eucharistic Action

Altar:
covered with one cloth, unless this comes at preparation rite
nearby: any candles, candlestands not carried in procession
nearby: stand for processional cross

Credence table:
large cup (can be covered by pall and/or white veil)
purificator
corporal
book stand, if needed
water in small cruet, if not in procession of gifts
basin, pitcher of water, towel
any bread, wine, not in procession of gifts
additional cups and purificators for the assembly (on tray)
additional patens for the assembly
pyx or ciborium, if extra hosts consecrated for the sick

Presider's chair:
nearby (on robe stand?): red chasuble if cope worn for procession
hymnal or booklet, if not carried in procession

Ministers' seats:
texts for concelebrants, if any
hymnals or booklets, if not carried in procession

Ambo:
lectionary with texts marked, if not carried in procession
psalm setting for cantor (unless carried there for this action)
books for singing the passion (or reading in parts), if used (secondary lecterns for those taking parts, or reading desks added to large ambo area)
general intercessions, if done here

Music stand (or secondary podium):
general intercessions, if done here

Sacristy

charcoal lit in thurible, then put in vesting room
extra charcoal (and tongs, matches) for adding during Mass
controls set for air, sound, lights
microphones put in place and turned on

VESTING ROOM

- vesture (see page 120); cope or chasuble, dalmatic of red
- lavaliere microphones, if any
- lectionary or gospel book with texts marked, if carried in procession
- local texts (dismissal of catechumens and elect, intercessions) inserted, other texts marked in sacramentary; reviewed prior to placement in (or procession to) special gathering area
- thurible, with lit charcoal
- vessel of incense, Lent scent
- processional cross, decorated with palm branches
- two or more candlesticks with lighted candles

ENTRANCE

Exterior:

- signs directing assembly to special gathering place
- arrangements made for procession: permit secured for use of public streets or sidewalks, traffic guards, special regulations for parking

Table with gifts:

- bread for all on one paten, more if needed, if in procession
- wine for all in one vessel, more if needed, if in procession
- water in small cruet, if in procession

Other:

- collection baskets ready
- booklets, bulletins, Triduum schedules or other handouts

CATECHUMENEON

- opened and prepared, if catechumens and/or elect present

CHAPEL OF EUCHARISTIC RESERVATION

- lamp lit
- key at tabernacle if eucharist for the sick will be added

OTHER GATHERING PLACE

- space set for entire assembly
- space set for instrumentalists, other leaders of music, presider, other ministers (near table/podium)
- palm branches for all, in baskets or other receptacles
- hymnals or booklets for all

On table or stand:

- vessel of water and sprinkler
- palms for presider and ministers who proceed from vesting room
- sacramentary (unless carried in procession from vesting room)

At podium:

- lectionary or gospel book (unless carried in procession from vesting room)

Chrism Mass

Place for Eucharistic Action

Seating:
hymnals or booklets

Open space:
table for the vessels of oil

Altar:
covered with one cloth, unless this comes at preparation rite
gospel book, if used and not carried in procession
nearby: any candles, candlestands not carried in procession
nearby: stand for processional cross

Credence table:
large spoon on dish (if bishop will mix fragrance and oil during rite)
large cup (can be covered by pall and/or white veil)
purificator
corporal
book stand, if needed
water in small cruet, if not in procession of gifts
basin, pitcher of water, towel
any bread, wine, not in procession of gifts
additional cups and purificators for the assembly (on tray)
additional patens for the assembly
pyx or ciborium, if Mass is prior to Holy Thursday and if eucharist for the sick is needed

Cathedra:
hymnal or booklet
places nearby for ministers assisting with miter, pastoral staff, sacramentary

Seating for concelebrants and other ministers:
texts for concelebrants
hymnals or booklets, if not carried in procession

Ambo:
lectionary with texts marked, if not carried in procession
psalm setting for cantor (unless carried there for this action)
(general intercessions replaced by texts in sacramentary for bishop)

Sacristy

charcoal lit in thurible, then put by procession gathering
extra charcoal (and tongs, matches) for adding during Mass
controls set for air, sound, lights
microphones put in places and turned on

VESTING ROOM(S)

vesture (see page 120); chasuble, dalmatics of white; if many deacons and presbyters are vesting, several rooms may be necessary—arranged so that the procession is duly formed

space for the bishop to address presbyters after Mass *(Ceremonial of Bishops, #294)*

space and equipment for the orderly distribution of oils (if not done during liturgy, may be in several rooms), for example: table for main vessels; pitchers for drawing off oils and setting up stations for distribution; at each station—table, three pitchers clearly labeled with oil's title, paper towels, trays for resting parish vessels and pouring, containers for receiving old oils, receptacles for paper towels, dishes of cut lemons for ministers' hands.

hymnals or booklets for concelebrants

lavaliere microphones, if any

lectionary or gospel book with texts marked, if carried in procession

local texts (dismissal of elect and catechumens?) inserted and other texts marked (blessing of oils) in sacramentary, for review prior to assistant carrying it

thurible, with lit charcoal

vessel of incense, Lent scent

processional cross

two or more candlesticks with lighted candles

ENTRANCE

Table with gifts:

three large vessels of olive oil (or two with oil, one with mixture of oil and fragrance)

vessel with chrism fragrance, unless already mixed in with oil that will be consecrated as chrism

bread for all on one paten, more if needed, if in procession

wine for all in one vessel, more if needed, if in procession

water in small cruet, if in procession

Other:

collection baskets ready

booklets, bulletins or other handouts

CATECHUMENEON

opened, if dismissal is scheduled

CHAPEL OF EUCHARISTIC RESERVATION

lamp lit

key at tabernacle if Mass is prior to Holy Thursday and eucharist for the sick will be added

Easter Triduum

THE THREE DAYS: Sacristans rarely need to be told of the Triduum's importance—or of its complexity! It is the privileged time for celebrating the primal event of salvation still present in our midst, still shaping us as church. It is the center of our year; its planning and preparation should never wait for late Lent. We will be less burdened when we recognize the Triduum events as annual repetitions of time-honored actions, not as fresh inventions each year. Notes from former years are enormously important as we enlist more volunteers and prepare requisites.

From the evening Mass of Holy Thursday through evening prayer on Easter Sunday, we will need to make changes in the physical environment of our buildings, utilize many implements seen but once a year, and serve more worshipers than at any other point in the year. Our responsibilities begin weeks or months ahead, making lists of requisites needed from careful reviews of the rites, and then finding or commissioning the most dignified materials possible. These artifacts are noted in the checklists that follow.

DECORATIONS: The church building is mostly stripped or barren for the first two days, then transformed with paradisal decorations at the Easter Vigil. There are some sub-plots:

–Thursday evening at the end of Mass: The place for the transfer of the eucharist is the tabernacle used all year, presuming that this is correctly separated from the celebration space. Its decoration this night should be simple, unlike many repositories of Tridentine and Baroque times. A few flowers (that are not explicitly "Easter") or something like small olive trees or branches can be combined with a few candles. Away from the chapel of reservation, everything is to be stripped or veiled: no crosses visible, no holy water in stoups or font, no covers or cloths on altar, no auxiliary furnishings like credence tables and kneelers. Only permanent furniture like the altar and the ambo should be visible, and they should be barren.

–Thursday midnight: All candles, except for one candle near the tabernacle, are extinguished, and all decorations are taken from the eucharistic chapel.

–Friday's celebration of the Lord's Passion: Only those items of furniture needed are set out, then removed after the rite. All else is bare. Any remaining eucharist is brought to a private place to be kept for viaticum. The cross (which was carried in during the celebration) is placed with lighted candles in a place conducive both to quiet prayer and to reverencing the cross with a touch or kiss—perhaps in the now-empty chapel of reservation.

–Saturday: The many artifacts and furnishings of the Vigil need to be placed as early as possible, but decorations should be delayed—so that the space is bare for the liturgy of the hours or for preparatory rites. Better yet, it should not be decorated during the day at all! The *Ceremonial of Bishops* (#48) reminds many older sacristans of hectic Vigils long ago: The rubrics ban the use of flowers from "Ash Wednesday until the Gloria at the Easter Vigil." For centuries, a reverent procession of flower bearers and veil removers took place at the Gloria. Thus, the decorative tasks of Holy Saturday include the delivery of decorations, temporary placement to see how they will look, and then an immediate removal of them to some place where a procession of flower-bearers will form during the Vigil. For this procession, the flowers can be placed in clusters or zones so that the right pots end up in the planned positions. A rehearsal of procession leaders can take place as the flowers are delivered and set. Meanwhile the enshrined cross remains in its place of honor. One other image can be introduced into the still-stripped environment: an image of Christ in the tomb, of the descent into hell, or of the sorrowful Virgin Mary.

Holy Thursday: Mass of the Lord's Supper

PLACE FOR EUCHARISTIC ACTION

Seating:
hymnals or booklets

Open space:
chairs for those whose feet will be washed
pedestals for the holy oils (after opening procession)
containers for gifts for the poor (unless at entrance)

Altar:
covered with one cloth, unless this comes at preparation rite
gospel book with text marked, if used and not carried in procession
nearby: any candles, candlestands not carried in procession
nearby: stand for processional cross

Credence table(s), in order of usage:
robe stand or place for resting chasuble during foot washing
linen apron (gremial), if used
large pitcher of warm water, basin, towels for drying feet
basin with soap, pitcher of water, towel for hand washing
corporal
large cup (can be covered by pall and/or white veil)
purificator
book stand, if needed
water in small cruet, if not in procession of gifts
additional cups and purificators for the assembly (on tray)
additional patens for the assembly
pyxes for hosts consecrated for the sick, unless these are held by the ministers who will leave from Mass for this ministry
humeral veils
candles and holders for all ministers to carry in procession at end

Presider's chair:
sacramentary (after review in vesting room)
hymnal or booklet, if not carried in procession

Ministers' seats:
texts for concelebrants, if any
hymnals or booklets, if not carried in procession

Ambo:
lectionary with texts marked, if not carried in procession
psalm setting for cantor (unless carried there for this action)
general intercessions, if done here

Music stand (or secondary podium):
general intercessions, if done here

SACRISTY

charcoal lit in thurible, then put in vesting room

extra charcoal (and tongs, matches) for adding during Mass

second thurible with charcoal to be lit later in Mass

controls set for air, sound, lights

microphones put in place and turned on

VESTING ROOM

vesture (see page 120); chasuble, dalmatic of white

lavaliere microphones, if any

lectionary or gospel book with texts marked, if carried in procession

local texts (reception of the holy oils, dismissal of catechumens and elect, intercessions) inserted and other texts marked in sacramentary, for review prior to placement by chair

thurible, with lit charcoal

vessel of incense

processional cross

two or more candlesticks with lighted candles

holy oils, in their vessels (for opening procession)

ENTRANCE

Exterior:
bells ready for ringing during Gloria

Table with gifts:
bread for all at this Mass on one paten, more if needed

bread for all on Good Friday in large pyx, ciborium

wine for all in one vessel, more if needed

water in small cruet, if in procession

container for gifts for the poor, unless all in assembly bring their gifts up

Other:
collection baskets ready

booklets, bulletins or other handouts

candles and holders for all, if used for procession at end

BAPTISTRY (OR WHERE REPOSITORY OF OILS IS LOCATED)

repository open for reception of oils during introductory rites

CATECHUMENEON

opened and prepared, if catechumens are present

CHAPEL OF EUCHARISTIC RESERVATION

lamp removed

tabernacle empty, unveiled, with doors open (and key at hand)

a few decorations, unlit candles in place

Good Friday & Holy Saturday: Tenebrae
Office of Readings Combined with Morning Prayer

Over the centuries preceding Vatican II, Tenebrae was the paschal title for the Office of Readings ("Vigils" or "Matins") combined with Morning Prayer ("Lauds") during which candles were extinguished as morning came. In recent centuries, despite the early-morning images, this was sometimes moved to Wednesday night, a sort of prelude to the Triduum. The reformed rites call for a return of the original Tenebrae. The combined office calls for these requisites:

Place for assembly

Seating:
hymnals or booklets

Open space:
large candelabrum for tenebrae can be positioned and lit, if used (old customs called for the extinguishing of candles at each psalm, until only one was left)

Altar, if hours celebrated in eucharistic space:
bare, nothing on it or near it

Presider's chair:
ritual book (after review in vesting room)
hymnal or booklet

Ministers' seats:
hymnals or booklets
candle snuffer (if used)

Ambo:
copies of the liturgy of the hours with texts marked, or passages marked in bible (with passage from early Christian literature in separate book)
text of intercessions, if done here

Music stand (or secondary podium):
text of intercessions, if done here

Sacristy

controls set for air, sound, lights
microphones put in places and turned on

Vesting Room

albs; stole for deacon/priest (red on Friday, violet Saturday)
lavaliere microphones, if any
texts marked in liturgy of the hours book or in special volume prepared with proper texts in correct order, for review before placement at chair

Entrance

booklets, bulletins or other handouts

Good Friday: Celebration of the Lord's Passion

Place for Assembly

Seating:
hymnals or booklets

Open space:
space set for prostration of presider and others

place set for later placement of two candles and cross (for example, processional cross base or simple stand for larger cross)

Altar:
completely bare

processional cross and stand put away

Credence table:
altar cloth

corporal

plates for the communion of all

Presider's chair:
sacramentary (after review in vesting room)

hymnal or booklet

nearby: robe stand for chasuble (if removed for veneration); shoe horn (if needed) for replacing shoes (if removed for veneration)

Ministers' seats:

hymnals or booklets

Ambo:
lectionary with texts marked, if not carried in procession

psalm setting for cantor (unless carried there for this action)

books for singing the passion or reading in parts, if used (secondary lecterns for those taking parts in proclamation of passion, or reading desks added to large ambo area)

text for the introduction or announcement of each intercession (unless announced from chair or music stand)

Sacristy

controls set for air, sound, lights

microphones put in place and turned on

Vesting Room

vesture (see page 120); chasuble, dalmatic of red

lavaliere microphones, if any

lectionary with texts marked, if carried in procession

local texts (dismissal of catechumens and elect?) inserted and other texts marked in sacramentary, for review prior to placement by chair

Entrance

cross (veiled or not, depending on ritual option selected)
two candles, candlesticks (able to stand on floor by cross)
matches
collection baskets ready
booklets, bulletins or other handouts

Catechumeneon

opened and prepared, if catechumens and elect are present

Chapel of Eucharistic Reservation

one candle lit by tabernacle
key at tabernacle
humeral veil (white or red)
two candles, candlesticks, able to stand to side of altar
matches

Holy Saturday: Preparation Rites for the Elect

The *Rite of Christian Initiation of Adults* (#185ff) calls for preparation rites this day: song and greeting, reading the word of God and homily, and celebrating certain rites ("giving back" the creed and/or the rite of *ephphetha).* Another preparatory service might take place this day, if infant baptism will be part of the Vigil—the reception of infants with exorcism and anointing with the oil of catechumens *(Rite of Baptism for Children,* #28.1). A service combining these two preparations is possible, uniting in one assembly the prayers and intense expectation of many elect and parents, sponsors and catechists.

Catechumeneon or Other Place for Assembly

Seating:
hymnals or booklets

Open space:
stand with oil of catechumens, if infants received

Altar, if rites celebrated in eucharistic space:
bare, nothing on it or near it

Credence table, if infants received:
basin with lemon, pitcher of water, towel

Presider's chair:
ritual book (after review in vesting room)
hymnal or booklet

Ministers' seats:
hymnals or booklets

Ambo:
Bible or lectionary with texts marked
psalm setting for cantor, if psalm used

Sacristy

controls set for air, sound, lights
microphones—if necessary—put in place and turned on

Vesting Room

albs; violet stole for deacon, presbyter
lavaliere microphones, if any
texts marked or inserted in ritual book in correct order, for review before placing at chair

Entrance

space set for reception of infants, if this rite scheduled
booklets, bulletins or other handouts

Easter Vigil

PLACE FOR EUCHARISTIC ACTION

Open space:
dedication candles, pew candles in place; lit in service

Altar:
covered with one cloth, unless this comes at preparation rite
gospel book with text marked, if used (not carried in tonight)
nearby: two or more candles, candlestands in place; lit in service
nearby: processional cross in stand

Credence table:
large cup (can be covered by pall and/or white veil)
purificator
corporal
book stand, if used
water in small cruet, if not in procession of gifts
basin, pitcher of water, towel
additional cups and purificators for the assembly (on tray)
additional patens for the assembly
pyx or ciborium, if extra bread consecrated for the sick

Presider's chair:
hymnal or booklet

Ministers' seats:
texts for concelebrants, if any
hymnals or booklets

Ambo:
lectionary with texts marked (not carried in tonight)
stand for the Easter candle
text of Exsultet (in special book)
psalm settings for cantor (unless carried there each time)
general intercessions, if done here

Music stand (or secondary podium):
general intercessions, if done here

SACRISTY

unlit charcoal placed in thurible and taken to gathering place
extra charcoal (and tongs, matches) for adding during Mass
controls set for air, sound
lights off (panel marked for times and numbers of changes)
microphones put in place and turned on

Vesting Room

vesture (see page 120); cope or chasuble, dalmatic of white or gold

lavaliere microphones, if any

local texts—intercessions, introductions, dismissal of catechumens not being baptized tonight and ritual texts (initiation) inserted in sacramentary, or all texts placed in correct order in special presider's book, for review prior to placement by fire or carrying by assistant

robes for neophytes; areas set for their drying and vesting

towels, clothes and change of vesture for presider if entering the font to baptize by immersion (If cope is used for procession and the liturgy of the word, it is taken off before presider enters the font. Chasuble is then used after presider dries.)

Entrance

Exterior:

bells ready for ringing during Gloria

signs directing assembly to special gathering place

(see also "Other Gathering Place" below)

Table(s) with gifts:

flowers and other decorations to be brought in during the Gloria, set up in correct order

bread for all on one paten, more if needed

wine for all in one vessel, more if needed

water in small cruet, if in procession

Other:

collection baskets ready

booklets, bulletins or other handouts

fire extinguishers near ushers

Baptistry

font full and warm

chrism in vessel

baptismal candles

towels for neophytes

basin with pieces of lemon, pitcher of water, towel, if needed, vessel(s) to be filled from font, and sprinkler(s)

Catechumeneon

opened and prepared, if catechumens not being baptized are present

Chapel of Eucharistic Reservation

lamp in place, lit after communion if communion for sick added

key at tabernacle if eucharist for the sick will be added

Other Gathering Place

large fire (receptacle, fuel, matches); other lights out
candles, bobeches, hymnals or booklets for all
places set for assembly, presider and ministers
fire extinguishers nearby

On table near place for presider and ministers:
Easter candle (unless carried from vesting room)
thurible with unlit charcoal
vessel of incense, Easter scent
material for decoration of candle: incense grains, stylus
wooden taper or other means of lighting Easter candle from fire
flashlight for illuminating texts for the presider
sacramentary or other presider's book
tongs for lighting charcoal

Easter Sunday: "Baptismal" Evening Prayer (Paschal Vespers)

The Triduum is recalled and concluded by a joyous celebration of evening prayer late on Easter Sunday. In the spaces where the sacraments have so recently been celebrated with such fervor, we gather to share once more in Easter light, psalms and water. This list presumes that the liturgy begins by the candle in the main assembly space, moving to the baptistry during the psalmody. For references to this renewed custom, see the *Ceremonial of Bishops*, #371, the *General Instruction of the Liturgy of the Hours*, #213, and the official texts of the hours.

PLACE FOR EUCHARISTIC ACTION

Seating:
hymnals or booklets
candles and bobeches for all

Open space:
dedication and pew candles in place, lit in service

Altar:
altar may be covered with one cloth or bare
nearby: processional cross may be in place

Presider's chair:
presider's book (after review in vesting room)
hymnal or booklet
candle and bobeche

Ministers' seats:
hymnals or booklets
candles and bobeches

Ambo:
nearby: Easter candle still burning in stand
cantor's setting of thanksgiving for light
cantor's psalm settings (unless carried there for that action)

SACRISTY

controls set for air, sound
lights off for beginning (panel marked with which lights to be turned on)
microphones put in places and turned on
charcoal lit in thurible (for use in later procession to baptistry and at the gospel canticle)
vessel of incense, Easter scent

VESTING ROOM

vesture (see page 120); cope, dalmatic of white or gold
lavaliere microphones, if any
Bible or liturgy of hours with reading marked, for review before placing in baptistry

texts inserted (prayer over the blessed Easter water, solemn Easter blessing) and marked in liturgy of the hours, or all texts placed in correct order in special presider's book, for review before placing at chair

ENTRANCE

candles and bobeches, booklets, bulletins or other handouts

BAPTISTRY

another stand for Easter candle

stand for thurible and vessel of incense between uses

At a podium:

Bible or liturgy of the hours with passage marked

texts of intercessions

Easter Season

THE SEASON: The Roman Calendar takes great care to show the unity of the days from Easter Day through Pentecost. (Easter Day is, uniquely, part of two seasons—Triduum and Eastertime.) The season is one great feast, one "great Sunday." It is the time for joyfully incorporating neophytes in the eucharistic assembly, for singing Alleluia, for feeling the pull on us of the new Jerusalem. Within the 50 days, two special times provide heightened awareness of certain Easter realities. The initial octave highlights the wonders of initiation; the concluding days from the Ascension to Pentecost kindle the fire of the Spirit.

VESTURE: There should not be one set of vesture for Easter Sunday and then another for the rest of the season. Let the clothing itself say that these days are one unit of time and celebration. The red days provide exceptions: apostles, martyrs and, of course, Pentecost.

DECORATIONS: The best decorations are not just pleasing ornaments. They are the central symbols, the elements of our interaction providing beauty and focus to our assembly. Thus the principal decoration is neither flowers nor banner, but the large Easter candle that was praised at Easter, that was plunged into the font, that provides light for all the baptized, that ties all the future days of this year to the Easter mystery. Nothing should compete with or diminish it, especially by hiding or muting its verticality and brightness. It should be kept lit for every gathering this season, burning brightly even before people gather. Once the candle is lit on Easter Eve, it is never extinguished publicly. Other candles can be lit from it, a gracious gesture at the beginning of any liturgy.

The newly baptized and their sponsors should occupy special places in the assembly throughout the Easter Season. Perhaps special seats could be reserved for them near the candle and ambo. Our tradition calls for using, throughout the season, the water blessed at the Vigil. Parishes with fonts in separate places sometimes display a large bowl of water somewhere near the front of the church. (Too often this looks like a punch bowl and not a sacred vessel.) It would be far more sensible to keep attention fixed on the font, no matter where it is located. During the sprinkling rite, maintain some association with the font, even if that means drawing Easter water from it and then carrying this water into the assembly for the prayer of thanksgiving over the water.

In an interesting parallel, synagogues follow a long tradition of using lilies for their 50-day celebration. Three other traditions of the Festival of Weeks may inspire Christian decorators. Texts highlight the apple tree with its beautiful blossoms (the tree is said to bear fruit 50 days after it blossoms); branches, boughs and greens are placed about the *bema* (ambo); and Torah scrolls are decorated with roses. Whatever patterns of decor are set on Easter Day, they should be followed with fresh blossoms throughout the 50 days.

With springtime wreaths on the church doors, with banners and bunting merrily waving, we announce our joy to the world. A chalk drawing of the Exodus or of the Jonah story on the front plaza will not soon be forgotten. This sidewalk art need not be framed in a side area between two shrubs. It might well spread over the entire parking lot!

Ordinary Time

ORDINAL TIME: Ordinary Time is not so much "ordinary" in the sense of undistinguished, but "ordinal" or counted time. It is simply the way that the church organizes liturgical texts, assigning each Sunday a number, counting each week one after the other. These 225 or so days do not form a season in the same way as do the 43 or so in Advent-Christmas, or the 96 in Lent-Triduum-Easter. They form the regular flow of the year, so that the five principal seasons stand out in their exceptional characteristics.

These weeks fill the intervals from the day after the feast of the Baptism of the Lord until the day before Ash Wednesday, and then from the day after Pentecost until the eve of Advent. As the seasons of nature outside the church change from winter to summer and fall, the changing colors and flowers may play a part in decorations. These are far less important, though, than attention to Sunday and the marking of varied solemnities and feasts.

VESTURE: The portion of Ordinary Time in winter reminds us, in most climates, of the need for coat rooms, even temporary areas for the coldest months (see page 86). The liturgical color for presiders on most Sundays is green, but on several Sundays solemnities eclipse the numbered day and call for white (or gold). Some planners prefer to see the green chasubles and dalmatics shift from darker to lighter shades as the weather warms, perhaps to correlate with the month's flowers. There are no exact regulations here, but we always should be on guard against making the robed persons into pieces of tableau environment.

DECORATIONS: This time between seasons lets us experience the place for worship unembellished, thus opening our eyes to the fixed elements of the place, teaching us to appreciate its inherent dignity. When the seasons to decorate arrive, this appreciation will make us more sensitive to the space and perhaps less apt to obscure the liturgical furnishings. Even in the simplicity of Ordinary Time, some flowers or other elements of color might be introduced, but they should not be "theme art" to display the given Sunday's scriptures. This inevitably leads to something too didactic, a symbol that needs to be explained, or (far worse) the impression that the altar or ambo area is a diorama instead of a place of action.

In the place where the eucharist is celebrated or in other parts of the church buildings, individual feasts and particular portions of Ordinary Time can be highlighted by temporary decor. For example: candles or flowers before images of saints on their feasts, special displays of volunteer opportunities in the entrance halls before Lent and Advent, the placement of a special book for inscribing the names of the dead near the baptistry in November.

On the exterior walls, or on surrounding grounds, the changing climate might suggest decorations. Especially recommended for any time of the year are those exterior embellishments that involve the participation of many members: ice sculptures and snow saints where winter reigns, doorways draped with festive colors for the dedication anniversary, gardens for flowers or vegetables. These should never become too contrived.

February 2, Presentation of the Lord: Blessing of Candles & Mass

The first form of the procession given in the sacramentary should be used in almost every circumstance, even when the feast falls on Sunday.

PLACE FOR EUCHARISTIC ACTION

Seating:
hymnals or booklets, unless distributed in other gathering area

Open space:
dedication and pew candles lit

Altar:
covered with one cloth, unless this comes at preparation rite
gospel book with text marked, if used and not carried in procession
nearby: any candles, candlestands not carried in procession
nearby: stand for processional cross

Credence table:
large cup (can be covered by pall and/or white veil)
purificator
corporal
book stand, if used
water in small cruet, if not in procession of gifts
basin, pitcher of water, towel
any bread, wine, not in procession of gifts
additional cups and purificators for the assembly (on tray)
additional patens for the assembly
pyx or ciborium, if extra bread consecrated for the sick

Presider's chair:
nearby (on robe stand?): white chasuble, if cope worn at start
hymnal or booklet, if not carried in procession

Ministers' seats:
texts for concelebrants, if any
hymnals or booklets, if not carried in procession

Ambo:
lectionary with texts marked, if not carried in procession
psalm setting for cantor (unless carried there for this action)
general intercessions, if done here

Music stand (or secondary podium):
general intercessions, if done here

SACRISTY

charcoal lit in thurible, then put in vesting room
extra charcoal (and tongs, matches) for adding during Mass

controls set for air, sound

lights turned off until after assembly's candles extinguished

microphones put in place and turned on

VESTING ROOM

vesture (see page 120); cope or chasuble, dalmatic of white

lavaliere microphones, if any

lectionary or gospel book with texts marked, if carried in procession

local texts inserted (dismissal of catechumens, intercessions) and other texts marked in the sacramentary, for review prior to placement in gathering area

thurible, with lit charcoal

vessel of incense

processional cross

two or more candlesticks with lighted candles

ENTRANCE

Exterior:
signs directing assembly to special gathering place

Table with gifts:
bread for all on one paten, more if needed, if in procession

wine for all in one vessel, more if needed, if in procession

water in small cruet, if in procession

Other:
collection baskets ready, if used

booklets, bulletins or other handouts

CATECHUMENEON

opened and prepared, if catechumens present

CHAPEL OF EUCHARISTIC RESERVATION

lamp lit

key at tabernacle if eucharist for the sick will be added

OTHER GATHERING PLACE

On table (unless held by ministers):
vessel of water and sprinkler

sacramentary

candles (as large as possible) for all, with bobeches

matches, or lit candle(s) from which to draw flame

Other:
hymnals or booklets for all

space reserved for instrumentalists and musical leaders

space reserved for presider and other ministers

February 3, Memorial of Saint Blase: Blessing of Throats in a Liturgy of the Word

Texts for the blessing of throats are found in chapter 51 of the *Book of Blessings*. This traditional sign of the struggle against illness can take place at Mass, at the liturgy of the hours, or in a liturgy of the word. This set-up list is for the last of these options, a fine liturgy led by a priest, a deacon, or a lay minister.

PLACE OF ASSEMBLY

Seating:
hymnals or booklets

Open area:
spaces designated for act of blessing

Altar, if blessing celebrated in eucharistic space:
altar cloth may be removed
candles can be lit in the area
stand with processional cross in place

Credence table:
two candles for each minister of blessing

Presider's chair:
Book of Blessings (after review in vesting room)
hymnal or booklet, if not carried in procession

Ministers' seats:
hymnals or booklets, if not carried in procession

Ambo:
Bible or *Book of Blessings,* with reading marked
psalm setting for cantor (unless carried there for this action)
intercessions on sheet or marked at #1645 of *Book of Blessings,* if done here

Music stand (or secondary podium):
intercessions on sheet or marked at #1645 of *Book of Blessings,* if done here

SACRISTY

controls set for air, sound, lights
microphones put in place and turned on

VESTING ROOM

vesture (see page 120); cope of red (or white) possible for presider
lavaliere microphones, if any
Book of Blessings for review prior to placement by chair

ENTRANCE

booklets, bulletins or other handouts

Solemnity of the Body and Blood of Christ: Mass and Procession

PLACE FOR EUCHARISTIC ACTION

Seating:
hymnals or booklets
candles and bobeches for all, if carried in procession and if not handed out upon arrival

Open space:
dedication candles, pew candles may be lighted

Altar:
covered with one cloth, unless this comes at preparation rite
gospel book with text marked, if used and not carried in procession
nearby: any candles, candlestands not carried in procession
nearby: stand for processional cross

Credence table:
vessel of water, when rite of sprinkling occurs
large cup (can be covered by pall and/or white veil)
purificator
corporal
book stand, if used
water in a small cruet, if not in procession of gifts
basin, pitcher of water, towel
any bread, wine, not in procession of gifts
additional cups and purificators for the assembly (on tray)
additional patens for the assembly
pyx or ciborium, if extra bread consecrated for the sick
monstrance and lunette (glass pyx in shape of host)
humeral veil
candles and bobeches for all ministers
"torches" or mounted candles for accompanying the eucharist

Presider's chair:
sacramentary (after review in vesting room)
hymnal or booklet, if not carried in procession
nearby (on robe stand): white or gold cope, if used

Ministers' seats:
texts for concelebrants, if any
hymnals or booklets, if not carried in procession
nearby: white copes for additional priests participating in procession, if any

Ambo:
lectionary with texts marked, if not carried in procession
psalm setting for cantor (unless carried there for this action)
general intercessions, if done here

Music stand (or secondary podium):
general intercessions, if done here

Sacristy

charcoal lit in thurible, then placed in vesting room
extra charcoal (and tongs, matches) for adding during Mass
second thurible prepared for closing procession
controls set for air, sound, lights
microphones put in place and turned on
portable canopy for use in procession, if customary

Vesting Room

vesture (see page 120); chasuble, dalmatic of white or gold
lavaliere microphones, if any
lectionary or gospel book with texts marked, if carried in procession
local texts (dismissal of catechumens, intercessions) inserted and other texts marked in sacramentary, for review prior to placement by chair
thurible, with lit charcoal
vessel of incense
processional cross
two or more candlesticks with lighted candles

Entrance

Exterior:
arrangements made for procession: permit for use of streets or sidewalks, traffic guards, special parking regulations, etc.

Table with gifts:
bread for all on one paten, more if needed, including host shaped to fit in lunette
wine for all in one vessel, more if needed
water in small cruet, if in procession

Other:
collection baskets ready
candles and bobeches, booklets, bulletins or other handouts

Catechumeneon

opened and prepared, if catechumens are present

Chapel of Eucharistic Reservation

lamp lit
key at tabernacle if eucharist for the sick will be added

Other Gathering Place

(destination of procession after communion: neighboring church, cemetery chapel, parish hall)
space for the processions' participants
altar covered, ready to receive monstrance
text of prayer before eucharistic benediction
key available at tabernacle for receiving the lunette

November 2: Mass and Parish Visitation of a Cemetery

Cemeteries are privileged places for liturgical prayer (cf. page 91). The *Book of Blessings* has an order for a liturgical visit to a nearby cemetery (chapter 57). This list is for the fullest form: Mass in church, procession, and Order for Visiting a Cemetery.

PLACE FOR EUCHARISTIC ACTION

Seating:
hymnals or booklets

Altar:
covered with one cloth, unless this comes at preparation rite
gospel book with text marked, if used and not carried in procession
nearby: any candles, candlestands not carried in procession
nearby: stand for processional cross

Credence table:
large cup (can be covered by pall and/or white veil)
purificator
corporal
book stand, if used
water in small cruet, if not in procession of gifts
basin, pitcher of water, towel
any bread, wine, not in procession of gifts
additional cups and purificators for the assembly (on tray)
additional patens for the assembly
pyx or ciborium, if extra bread consecrated for the sick

Presider's chair:
sacramentary (after review in vesting room)
hymnal or booklet, if not carried in procession

Ministers' seats:
texts for concelebrants, if any
hymnals or booklets, if not carried in procession

Ambo:
lectionary with texts marked, if not carried in procession
psalm setting for cantor (unless carried there for this action)
general intercessions, if done here

Music stand (or secondary podium):
general intercessions, if done here

SACRISTY

charcoal in thurible lit, then put in vesting room
extra charcoal (and tongs, matches) for adding during Mass
controls set for air, sound, lights
microphones put in place and turned on

Vesting Room

vesture (see page 120); chasuble, dalmatic of white, violet or black

lavaliere microphones, if any

lectionary or gospel book with texts marked, if carried in procession

local texts (intercessions) inserted and other texts marked in sacramentary, for review prior to placement by chair

thurible, with lit charcoal

vessel of incense

processional cross

two or more candlesticks with lighted candles

Entrance

Exterior:
arrangements made for procession: permit for use of street, traffic guards, special parking regulations.

Table with gifts:
bread for all on one paten, more if needed, if in procession

wine for all in one vessel, more if needed, if in procession

water in small cruet, if in procession

Other:
booklets, bulletins or other handouts

Baptistry

book, on standing desk or stand, for parish members to inscribe the names of the deceased (in place from the eve of All Saints to the day before Advent)—can be located near lit Easter candle in baptistry or elsewhere

pens for inscriptions

Chapel of Eucharistic Reservation

lamp lit

key at tabernacle if eucharist for the sick will be added

Cemetery

scripture text marked in *Book of Blessings* or funeral rite or Bible

psalm setting and litany text for cantor

Book of Blessings, with texts marked

vessel of baptismal water and sprinkler

thurible with lit coals and vessel of incense (carried from Mass)

additional booklets for those who join only at cemetery

area designated for presider, musical leaders, other ministers (perhaps near cross at center or near entrance of cemetery)

Local Solemnities: Title of Parish, Anniversary of Dedication

THE DAYS: These wonderful celebrations help us feel more intensely these fundamental realities: that the local community, the people here gathered, are the holy people of God; that these buildings built by our ancestors and ourselves are privileged places of sacred mysteries; that our cherished patrons and parish names help to form us in the image of Christ. We are incomplete communities if we just adhere to the universal calendar, as wondrous as that might be. We need these local days to see our own particular living in sacramental unity.

The anniversary of dedication is celebrated on the actual date only by those communities, like monasteries, that can spend this together as a full solemnity. Most, if not all, parishes should observe the anniversary on the preceding Sunday (if this is a Sunday in Ordinary Time) or on the Sunday before All Saints. This latter day, the observed dedication anniversary for all churches whose buildings were dedicated in the liturgical seasons (any time outside Ordinary Time), shows the profound unity of the holy ones on earth and all the saints in heaven.

The solemnity of the title (name or patron) of the parish takes place in closer proximity to the date of the feast, because we celebrate this date in unity with many other churches. The actual date is more than likely related to the death date (birthday into heaven) of the saint or the dedication of an early church in honor of this title. If in Ordinary Time, parishes should move the observance to the previous Sunday.

DECORATIONS: As always, the best decorations arise from or are deeply related to the actual rites being celebrated. Events unfolding on the local feast should be reviewed when considering the best decorations. An outdoor procession with an image of the patronal saint might suggest the strewing of the path with seasonal flowers. A procession of all to the font for a signing with baptismal water might indicate the hanging of wonderful garlands over the entrance area of the baptistry. A candlelight vigil would require enough candles. The intense interest of children—after preparing a skit on the history of the parish, or completing a catechetical unit on the life of the saint—also could be expressed by their work on a large, temporary mural celebrating local faith. In addition to events, the images presented by the dedication anniversary texts and by the title or saint can help form ideas for the decor.

These celebrations, especially the anniversary of dedication, should motivate us to look at the entire building. We need more than sanctuary flowers and an historical diorama near the entranceway. Instead, we might concentrate on the walls and corners, on the outlines of the building itself. Dedication candles (page 39) should certainly be lit at all local solemnities, for they provide the embrace of Christ's light for the whole people. The four corners of the assembly hall (and not the central furnishings) might be marked by brilliant arrangements of flowers.

A rediscovery of patronal or titular days should motivate a parish to review its iconography. Does the name of the parish find expression in a suitable image? Can one be commissioned? Can one owned by the parish be brought out of storage? Is it properly located to attract veneration but not to interfere with the celebration of the sacred mysteries?

Decorations should be provided outdoors—around doorways, to the outline of the structure or to the tower. Everyone who passes it should know that this parish is celebrating. Luminarias (farolitos) might surround any outdoor image of the title at ground level.

34◆ Checklists for Other Rites

Relationship to the Liturgical Year

Celebrations of the Mass and the hours are, by far, the most frequent actions prepared for by sacristans. Our liturgical heritage, however, provides us with many other rites to celebrate passages in human life, to maintain and deepen our life in Christ. The various lists in this section highlight the requisites for some of the most important rituals.

These other rites—initiation, marriage, holy orders, the care of the sick, blessings and funerals—often occur in the context of a eucharistic celebration. Whether in or outside of Mass, they all should reflect our annual passage through seasons. To cite but two examples, a funeral in Advent can draw on the rich texts of Isaiah and the expectation of the final coming. Celebrations of marriage in the Easter Season can use the texts about the wedding feast of the Lamb.

On some days, the importance of the festival has brought about rules forbidding or restraining certain rites. These are usually listed in the ordo, and can be ascertained from a careful study of the general introduction printed at the start of each rite. Days for the rites related to the catechumenate and adult initiation are generally set by the rite itself. On certain days, funerals are restricted to rites outside of Mass (holy days of obligation, Holy Thursday and the Easter Triduum, Sundays of Advent, Lent and the Easter Season). On certain days, marriage rites are forbidden (for example, Holy Saturday); on several others the texts of sacramentary and lectionary must be from the seasonal day (for example, Pentecost). Many rites have particular texts identified as "Easter Season"; many other texts of scripture or prayers are easily related to particular seasons (for example, Isaiah in Advent, Revelation in Easter). These can be identified by reviewing the texts on surrounding days beside those in the ritual book.

In such ways, all of the rites in a parish show our tradition's enormous respect for seasons and solemnities. Our worship is not just a random grouping of nice texts. It is a liturgy of repeated days and seasons and rites and smells and sounds, so that its rhythm can become ours. In every way possible, we should collaborate with other planners so that decorations and texts, music and vestments, altar cloths and volunteer schedules work for the full experience of the liturgical year.

Using the Checklists

A general list for the liturgy of the hours, especially morning prayer and evening prayer, is given first. These actions should be part of every parish's life, the veritable breathing of the body. Their rare observance is a matter of considerable concern. This is followed by several lists for actions found in the *Roman Ritual.* (See page 103 for a list of all the ritual books grouped under the *Roman Ritual.*) Finally, there are checklists for some of the liturgies at which a bishop presides. The events normally linked to a particular day in the liturgical year are found in the lists of the previous chapter, for example initiation of adults at the Easter Vigil.

Quite obviously, these are general charts, not local lists. A given celebration of evening prayer can involve 10 or 1,000 persons, with grand ceremonial or minimal action. The lists here presume the fuller forms of the rites, and simpler forms will simply mean the omission of certain elements from the lists (for example, incense). Local plans and customs, the particular circumstances of each rite, will always call for adaptations. The lists here are meant as starters. Local lists should be prepared with presiders and planners, long before the day of celebration.

Liturgy of the Hours

PLACE OF ASSEMBLY

Seating:
hymnals or booklets, with all appropriate texts for assembly

flexible seating best arranged with assembly in facing rows

(at evening prayer, with full service of light: candles, bobeches for all)

Open space:
at solemn evening prayer, with a service of light, especially on Sundays: the Easter candle may be positioned so that all may light their candles from it; or evening prayer could be celebrated in the baptistry itself; or other candles may provide the light if the Easter candle remains in the baptistry and the assembly is elsewhere. In Advent, the candles of the wreath provide light

Altar, if hours celebrated in eucharistic space:
the altar cloth may be removed

nearby: processional cross may be in place, if not in procession

Presider's chair:
presider's book (after review in vesting room)

hymnal or booklet

at evening prayer with full service of light: candle, bobeche

Ministers' seats:
hymnals or booklets

at evening prayer with full service of light: candles, bobeches

Ambo:
Bible or liturgy of the hours with reading(s) marked

cantor's book with psalms (unless carried there for this action)

text of intercessions, if done here

Music stand (or secondary podium):
text of intercessions, if done here

SACRISTY

charcoal lit in thurible, then placed in vesting room

extra charcoal (and tongs, matches), if more to be added later; controls set for air, sound, lights

lights off, if evening prayer begins with service of light

microphones—if necessary—put in places and turned on

VESTING ROOM

albs for ministers; stole if presider is ordained; feasts: cope/dalmatic optional

lavaliere microphones, if any

texts marked in liturgy of the hours or inserted in presider's book, for review prior to placement by chair

thurible, with lit charcoal
vessel of incense, seasonal scent
(at solemn celebrations: processional cross)
(at solemn celebrations: two candles, candlesticks)

Entrance

booklets, bulletins or other handouts
(at evening prayer with full service of light: candles, bobeches for all, if not placed in seats)

Rite of Acceptance into the Order of Catechumens

This list presents the general requisites for this rite when it is celebrated at the parish's Sunday gathering for eucharist. This rite may also be combined with the rite of welcoming baptized but previously uncatechized adults.

Place for Eucharistic Action

Seating:
hymnals or booklets, unless in other gathering place

Open space:
solemnities outside Lent: dedication candles, pew candles lit

Altar:
gospel book on altar, if used (rite calls for lectionary to be carried in procession)
covered with one cloth, unless this comes at preparation rite
nearby: any candles, candlestands not carried in procession
nearby: stand for processional cross

Credence table:
Bibles or books of gospels for new catechumens (and candidates)
large cup (can be covered by pall and/or white veil)
purificator
corporal
book stand, if needed
water in a small cruet, if not in procession of gifts
basin, pitcher of water, towel
any bread, wine, not in procession of gifts
additional cups and purificators for the assembly (on tray)
additional patens for the assembly
pyx or ciborium, if extra bread consecrated for the sick

Presider's chair
nearby, on robe stand: chasuble if cope worn at start
hymnal or booklet, if not carried in procession

Ministers' seats:
texts for concelebrants, if any
hymnals or booklets, if not carried in procession

Ambo:
psalm setting for cantor (unless carried there for this action)
text of intercessions for the catechumens (and the candidates), if done here
general intercessions, if done here

Music stand (or secondary podium):
text of intercessions for the catechumens (and candidates), if done here
general intercessions, if done here

Sacristy

charcoal lit in thurible, then put in vesting room
extra charcoal (and tongs, matches) for adding during Mass
controls set for air, sound, lights
microphones put in places and turned on

Vesting Room

vesture (see page 120); cope or chasuble, dalmatic of day's color
lavaliere microphones, if any
lectionary with texts marked, for carrying in procession
texts from the rite of acceptance or from the combined rite of acceptance/welcome, and local texts (general intercessions) inserted and other texts marked in sacramentary; or all texts placed in order in special presider's book—for review prior to placement at gathering area
thurible, with lit charcoal
vessel of incense, seasonal scent
processional cross
two or more candlesticks with lighted candles

Entrance

Exterior:
signs indicating area for initial gathering

Table with gifts:
bread for all on one paten, more if needed
wine for all in one vessel, more if needed
water in small cruet, if in procession

Other:
collection baskets ready
programs, bulletins or other handouts

Catechumeneon

opened and prepared

Chapel of Eucharistic Reservation

lamp lit
key at tabernacle if eucharist for the sick will be added

Other Gathering Place

Outside the church, in the entrance hall or elsewhere:
sacramentary with texts inserted, or ritual book, or special presider's book, after review in vesting room
hymnals for entire assembly, unless all will first gather in place of eucharistic assembly and then go in procession with hymnals to this gathering area
space set for candidates and sponsors
space set for instrumentalists and other leaders of music
space set for presider and other ministers

Rite of Baptism for Several Children

This list is designed for a Sunday afternoon celebration of the baptismal liturgy apart from Mass. This rite is for children younger than "catechetical age." (Those older take part in the stages of catechumenate described in the *Rite of Christian Initiation of Adults.)* This rite may also be celebrated at the parish's gathering for Sunday eucharist, with ritual adaptations explained at #29 of the rite.

PLACE FOR EUCHARISTIC ACTION

Seating:
arranged as close to ambo as circumstances allow
hymnals or booklets

Altar:
altar cloth may be removed
nearby: processional cross may be in place

Presider's chair:
hymnal or booklet, if not carried in procession

Ministers' seats:
hymnals or booklets, if not carried in procession

Ambo:
ritual book, lectionary, or Bible with texts marked
psalm settings for cantor (unless carried there for this action)
nearby: stand with vessel of oil of catechumens, if used
text of intercessions, if done here

Music stand (or secondary podium):
text of intercessions, if done here

SACRISTY

controls set for air, sound, lights
microphones, if necessary, put in place and turned on

VESTING ROOM

vesture (see page 120); cope, dalmatic of white or of day's color
lavaliere microphones, if any
local texts inserted (names of children for the invocation of saints) and other texts marked in *Rite of Baptism for Children,* for review prior to placement by entranceway

ENTRANCE

space set for parents, godparents, children
space set for instrumentalists and other leaders of music
space set for presider and other ministers
space set for rest of assembly
hymnals or booklets for all

table for checking names and detailed information

ritual book for presider (unless carried there)

BAPTISTRY

font full of warm water

Easter candle lit

spaces set for parents, sponsors, children, instrumentalists, other leaders of music, presider, other ministers

table or other place set for drying and vesting (in christening clothes) of infants after immersion baptism

On other table:

shell for pouring, if used

towels

baptismal candles

candlelighter for passing light from Easter candle

vessel of chrism (unless in nearby repository)

CATECHUMENEON

provisions for the care of infants/children (rite #14, 43)

DEVOTIONAL AREAS

Marian shrine lit, if custom calls for bringing infants there

Reception of Baptized Christians into the Full Communion of the Catholic Church

This rite, found at Part II:5 of the *Rite of Christian Initiation of Adults,* is usually celebrated at Mass. When it is part of the Easter Vigil, see the checklist on page 215. On other days, at a regularly scheduled parish Mass or at another gathering for the eucharist, the following list can be used.

Place for Eucharistic Action

Open space:

solemnities outside Lent: dedication candles, pew candles lit

place designated for the act of reception (and confirmation)

pedestal or stand with vessel of chrism (if confirmation included in rite)

Seating:

hymnals or booklets

designated seating for those to be received and their sponsors, if reserved

Altar:

gospel book on altar, if used and not carried in procession

covered with one cloth, unless this comes at preparation rite

nearby: any candles, candlestands not carried in procession

nearby: stand for processional cross

Credence table:

smaller vessel from which chrism can be administered (if confirmation included in rite)

basin, pitcher of water, towel (with lemon pieces if confirmation included in rite)

large cup (can be covered by pall and/or white veil)

purificator

corporal

book stand, if necessary

water in small cruet, if not in procession of gifts

any bread, wine, not in procession of gifts

additional cups and purificators for the assembly (on tray)

additional patens for the assembly

pyx or ciborium, if extra hosts consecrated for the sick

Presider's chair

sacramentary, after review in vesting room

ritual book, after review in vesting room, unless copies of these texts inserted in sacramentary

hymnal or booklet, if not carried in procession

Ministers' seating:

texts for concelebrants, if any

hymnals or booklets, if not carried in procession

Ambo:

lectionary with texts marked, if not carried in procession
psalm setting for cantor (unless carried there for this action)
general intercessions, if done here

Music stand (or secondary podium):
general intercessions, if done here

SACRISTY

charcoal lit in thurible, then put in vesting room
extra charcoal (and tongs, matches) for adding during Mass
controls set for air, sound, lights
microphones put in place and turned on

VESTING ROOM

vesture as on page 120; chasuble, dalmatic of day's color
lavaliere microphones, if any
gospel book or lectionary with texts marked, for carrying in procession
texts from the rite of reception and local texts inserted and other texts marked in sacramentary; or all texts placed in order in special presider's book; or both sacramentary and ritual book marked, for review prior to placement at presider's chair
thurible, with lit charcoal
vessel of incense, seasonal scent
processional cross
two or more candlesticks with lighted candles

ENTRANCE

Table with gifts:
bread for all on one paten, more if needed
wine for all in one vessel, more if needed
water in small cruet, if in procession

Other:
collection baskets ready
programs, bulletins or other handouts

CATECHUMENEON

opened and prepared, if catechumens present

CHAPEL OF EUCHARISTIC RESERVATION

lamp lit
key at tabernacle, if eucharist for the sick will be added

Funerals: Vigil for the Deceased with Reception at the Church

PLACE OF VIGIL

Place for eucharistic action, catechumeneon, baptistry or other chapel

Open space:
space arranged for placement of casket on casket stand, on bed of flowers or herbs, or on floor in place of honor

Easter candle or other candles placed nearby

Seating:
for presider, ministers, assembly

hymnals or booklets

SPACE FOR LEADERS OF MUSIC

Altar, if vigil in eucharistic space:
altar cloth may be removed

nearby: processional cross may be in place

Ambo (or other lectern, if vigil not in main assembly place):
ritual book, Bible, or lectionary with texts marked

psalm setting for cantor (unless carried there for this action)

text of litany/intercessions, if done here

Music stand (or secondary podium):
text of litany/intercessions, if done here

SACRISTY

controls set for air, sound, lights

microphones, if necessary, put in place and turned on

VESTING ROOM

albs; cope (white, violet, black), if used; stole for deacon or presbyter (white, violet or black)

lavaliere microphones, if any

local texts inserted and other texts marked in *Order of Christian Funerals* (#82–97), for review prior to placement by entry (unless carried there)

ENTRANCE

hymnals or booklets for all

area for presider, ministers, assembly to receive body

vessel with baptismal water, sprinkler

casket pall, if casket closed

symbol of Christian life—book of gospels, Bible, cross—if used

ritual book for presider (unless carried there)

Funerals: Funeral Mass with Reception of the Body

PLACE FOR EUCHARISTIC ACTION

Seating:
hymnals or booklets, unless distributed at entrance

Open space:
space arranged for placement of casket on casket stand, on bed of flowers or herbs, or on floor in place of honor
Easter candle or other candles placed nearby

Altar:
covered with one cloth, unless this comes at preparation rite
nearby: any candles, candlestands not carried in procession
nearby: stand for processional cross

Credence table:
large cup (can be covered by pall and/or white veil)
purificator
corporal
sacramentary, after review in vesting room
book stand, if used
water in small cruet, if not in procession of gifts
basin, pitcher of water, towel
any bread, wine, not in procession of gifts
additional cups and purificators for the assembly (on tray)
additional patens for the assembly
pyx or ciborium, if extra bread consecrated for the sick

Presider's chair:
hymnal or booklet, if not carried in procession

Ministers' seats:
texts for concelebrants, if any
hymnals or booklets, if not carried in procession

Ambo:
lectionary with texts marked, if not carried in procession
psalm setting for cantor (unless carried there for this action)
ritual book, or other sheet with general intercessions, if done here

Music stand (or secondary podium):
ritual book, or other sheet with general intercessions, if done here

SACRISTY

charcoal lit in thurible, then placed in vesting room
extra charcoal (and tongs, matches) for adding during Mass
controls set for air, sound, lights
microphones, if necessary, put in place and turned on

Vesting Room

- vesture (see page 120); chasuble, dalmatic of white, violet or black
- lavaliere microphones, if any
- lectionary or gospel book with texts marked, if carried in procession
- texts marked in sacramentary, for review prior to placement on credence table
- local texts inserted and other texts marked in *Order of Christian Funerals,* before placement by entrance (unless carried there)
- thurible, with lit charcoal
- vessel of incense
- processional cross
- two or more candlesticks with lighted candles

Entrance

- hymnals or booklets for all
- area for presider, ministers, assembly to receive body
- vessel with baptismal water, sprinkler
- casket pall, if used
- symbol of Christian life—book of gospels, Bible, cross—if used
- ritual book for presider (unless carried there)

Table with gifts:

- bread for all on one paten, more if needed, if in procession
- wine for all in one vessel, more if needed, if in procession
- water in small cruet, if in procession

Chapel of Eucharistic Reservation

- lamp lit
- key at tabernacle, if eucharist for the sick will be added

Cemetery

- processional route cleared to parish cemetery
- spaces set at grave site for assembly
- burial plot prepared for committal
- shovels or other equipment for act of committal (rite calls for this to occur during or at conclusion of rite)
- flowers or other materials for gesture of leave-taking
- hymnals or booklets, if not brought by assembly from church
- ritual book for presider, unless carried from church
- ritual book or other sheet with intercessions, for assistant

Funerals: Rite of Committal

It is most highly recommended that this take place at the actual site of burial, so that the action of committal can occur as part of the service.

By the Burial Site

- spaces set for assembly
- burial plot opened, prepared for committal
- shovels or other equipment for act of committal (rite calls for this to occur during or at conclusion of rite)
- flowers or other materials for gesture of leave-taking
- hymnals or booklets, if not brought by assembly from church
- ritual book for presider, unless carried from church
- ritual book or other sheet with intercessions, for assistant

Nearby

- vesture, if used (alb for any minister; alb and stole, with optional cope for deacon or priest—white, violet or black)

Rite of Marriage: Celebration of Marriage during Mass

PLACE FOR EUCHARISTIC ACTION

Seating for assembly:
hymnals or booklets
carpet/runner for aisle installed, if used

Open space:
pew candles lighted if customary
space set for exchange of consent and rings
seating and hymnals or booklets for bride, groom, witnesses (without turning their backs to assembly, perhaps just to one side or another, or near presider's chair; not necessarily a few feet in front of altar, since the ambo may not be visible from there); kneelers provided only if customary for all to kneel at eucharistic prayer
stand/pedestal with dish holding rings
nearby (or on credence): vessel of baptismal water, sprinkler

Altar:
covered with one cloth, unless this comes at preparation rite
gospel book, if used and not carried in procession
nearby: any candles, candlestands not carried in procession
nearby: stand for processional cross

Credence table:
vessel of baptismal water and sprinkler
large cup (can be covered by pall and/or white veil)
purificator
corporal
book stand, if used
water in small cruet, if not in procession of gifts
basin, pitcher of water, towel
any bread, wine, not in procession of gifts
additional cups and purificators for the assembly (on tray)
additional patens for the assembly
pyx or ciborium, if extra bread consecrated for the sick

Presider's chair:
sacramentary, after review in vesting room
hymnal or booklet, if not carried in procession

Ministers' seats:
texts for concelebrants, if any
hymnals or booklets, if not carried in procession

Ambo:
lectionary with texts marked, if not carried in procession
psalm setting for cantor (unless carried there for this action)
general intercessions, if done here

Music stand (or secondary podium):
general intercessions, if done here

SACRISTY

charcoal lit in thurible, then put in vesting room
extra charcoal (and tongs, matches) for adding during Mass
controls set for air, sound, light
microphones put in places and turned on

VESTING ROOM

vesture (see page 120); chasuble, dalmatic of white or day's color
lavaliere microphones, if any
sheet from planning meeting with list of selected texts
lectionary or gospel book with texts marked, if carried in procession
local texts (intercessions) inserted and other texts marked in sacramentary, for review prior to placement by chair
local texts (words of welcome) inserted and other texts marked in *Rite of Marriage,* for review before placing at entrance
thurible, with lit charcoal
vessel of incense
processional cross
two or more candlesticks with lighted candles

ENTRANCE

space set for rite of welcome (bride, groom, parents, witnesses, some or all of assembly)
space set for presider, other ministers (crossbearer, candlebearers, incensebearer)
ritual book for presider (unless carried there)
hymnals or booklets for all

Table with gifts:
bread for all on one paten, more if needed, if in procession
wine for all in one vessel, more if needed, if in procession
water in small cruet, if in procession

CHAPEL OF EUCHARISTIC RESERVATION

lamp lit
key at tabernacle, if eucharist for the sick will be added

Rite of Marriage: Celebration of Marriage outside Mass

PLACE OF ASSEMBLY

Place for eucharistic action, or other chapel

Seating:
hymnals or booklets
carpet/runner for aisle installed, if used

Open space:
pew candles lighted if customary
space set for exchange of consent and rings
seating and hymnals or booklets for bride, groom, witnesses (without turning their backs to assembly, perhaps just to one side or another, or near presider's chair; not necessarily a few feet in front of altar, since the ambo may not be visible from there); kneelers unnecessary
stand/pedestal with dish holding rings
nearby: vessel of baptismal water, sprinkler

Altar, if rite celebrated in eucharistic space:
altar cloth may be removed
gospel book with text marked, if used and not carried in procession
nearby: processional cross may be in place, if not in procession

Presider's chair:
hymnal or booklet, if not carried in procession

Ministers' seats:
hymnals or booklets, if not carried in procession

Ambo:
lectionary with texts marked, if not carried in procession
psalm setting for cantor (unless carried there for this action)
general intercessions, if done here

Music stand (or secondary podium):
general intercessions, if done here

SACRISTY

charcoal lit in thurible, if used, then put in vesting room
controls set for air, sound, lights
microphones put in place and turned on

VESTING ROOM

vesture (see page 120); cope, dalmatic of white or of day's color
lavaliere microphones, if any
sheet from planning meeting with list of selected texts
lectionary or gospel book with texts marked, if carried in procession

local texts (words of welcome) inserted and other texts marked in *Rite of Marriage,* for review before placing at entrance

thurible, with lit charcoal, if used in procession

vessel of incense, if used in procession

processional cross, if used in procession

two candlesticks with lighted candles, if used in procession

ENTRANCE

space set for rite of welcome (bride, groom, parents, witnesses, some or all of assembly)

space set for presider, other ministers (crossbearer, candlebearer, incense-bearer)

ritual book for presider (unless carried there)

hymnals or booklets for all

Pastoral Care of the Sick: Communion of the Sick at Home, Hospital or Nursing Home

This rite is chapter 3 of the *Pastoral Care of the Sick*. See #74 of that rite and page 78 of this manual in regards to bringing eucharistic wine to the sick.

PLACE OF GATHERING

Depending upon the number and condition of the sick, this rite may take place in the sitting room of a nursing home, or a similar gathering place within a hospital. There several of the sick and their relatives and friends might gather.

Open space:
space designated and proper furnishings provided for the sick

space for relatives, friends and any representatives of the local church

hymnals or booklets for all

scripture text provided for reader (from #84 of rite or from Bible)

text of intercessions, if these will be read by other minister

Small table:
May be prepared by those who are with the sick, before the minister's arrival

linen cloth cover on table

lighted candles

space designated for the dignified placement of pyx and/or vessel of eucharistic wine

vessel of baptismal water, if used; may be in place or brought by minister

ritual book, usually brought by minister

small container of water, if eucharistic vessel(s) will be cleansed there

LOCAL CHURCH BUILDING

Before the minister departs for the place of celebration:
texts marked in *Pastoral Care of the Sick*

baptismal water in closed carrying vessel prepared, if used

if communal celebration in nursing home or hospital, minister may bring alb and, if ordained, stole

Chapel of Eucharistic Reservation:
pyx with eucharistic bread prepared, with sufficient amount for all the sick and relatives who will receive

vessel with eucharistic wine prepared, if used (see page 78)

Pastoral Care of the Sick: Anointing of the Sick within Mass

PLACE FOR EUCHARISTIC ACTION

Seating:
hymnals or booklets

Open space:
space designated for the sick to step forward for anointing (or else their seating positioned with room for ministers to move among them)
stand/pedestal with vessel of oil of the sick

Altar:
covered with one cloth, unless this comes at preparation rite
gospel book with text marked, if used and not carried in procession
nearby: any candles, candlestands not carried in procession
nearby: stand for processional cross

Credence table:
small bowls or other vessels for minister(s) of anointing to carry oil to sick
cards with text for anointing action, for ministers
basin(s) and lemon, pitcher(s) of water, towel(s) for ministers
large cup (can be covered by pall and/or white veil)
purificator
corporal
book stand, if necessary
water in small cruet, if not in procession of gifts
any bread, wine, not in procession of gifts
additional cups and purificators for the assembly (on tray)
additional patens for the assembly
pyx or ciborium, if bread consecrated for the absent sick

Presider's chair:
sacramentary, after review in vesting room
ritual book, after review in vesting room, unless copies of these texts inserted into sacramentary
hymnal or booklet, if not carried in procession

Ministers' seats:
(texts for concelebrants, if any)
hymnals or booklets, if not carried in procession

Ambo:
lectionary with texts marked, if not carried in procession
psalm setting for cantor (unless carried there for this action)
litany (#138 in rite), if done here

Music stand (or secondary podium):
litany (#138 in rite), if done here

Sacristy

charcoal lit in thurible, then put in vesting room

extra charcoal (and tongs, matches) for adding during Mass

controls set for air, sound, lights

microphones put in place and turned on

Vesting Room

vesture (see page 120); chasuble, dalmatic of white or day's color

lavaliere microphones, if any

lectionary or gospel book with texts marked, if carried in procession

local texts (dismissal of catechumens) inserted and other texts marked in sacramentary, for review prior to placement by chair

texts also marked in *Pastoral Care of the Sick,* #135–142, unless these are copied and inserted in the sacramentary, for review prior to placement by chair or assistant minister's chair or credence table

thurible, with lit charcoal

vessel of incense

processional cross

two or more candlesticks with lighted candles

Entrance

Table with gifts:

bread for all on one paten, more if needed, if in procession

wine for all in one vessel, more if needed, if in procession

water in small cruet, if in procession

Other:

collection baskets ready, if used

booklets, bulletins or other handouts

Chapel of Eucharistic Reservation

lamp lit

key at tabernacle, if eucharist for absent sick will be added

Rite of Reconciliation of Several Penitents with Individual Confession and Absolution

The Rite of Penance contains several ritual orders, with or without sacramental absolution, for a variety of pastoral circumstances. Each of these orders or rites is a liturgy, with particular artifacts and furnishings that facilitate the communal action. This is true even for the rite for reconciliation of individual penitents, what many commonly call "confession"—even with just two present, it is the act of Christ and church.

This list is for the order that is most often used in the United States, what has usually come to be called a "penance service."

Place of Celebration

Seating for assembly:
- hymnals or booklets
- space designated for other priests to gather near presiding priest after individual confession and absolution

Altar, if celebration is in eucharistic space:
- cloth can be removed, if desired
- nearby: candlestands, if candles will be carried in procession
- nearby: processional cross may be in stand, or may be carried in procession

Presider's chair:
- ritual book, after review in vesting room
- hymnal or booklet, if not carried in procession

Ministers' seating:
- places designated for other priest confessors
- hymnals or booklets, if not carried in procession

Ambo:
- lectionary or ritual book or Bible, with texts marked, if not carried in procession
- psalm setting for cantor (unless carried there for this action)

Music stand (or secondary podium):
- text of examination of conscience, if used
- text for general confession and litany, read by deacon or other minister

Places for Individual Confession and Absolution

This may be space designated within the main gathering place, or regular chapels of reconciliation. At each designated place or chapel:
- chair for confessor
- text of absolution, if needed
- chair for penitent
- screen and kneeler, if possible; arranged so that penitent approaches place and can choose kneeler or chair before the priest sees him or her

Sacristy

controls set for lights, air, sound
microphones put in place

Vesting Room

vesture: for presiding priest—alb and stole (with cope), violet or color of day; other priests: alb and stole

lavaliere microphones, if any

lectionary or Bible, if carried in procession

local texts inserted and other texts marked in *The Rite of Penance*, for review before placing at chair

processional cross, if carried in procession

two lighted candles, if carried in procession

Rite of Eucharistic Exposition and Benediction

Solemn or lengthy exposition should begin after the prayer after communion of the Mass at which the host for exposition is consecrated. This list is for exposition taking place at a time removed from the celebration of the eucharist.

Place for Eucharistic Action

Seating:
hymnals or booklets

Altar:
covered with one cloth
nearby: two or four candlestands, with lit candles
nearby: processional cross may be in stand
nearby: space set for presider and ministers to kneel and to incense the eucharist
nearby: ritual book, hymnal, after review in sacristy

Credence table:
monstrance
stand with thurible and vessel of incense nearby

Presider's chair:
hymnal or booklet, if not carried in procession

Ministers' seats:
hymnals or booklets, if not carried in procession

Ambo:
lectionary, Bible or *Holy Communion and Worship of the Eucharist outside Mass,* with readings marked
psalm settings for cantor (or carried there for this action)

Music stand (or secondary podium):
texts of litanies, intercessions or other prayers used

Sacristy

thurible, with lit charcoal, ready for incensation near beginning and end of exposition (or on stand accessible from altar)
vessel of incense
controls set for air, sound, lights
microphones, if necessary, put in place and turned on

Vesting Room

vesture (see page 120); cope, dalmatic of white
lavaliere microphones, if any
local texts for exposition inserted and other texts marked in ritual book *(Holy Communion and Worship of the Eucharist outside Mass),* for review prior to placement either at presider's chair or in place for kneeling

ENTRANCE

booklets, bulletins or other handouts

CHAPEL OF EUCHARISTIC RESERVATION

lamp lit

key at tabernacle

lunette (glass pyx that fits monstrance) in tabernacle, holding host consecrated at prior Mass

white humeral veil for transfer of eucharist to altar

two candlestands and candles to accompany transfer, then joining other two or four candles near altar

Blessings: Order for the Blessing of Animals

The *Book of Blessings* has 71 chapters with orders of blessing for families, buildings, objects, parish members and more. Its introduction should be read for an appreciation of what "blessing" means here—praise of God and intercession for those who use elements of God's creation. Most of the rites contain a liturgy of the word before a prayer of praising God. The list given here presumes a large gathering of parishioners and animals in an outdoor place. The service is led by a priest, deacon, or lay minister.

Place of Assembly

Seating:

folding chairs from parish hall, blankets or lawn chairs brought from homes, or no formal seating

booklets for all

room for pet carriers, or similar assistance for all animals

Presider's chair or place to stand:

Book of Blessings, after review in vesting room

booklet

sound system, if necessary

Small table:

vessel of baptismal water and sprinkler (several, if other ministers will also circulate for full sprinkling action)

Ministers' seats or places to stand:

booklets

Lectern (reserved for readings, homily—presider's prayer should be from his or her position):

lectionary, Bible or *Book of Blessings,* with text marked

psalm setting for cantor (unless carried there for this action)

intercessions

sound system, if necessary

Place for instrumentalists and other leaders of music:

sound system, if necessary

music stands, as needed

Vesting Room

albs for assisting ministers; alb and cope for presider; stole under cope for ordained presider—of white or day's color

lavaliere microphones, if usable with outdoor sound system

texts marked in *Book of Blessings,* for review prior to placement

Entrance

signs directing participants to correct place

Devotions: Stations of the Cross

Because this devotional practice is not part of the liturgy, there are neither official texts nor exact lists of requisites. There are even different lists for setting the titles of the 14 stations. See page 81 for a description of the installation of crosses and images for this devotion.

This list is for a public gathering that includes hymn-singing and the procession of participants from station to station.

Place of Assembly

At the start of the processional route, near station one:
hymnals or booklets for all

places designated for musicians, leader and other ministers (for example, cross bearer and two candle bearers)

Processional route, by 14 stations:
lighting, as appropriate

places designated for assembly and ministers

14 images or crosses set in place, if not permanently positioned

Sacristy

controls set for lights, air, sound

microphones put in place, if used

Vesting Room

vesture: alb (and cope, red or color of day) for any leader; alb and stole (and cope) for ordained leader, in red or color of day

lavaliere microphones, if used

texts marked or inserted in appropriate books for all who will read or lead prayer

processional cross, if used in procession

two lighted candles, if used in procession

Entrance

sign indicating location of celebration, if in separate or outdoor place

35◆ Checklists for Rites at Which a Bishop Presides

Pastoral Visitation of the Bishop

The *Ceremonial of Bishops* (#1177ff) warns bishops that their visits to parishes should never be purely an administrative duty. The visitation should allow parishioners to interact with the chief herald of the gospel, a shepherd and loving teacher. Sacristans, meanwhile, focus neither on the administrator nor the shepherd. Instead, the bishop is all too often perceived as the man whose presence brings unusual and often confusing demands on the sacristy. This need not be so. The rites at which the bishop presides might involve larger assemblies, an important opportunity to involve more volunteers in the sacristy. Some events might be unfamiliar locally, for example an ordination service, but the representatives of the bishop (and he himself) always want to plan details far in advance. Bishops wear the same vestments as priests, and their specific insignia are explained on page 134. Their presidency at liturgy is often the same as priests, but they do have some roles reserved to bishops (and explained in the *Ceremonial of Bishops).* If there are any questions in the sacristy, they should be forwarded to the diocesan office well in advance of the bishop's visit.

The visitation, preceded in the parish by times of catechesis, might include all or some of these events: a formal rite of welcoming (see paragraph just below), dedication of the church (list at page 268), Mass (same as any eucharist), liturgy of the hours, confirmation (list at page 259), ordination (lists on pages 261–267) visits to the sick (list at page 249), celebration of the word of God, and a liturgical visit with parishioners to the cemetery (list at page 227).

SPECIFIC CUSTOMS: A visitation that begins with a formal reception or liturgical welcome *(Ceremonial of Bishops,* #1180) may necessitate these items:

Vesting room:
cope, stole, alb for pastor

Entrance hall:
space for assembly
space for pastor and bishop
a small crucifix (or processional cross) for veneration
vessel of baptismal water and sprinkler

Presider's chair:
sacramentary with texts marked

Rite of Confirmation within Mass

Those baptized as infants are normally confirmed by the bishop, at their first eucharist or later. (See the Easter Vigil list, page 215, for the confirmation by presbyters of adults baptized or received into the church.)

Place for Eucharistic Action

Seating:
hymnals or booklets
designated seating for candidates and sponsors

Open space:
dedication candles, pew candles may be lighted
pedestal or stand with vessel of chrism
space set for candidates and sponsors when called forward

Altar:
covered with one cloth, unless this comes at preparation rite
gospel book with text marked, if used and not carried in procession
nearby: any candles, candlestands not carried in procession
nearby: stand for processional cross

Credence table:
smaller vessel(s) from which chrism can be administered
basin(s) with lemon pieces, pitcher(s) of water, towels
large cup (can be covered by pall and/or white veil)
purificator
corporal
water in small cruet, if not in procession of gifts
book stand, if necessary
additional cups and purificators for the assembly (on tray)
additional patens for the assembly
pyx or ciborium, if extra bread consecrated for the sick

Presider's chair:
nearby: seats for servers assisting the bishop
nearby: the server assisting with the book has the sacramentary and ritual book (Roman Pontifical or the rite of confirmation excerpted from it)
hymnal or booklet

Ministers' seats:
texts for concelebrants, if any
hymnals or booklets

Ambo:
lectionary with texts marked, if not carried in procession
psalm setting for cantor (unless carried there for this action)
general intercessions, if done here

Music stand (or secondary podium):
names of candidates to be presented
general intercessions, if done here

SACRISTY

charcoal lit in thurible, then put in vesting room
extra charcoal (and tongs, matches) for adding during Mass
controls set for air, sound, lights
microphones put in places and turned on

VESTING ROOM(S)

(Several rooms may be necessary, especially if candidates will wear robes and if they will be in opening procession.)
robes for candidates, set up in order agreed at rehearsal, preferably albs, their baptismal robes
space set for candidates' gathering before the procession
albs (with cinctures and amices if necessary) for all ministers, stoles and chasubles for concelebrants, normally red
stoles and dalmatics for deacons, normally red
stole, chasuble, miter, pastoral staff for bishop
lavaliere microphones, if any
lectionary or gospel book with texts marked, if carried in procession
local texts (dismissal of catechumens, intercessions) inserted and other texts marked in sacramentary and in ritual book, for review prior to placement by chair
thurible, with lit charcoal
vessel of incense
processional cross
two or more candlesticks with lighted candles

ENTRANCE

Table with gifts:
bread for all on one paten, more if needed
wine for all in one vessel, more if needed
water in small cruet, if in procession

Other:
collection baskets ready, if used
booklets, bulletins or other handouts

CATECHUMENEON

opened and prepared, if catechumens present

CHAPEL OF EUCHARISTIC RESERVATION

lamp lit
key at tabernacle, if eucharist for the sick will be added

Ordination of Deacons

PLACE FOR EUCHARISTIC ACTION

Seating:
hymnals or booklets
reserved seating, if necessary, kept to a minimum, must be well marked

Open space:
dedication candles, pew candles may be lighted
seating for candidates (not blocking sightlines between members of the assembly, between assembly and altar)

Altar:
covered with one cloth, unless this comes at preparation rite
nearby: any candles, candlestands not carried in procession
nearby: stand for processional cross

Credence table(s):
Sunday: vessel of baptismal water and sprinkler, if used
stoles and dalmatics for newly ordained (arranged with names if in specific sizes)
book of gospels for each new deacon, if individual ones given
large cup (can be covered by pall and/or white veil)
purificator
corporal
book stand, if necessary
water in small cruet, if not in procession of gifts
basin, pitcher of water, towel
additional cups and purificators for the assembly (on tray)
additional patens for the assembly
pyx or ciborium, if extra bread consecrated for the sick

Presider's chair (cathedra):
nearby: chairs for assistants with miter, pastoral staff, books (hymnal or booklet, sacramentary, Roman Pontifical)
space nearby where candidates can stand without blocking sightlines of assembly, and can prostrate themselves

Ministers' seats:
special seating for vested deacons
texts for concelebrants
hymnals or booklets

Ambo:
lectionary with texts marked
psalm setting for cantor (unless carried there for this action)

Music stand (or secondary podium):
names of candidates to be called

text for presentation of candidates

litany of the saints text for cantor, with interpolations (patrons, titular, petitions)

Sacristy

charcoal lit in thurible, then put in vesting room

extra charcoal, tongs and matches for adding during Mass

controls set for air, sound, lights

microphones put in place and turned on

Vesting Room(s)

(The vesting can take place in any room(s) of the complex, as long as it is large enough.)

albs (with cinctures and amices, if necessary) for all ministers, including those to be ordained

stoles and dalmatics for those who are already deacons (vesture in color of day or white)

stoles (and chasubles) for concelebrants

stole (dalmatic), chasuble, miter, pastoral staff (pallium) for bishop

lavaliere microphones, if any

gospel book with text marked

texts marked in sacramentary and in Roman Pontifical, for review prior to placement by chair

thurible, with lit charcoal

vessel of incense

processional cross

two or more candlesticks with lighted candles

place for ministers to gather for procession

Entrance

bread for all on one paten, more if needed

wine for all in one vessel, more if needed

water in small cruet, if in procession

Chapel of Eucharistic Reservation

lamp lit

key at tabernacle, if eucharist for the sick will be added

Ordination of Presbyters (Priests)

Place for Eucharistic Action

Seating:
hymnals or booklets
reserved seating, if necessary, kept to a minimum, must be well marked

Open space:
dedication candles, pew candles may be lighted
seating for candidates (not blocking sightlines between members of the assembly or between assembly and altar); may be seated with other deacons
stand or pedestal for vessel of chrism

Altar:
covered with one cloth, unless this comes at preparation rite
nearby: any candles, candlestands not carried in procession
nearby: stand for processional cross

Credence table(s):
Sunday: vessel of baptismal water and sprinkler, if used
stoles for presbyters not concelebrating who will lay on hands
chasubles (and stoles, if these will be changed) for newly ordained (arranged with names if in specific sizes)
linen apron (gremial)
vessel for anointing with chrism
basin(s) with lemon pieces, pitcher(s) of water, towel(s) for newly ordained and bishop
purificator
corporal
book stand, if necessary
additional cups and purificators for the assembly (on tray)
additional patens for the assembly
pyx or ciborium, if extra bread consecrated for the sick

Presider's chair (cathedra):
nearby: chairs for assistants with miter, pastoral staff, books (hymnal or booklet, sacramentary, Roman Pontifical)
space nearby where candidates can stand without blocking sight lines of assembly, can prostrate themselves, and can kneel for presbyters to lay on hands
space for all presbyters to gather about the bishop after laying on of hands

Ministers' seats:
for newly ordained during preparation of altar and after communion
for vested priests, texts for concelebrants
for vested deacons
hymnals or booklets

Ambo:
lectionary with texts marked
psalm setting for cantor (unless carried there for this action)

Music stand (or secondary podium):

names of candidates to be called
text for presentation of candidates
litany of the saints text for cantor, with interpolations (patrons, titular, petitions)

SACRISTY

charcoal lit in thurible, then put in vesting room
extra charcoal (and tongs, matches) for adding during Mass
controls set for air, sound, lights
microphones put in places and turned on

VESTING ROOM(S)

(The vesting can take place in any room(s) of the complex, as long as it is large enough.)
albs (with cincture and amices, if necessary) for all ministers
diaconal stoles for all to be ordained (vesture in color of day or white)
stoles and dalmatics for deacons
stoles (and chasubles) for concelebrants
stole (dalmatic), chasuble, miter, pastoral staff (pallium) for bishop
lavaliere microphones, if any
gospel book with text marked
texts marked in sacramentary and in Roman Pontifical, for review prior to placement by chair
thurible, with lit charcoal
vessel of incense
processional cross
two or more candlesticks with lighted candles
place for ministers to gather for procession

ENTRANCE

bread for all on one paten, more if needed
large cup with wine, mixed with a little water
other vessels of wine, if the one cup is insufficient for all

CHAPEL OF EUCHARISTIC RESERVATION

lamp lit
key at tabernacle if eucharist for the sick will be added

Ordination of a Bishop

Place for Eucharistic Action

Seating:
hymnals or booklets
reserved seating, if necessary, kept to a minimum, must be well marked

Open space:
dedication candles, pew candles may be lighted
stand or pedestal for vessel of chrism

Altar:
covered with one cloth, unless this comes at preparation rite
nearby: any candles, candlestands not carried in procession
nearby: stand for processional cross

Credence table(s):
Sunday: vessel of baptismal water and sprinkler, if used
linen apron (gremial)
vessel for anointing with chrism
basin with lemon pieces, pitcher of water, towel
ring, pastoral staff, miter for bishop-elect
large cup (can be covered by pall and/or white veil)
purificator
corporal
water in small cruet, if not in procession of gifts
book stand, if necessary
additional cups and purificators for the assembly (on tray)
additional patens for the assembly
pyx or ciborium, if extra bread consecrated for the sick

Presider's chair (cathedra):
nearby: chairs for assistants with miter, pastoral staff, books (hymnal or booklets, sacramentary and Roman Pontifical)
space nearby where bishop-elect can stand without blocking sight lines of assembly, can prostrate himself, and can kneel for laying on of hands

Ministers' seats:
near the cathedra: prominent chair for use by newly ordained bishop or by principal consecrator after the ordination
near the cathedra: chairs for other bishops (a minimum of two), with copies of the consecratory prayer
for the bishop-elect, and two assisting priests
for priest who will present bishop-elect
for concelebrating priests
for vested deacons
for assisting ministers
for lectors

for college of diocesan consultors and chancellor
for ecumenical and interfaith representatives
hymnals or booklets at all these chairs

Ambo:
lectionary with texts marked
psalm setting for cantor (unless carried there for this action)
the apostolic letter

Music stand (or secondary podium):
text of presentation
litany of the saints text for cantor, with interpolations (patrons, titular, petitions)

Sacristy

charcoal lit in thurible and then put in vesting room
extra charcoal (and tongs, matches) for adding during Mass
controls set for air, sound, lights
microphones put in places and turned on

Vesting Room(s)

(The vesting can take place in any room(s) of the complex, as long as it is large enough.)
albs (with cinctures and amices, if necessary) for all ministers
stoles and dalmatics for deacons (vesture in color of day or white)
stoles (and chasubles) for concelebrating priests
stoles and copes for priests assisting bishop-elect, if they do not concelebrate
pectoral cross, stole, dalmatic, chasuble for bishop-elect
stoles, chasubles, miters for concelebrating bishops
stole (dalmatic), chasuble, miter, pastoral staff (pallium) for principal consecrator
hymnals or booklets for all
lavaliere microphones, if any
gospel book with text marked
texts marked in sacramentary and in Roman Pontifical, for review prior to placement by cathedra
thurible with lit charcoal
vessel of incense
processional cross
two or more candlesticks with lighted candles
place for ministers to gather for procession

Entrance

bread for all on one paten, more if needed
one or more vessels of wine
water in small cruet, if in procession

Chapel of Eucharistic Reservation

lamp lit
key at tabernacle if eucharist for the sick will be added

Dedication of a Church

PLACE FOR EUCHARISTIC ACTION

Open space:
dedication candles on walls, unlit
small table for resting reliquary, if needed

Altar, completely bare (with aperture for relics)

Credence tables:
vessel of water and sprinkler
sealant or cement to close the cover of the aperture in the altar (over relics)
linen apron (gremial)
vessel of chrism (with smaller bowl if necessary)
basins with lemon pieces, pitchers of water, towels
brazier with charcoal briquettes, and vessel of incense; small candle and matches
several thuribles and charcoal, with vessel of incense
linen towels for altar (and waterproof cover, or cerecloth—linen waxed on both sides)
altar cloth
four, six or seven candlestands and candles
stand for processional cross
small candle, matches to begin lighting of altar candles, then dedication candles
candlelighter, if needed
large cup (can be covered by pall and/or white veil)
purificator
corporal
water in small cruet, if not in procession of gifts
book stand, if necessary
additional cups and purificators for the assembly (on tray)
additional patens for the assembly
pyx or ciborium for extra bread consecrated for the sick
humeral veil

Presider's chair:
nearby: seats for ministers assisting with miter, pastoral staff, books (dedication rite, sacramentary, hymnal or program)

Ministers' seats:
texts for concelebrants, if any
hymnals or booklets

Space for leaders of music:
psalm setting to be carried by cantor to ambo
special text of litany of the saints with local interpolations

Ambo, completely bare

SACRISTY

controls set for air, sound, lights (generally off, until lighting of the altar rite)

microphones put in place and turned on

ENTRANCE

Exterior:

signs direct assembly to preliminary assembly place

procession route arranged: permits for use of streets or sidewalks, traffic guards.

Doors:

closed; no one enters church building before procession

Table with gifts:

bread for all on one paten, more if needed

wine for all in one vessel, more if needed

water in small cruet, if in procession

CHAPEL OF EUCHARISTIC RESERVATION

lamp in place, unlit

key at tabernacle

VESTING ROOM

(Room is distinct from church, near gathering place.)

albs (with cinctures and amices, if necessary) for all ministers

stoles and dalmatics of white for deacons (red if carrying martyr's relics)

stoles and chasubles of white for priests

stole (dalmatic), chasuble of white, miter, pastoral staff (pallium) for bishop

lavaliere microphones, if any

lectionary with texts marked, to be carried by lector

texts marked in sacramentary and in dedication ritual book, for review prior to carrying by assistant

processional cross

OTHER GATHERING PLACE

(A neighboring church or other suitable place will do.)

relics of saints in reliquary, with flowers and candles

booklets for all

space for entire assembly

spaces set for instrumentalists, other leaders of music, bishop, other ministers

ABOUT THE ILLUSTRATIONS

The Cover

Our pre-Christian ancestors carved depictions of peacocks to symbolize immortality. They were convinced, even to the time of St. Augustine of Hippo, that this animal's flesh never decayed. "It happened at Carthage that a bird of this kind was cooked and served up to me, and, taking a suitable slice of flesh from its breast, I ordered it to be kept, and when it had been kept as many days as make other flesh stinking, it was produced and set before me, and emitted no offensive smell. And after it had been laid by for 30 days and more, it was still in the same state; and a year after, the same still, except that it was a little more shrivelled and drier." *City of God,* 21:4.

The peoples allied with Rome also associated the peacock with Juno, their highest goddess and highest expression of the feminine. Thus peacocks were released upon the death of empresses, the time of their transformation to immortal deities. With these meanings, it is no surprise that peacocks came to be depicted on all manner of funereal objects—lamps, tombs, memorials. Early Christians did not forget or fight the earlier associations. They freely used peacock imagery precisely to evoke the old feelings of immortality and the feminine. These feelings were then given fresh interpretation within the paschal mystery.

The classical form of two peacocks, or of a peacock and peahen, drinking from each side of a vessel, came to connote so much—the water of life at baptism, the eucharistic drink that brings immortality, the divinization of all women and men in the church. Despite the changes of cultures and images, we too prepare vessels so that the church may drink of immortality.

1. The Church

"We now anoint this altar and this building.
May God in his power make them holy,
visible signs of the mystery of Christ and his Church."
Dedication of a Church and an Altar, Dedication of a Church, #64.

2. History of the Sacristy

"A sacristy or vesting space should be located to favor the procession of cross, candles, book, and ministers through the midst of the congregation to the altar area." National Conference of Catholic Bishops, Bishops' Committee on the Liturgy, *Environment and Art in Catholic Worship, #82.*

3. The Sacristan

"Another story was told me by a fellow bishop of mine who had been a monk in the city of Ancona. . . . The sacristan of this church, a pious man named Constantius, was known far and wide for his sanctity. Having renounced the things of this world completely, he directed his soul heavenward with all the powers of his mind. One day the church's oil supply ran out, and Contantius had nothing with which to fill the lamps. So he took water, poured some into each lamp, and fixed a wick in the middle as usual. Then he lighted the lamps and they all began to burn as if they were fed with oil." Gregory the Great (sixth-century bishop of Rome), *Dialogues* I:5.

4. Sacred Mysteries and Liturgical Art

"God our creator,
the heavens declare your glory,
and earth proclaims your handiwork.
We praise you for the work of creation,
manifest in the imagination and skill of artists and craftspeople
who bring beauty and delight,
challenge and vision to our lives.
May your blessing be upon all who share this work:
May we become heralds of your reign
when beauty shall be the companion of justice and peace."
National Conference of Catholic Bishops, Bishops' Committee on the Liturgy, *Catholic Household Blessings and Prayers*, "Blessing of the Work of an Artist or Craftsperson," p. 307.

5. A Place for the Eucharistic Assembly

"Through his death and resurrection, Christ became the true and perfect temple of the New Covenant and gathered together a people to be his own. This holy people, made one as the Father, Son, and Holy Spirit are one, is the Church, that is, the temple of God built of living stones, where the Father is worshiped in spirit and in truth. Rightly, then, from the early times 'church' has also been the name given to the building in which the Christian community gathers to hear the word of God, to pray together, to receive the sacraments, and to celebrate the eucharist. Because the church is a visible building, it stands as a special sign of the pilgrim Church on earth and reflects the Church dwelling in heaven." *Dedication of a Church and an Altar,* Dedication of a Church, #1–2a.

The upper part of the image depicts the new Jerusalem (Revelation 21:1–23).

6. The Presider's Chair

"After three days they found him in the temple, sitting among the teachers, listening to them and asking them questions." Luke 2: 46.

The lower part of the illustration depicts one form of seating for liturgical presiders and their colleagues, prevalent most especially in the early Christian era.

7. The Altar

"Then Jacob woke from his sleep and said, 'Surely the Lord is in this place—and I did not know it!' And he was afraid, and said, 'How awesome is this place! This is none other than the house of God, and this is the gate of heaven.' So Jacob rose early in the morning, and he took the stone that he had put under his head and set it up for a pillar and poured oil on the top of it." Genesis 28:16–18. See the whole story, Genesis 28:11–22.

The altar shown on the lower level uses motifs popular from the fifth to eleventh centuries in what would later be southern France—for example the ancient altar still used at S. Sernin, Toulouse.

8. The Ambo

Ezra "read from [the book of the law of Moses] facing the square before the Water Gate from early morning until midday, in the presence of the men and women and those who could understand; and the ears of all the people were attentive to the book of the law. The scribe Ezra stood on a wooden platform that had been made for the purpose." Nehemiah 8:3–4a. See the whole episode narrated in Nehemiah 8:1–12. This passage is proclaimed as the first reading in a new church or at a new ambo.

The ambo on the lower level reflects shapes and iconography prevalent in some early Christian and early medieval ambos. Many still serve the churches of Italy, particularly in the Campania region.

9. The Sanctuary

Chapters 25–31 of Exodus describe the wilderness dwelling of Israel. Through the massive amount of detail of these chapters, those who prepare for liturgy in our own day can still thrill to the selection of artisans such as Bezalel (31:2), still recognize how the furnishings and shapes of a worship site contribute to the identity of a holy people.

The lower level depicts an ancient system for arranging altar, ambo and paschal candlestand in the midst of ministers and assembly. From early Christian roots, the system continued through medieval modifications—as here at San Clemente, Rome (twelfth century).

10. A Place for Instrumentalists and Leaders of Music

"Jesse made seven of his sons pass before Samuel, and Samuel said to Jesse, 'The Lord has not chosen any of these.' Samuel said to Jesse, 'Are all your sons here?' And he said, 'There remains yet the youngest, but he is keeping the sheep.'" 1 Samuel 16:10–11a. Throughout chapter 16 (and later), the narrator describes the rise of a lyre-playing David. The lyre was esteemed by many ancient peoples as the most fitting instrument for worship.

11. The Baptistry

"Now in Jerusalem by the Sheep Gate there is a pool, called in Hebrew Bethzatha (Bethesda), which has five porticoes. In these lay many invalids—blind, lame, and paralyzed. One man was there who had been ill for 38 years. When Jesus saw him lying there and knew that he had been there a long time, he said to him, 'Do you want to be made well?' The sick man answered him, 'Sir, I have no one to put me into the pool when the water is stirred up; and while I am making my way, someone else steps down ahead of me.' Jesus said to him, 'Stand up, take your mat and walk.'" John 5:2–8.

The earliest commentators and homilists saw in this passage an image of their fonts—pools of healing water, stirred up now for all neophytes. The new pools took on various shapes as Christianity spread through various cultures. Often the shape was polygonal, for example a hexagon with its perceived relationship to the sixth day of the week and death to sin.

12. The Catechumeneon

As Jesus "walked by the Sea of Galilee, he saw two brothers, Simon, who is called Peter, and Andrew his brother, casting a net into the sea—for they were fishermen. And he said to them, 'Follow me, and I will make you fish for people.'" Matthew 4:18–19.

13. Chapel of Reconciliation

"And when they could not bring him to Jesus because of the crowd, they removed the roof above him; and after having dug through it, they let down the mat on which the paralytic lay. When Jesus saw their faith, he said to the paralytic, 'Son, your sins are forgiven.'" Mark 2:4–5.

14. Chapel for the Reservation of the Eucharist

Jesus "took her by the hand and said to her, 'Talitha cum,' which means, 'Little girl, get up!' And immediately the girl got up and began to walk about (she was twelve years of age). At this they were overcome with amazement. He strictly ordered them that no one should know this, and he told them to give her something to eat." Mark 5:41–43.

"The primary and original reason for reservation of the eucharist outside Mass is the administration of viaticum." *Holy Communion and Worship of the Eucharist outside Mass, #5.*

15. Shrines and Other Areas for Private Devotions

Jesus "called his disciples and said to them, 'Truly I tell you, this poor widow has put in more than all those who are contributing to the treasury. For all of them have contributed out of their abundance; but she out of her poverty has put in everything she had, all that she had to live on.'" Mark 12:43–44.

16. Entrance Area

"They shall take some of the blood and put it on the two doorposts and the lintel of the houses in which they eat it." Exodus 12:7.

The entranceway depicted is at the twelfth-century basilica of Vezelay (Burgundy, France).

17. Gathering Place

"People were bringing little children to him in order that he might touch them; and the disciples spoke sternly to them. But when Jesus saw this, he was indignant and said to them, 'Let the little children come to me; do not stop them; for it is to such as these that the kingdom of God belongs.'" Mark 10:13–14.

18. Cemetery

"He cried with a loud voice, 'Lazarus, come out!'" John 11:43b.

19. Sacristy Furnishings

Jesus "sent two of his disciples, saying to them, 'Go into the city, and a man carrying a water jar will meet you; follow him, and wherever he enters, say to the owner of the house, "The teacher asks, Where is my guest room where I may eat the Passover with my disciples?" He will show you a large room upstairs, furnished and ready. Make preparations for us there.'" Mark 14:13–15.

20. Liturgical Books

Jesus "rolled up the scroll, gave it back to the attendant, and sat down. The eyes of all in the synagogue were fixed on him. Then he began to say to them, 'Today this scripture has been fulfilled in your hearing.'" Luke 4:20–21.

21. Liturgical Vessels

"And a woman in the city, who was a sinner, having learned that [Jesus] was eating in the Pharisee's house, brought an alabaster jar of ointment. She stood behind him at his feet, weeping, and began to bathe his feet in her tears and to dry them with her hair. Then she continued kissing his feet and anointing them with the ointment." Luke 7:37–38.

22. Liturgical Vestments

"The son said to him, 'Father, I have sinned against heaven and before you; I am no longer worthy to be called your son.' But the father said to his slaves, 'Quickly, bring out a robe—the best one—and put it on him; put a ring on his finger and sandals on his feet. And get the fatted calf and kill it, and let us eat and celebrate.'" Luke 15:21–23.

23. Linens and Textiles Other Than Vesture

"Do not be alarmed; you are looking for Jesus of Nazareth, who was crucified. He has been raised; he is not here. Look, there is the place they laid him." Mark 16:6.

24. Candles and Their Equipment

"Christ is the light of the nations
and the glory of Israel his people."
Antiphon for procession, with all bearing lit candles on the Solemnity of the Presentation of the Lord, February 2. See Luke 2:32.

25. Incense and its Implements

"On entering the house, they saw the child with Mary his mother; and they knelt down and paid him homage. Then, opening their treasure chests, they offered him gifts of gold, frankincense, and myrrh." Matthew 2:11.

26. Flowers

"Many people spread their cloaks on the road, and others spread leafy branches that they had cut in the fields." Mark 11:8.

27. Maintenance and Housekeeping

"And all ate and were filled. What was left over was gathered up, twelve baskets of broken pieces." Luke 9:17.

28. Security and Health

"She had heard about Jesus, and came up behind him in the crowd and touched his cloak, for she said, 'If I but touch his clothes, I will be made well.'" Mark 5:27–28.

29. Mechanical Systems

Zacchaeus "was trying to see who Jesus was, but on account of the crowd he could not, because he was short in stature. So he ran ahead and climbed a sycamore tree to see him." Luke 19:3–4.

30. Liturgical Items No Longer in General Use

"Therefore every scribe who has been trained for the kingdom of heaven is like the master of a household who brings out of his treasure what is new and what is old." Matthew 13:52.

INDEX